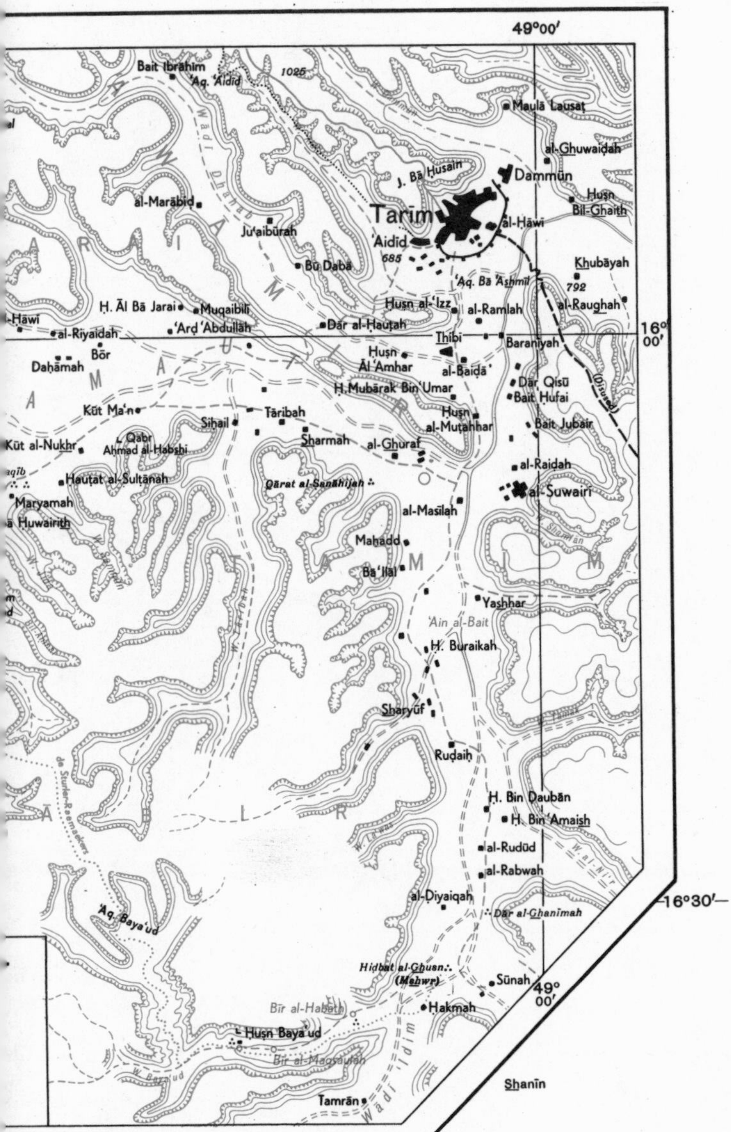

49°00′
Bait Ibrahim
'Aq. 'Aidid
1025
Wadi Dhahab
Maulā Lausaṭ
al-Ghuwaiḍah
J. Bā Husain
Dammūn
Ḥuṣn Bil-Ghaith
al-Marābiḍ
Tarīm
al-Ḥāwī
Ju'aibūrah
'Aidīd
685
Khubāyah
Bū Dabā
'Aq. Bā 'Ashmīl
792
al-Raughah
Ḥ. Āl Bā Jarai
Muqaibilī
'Arḍ 'Abdullāh
Ḥuṣn al-'Izz
al-Ramlah
Dār al-Ḥauṭah
al-Riyaiḍah
Thibī
Baraniyah
16° 00′
Bōr
Dahāmah
Ḥuṣn Āl 'Amhar
al-Baiḍā'
Dār Qisū
Bait Hufai
Ḥ. Mubārak Bin 'Umar
(Disused)
Kūt Ma'n
Ḥuṣn al-Muṭahhar
Sihail
Tāribah
Bait Jubair
Kūt al-Nukhr
Qabr Aḥmad al-Habshi
Sharmah
al-Ghuraf
al-Raidah
Ḥauṭat al-Sulṭānah
Qārat al-Sanāhijah
al-Suwairī
Maryamah
al-Masīlah
Huwairith
Mahadd
Bā 'Ilal
Yashhar
'Ain al-Bait
Ḥ. Buraikah
Sharyūf
Ruḍaiḥ
Ḥ. Bin Daubān
Ḥ. Bin 'Amaish
al-Rudūd
al-Rabwah
al-Ḍiyaiqah
Dār al-Ghanīmah
16°30′
'Aq. Baya'ud
Hidbat al-Ghusn
(Mahwr)
Sūnah
49° 00′
Hakmah
Bīr al-Habath
Ḥuṣn Baya'ud
Bīr al-Maqsaulah
W. Baya'ud
Wadi 'Idim
Shanīn
Tamrān
48°00′

A horseman and bowman hunting the ibex—a rock graffito at the side of the track at the top of the Wādī Sirr of Banī Ḥushaish, E. of Ṣan'ā'. The lighter flecks on the left are bullet marks.

[*Frontispiece*

South Arabian Hunt

by R. B. Serjeant

London 1976
LUZAC

First Published 1976 by Luzac & Company Ltd.
46 Great Russell Street,
London WC1B 3PE

SBN 7189 0172 X

PRINTED IN GREAT BRITAIN BY HEADLEY BROTHERS LTD
109 KINGSWAY LONDON WC2B 6PX AND ASHFORD KENT

CONTENTS

	Page
Introduction	1
Ritual Hunting in Arabic Literature?	4
The *Talbiyah* Stanzas of the God al-Nasr and the Hunt ...	9
Hunting in Ḥaḍramawt in the early ᶜAbbāsid Period ...	13
Popular Conceptions of the Hunt	14
Saiyid Opposition to the Hunt	18
Quarter Hunting Processions in Mediaeval Baghdād ...	23
The Hunt at Tarīm	25
Division of the Meat	30
The Hunt at Dammūn	32
The Hunt at ᶜĪnāt	32
Hunters at Qaᶜūḍah, etc.	33
Hunting in Wāḥidī Territory	34
Hunting Poems	39
Hunting at Madūdah	41
The Madūdah Document, Methods and Text	43
The Hunting Customs of the Villagers of Madūdah... ...	44
The Granting of Permission to Hunt	45
The Great Soirée	48
The Hunting Expedition	50
After the Hunt	55
Laws in Usage relating to the Killing of the Game	56
Hunting Case (No. 1)	57
Hunting Case (No. 2)	58
Hunting Case (No. 3)	59
Commentary	60
Recent Archaeological Evidence of the Ritual Hunt ...	64
The God Ta'lab	74
Ṣirwāḥ and Northern Yemen	77
Interpretation of the Antique by Reference to the Present ...	80
Appendix: Comparisons of the Hunt of the Baggārah Ḥumr Tribe of South-west Kordofan	82
Summary	84

References 86
Supplementary Notes 116
Glossary 117
Index of Proper Names 131
Index of Gods 137
Geographical Index 139

LIST OF ILLUSTRATIONS

FRONTISPIECE	Hunting the ibex, graffito from Wādī Sirr.
PLATE 1	Bronze lamp with ibex and hunting dog.
PLATE 2	Hunting net at Madūdah village.
PLATE 3	Picnic of the Baqqārah at Tarīm.
PLATE 4	Doorway flanked by ibex horns.
PLATE 5	Frieze of bulls' heads from Shabwah.
PLATE 6	Winged alabaster figure from Ma'rib.
PLATE 7	Tomb of Sa'id b. Sālim Bā Buraik, Shabwah.
PLATE 8	Winged figure in bronze.
PLATE 9	Capital of column from Ḥuṣn al-'Urr.
PLATE 10	Door jamb—front side, Ḥuṣn al-'Urr.
PLATE 11	Door jamb—side view, Ḥuṣn al-'Urr.
PLATE 12	Hunters with ibex heads at Tarīm.
PLATE 13	Family of ibexes, Saiwūn.
PLATE 14	Ibex horns set over a siqāyah.
PLATE 15	House with ibex horns, Ṣa'dah.
PLATE 16	Oryx from Shaikh Jāsim Āl Thānī's herd.
PLATE 17	House wall with animal figure, Wādī Rijām.
PLATE 18	Shield of Indian origin from Upper Yāfi'.

INTRODUCTION

While preparing a group of Ḥaḍramī hunting poems for publication, Professor Beeston's important article, "The Ritual Hunt", i.e. the ancient South Arabian Hunt, came into my hands.[1] The close link between the inscriptional material which he had examined, and my own findings in Tarīm was immediately evident to me, but I was not able to explore this topic more extensively until I re-visited Ḥaḍramawt in 1953–54 armed with his article. I completed the first draft of this study in 1955, but intending to publish it along with others, I made no attempt to print it at the time, and since then have added much to it. A few weeks before his death, the late H. St. J. B. Philby was kind enough to look through the draft; Professor Beeston also saw it at an earlier stage; and I am indebted to my one-time colleague Professor Maḥmūd ᶜAlī al-G͟hūl for several useful suggestions, as well as to other persons whose names appear below as having contributed information. The whole study itself was dependent on the goodwill and aid of Ḥaḍramī friends in those happy days when Ḥaḍramawt enjoyed British protection and peace and prospered greatly. In revising the final draft, and adding a few notes from my 1972 visit to Ṣanᶜā' and the north I have not attempted to bring up to date the politico-geographical references and substitute such words as the contemporary "governate" for "sulṭanate", and indeed the country might well revert to something like the older system again. New archaeological evidence provided by two Egyptian scholars is discussed *infra*, and I have added some data I collected while on my two tours in Royalist, i.e. Imāmic, Yemen, though on account of the war I was unable to make very serious detailed enquiries. The honour of first remarking and recording the existence of the organised Hunt in Ḥaḍramawt belongs of course to Mr. and Mrs. W. H. Ingrams who suggested that it must be pre-Islāmic in its origins.[2] The evidence of this study will, I think, demonstrate how correct their surmise was. I am indebted to the Department of Oriental Studies in Manchester for re-typing my final version.

* * *

It is, of course, of the organised Hunt with some religious association that this study treats, and it seems to be confined to a special limited area. The Hunt I am about to describe differs from the type of hunting, for instance, reported by ᶜAbd al-Wāsiᶜ[3] as existing among the Zarānīq. The Tihāmah has many gazelles, he says, and this tribe pursues them throughout the heat of the day even, running on foot, chasing the gazelle for as much as four hours until it is worn out, for it seems that it cannot last longer than this before it weakens and lies down on the ground—in the position, I might add, in which the oryx is shown in the east Yemenite stelae (see Fig. No. I). These "Bedouin" do not even drink during the chase or they would be unable to continue running, nor do they eat bread, but carry a few grains of millet in a cloth and chew at these when they feel hunger. I dare say that tribesmen might be found in eastern Yemen who hunted after a like fashion, but for the last two decades the arrival of the motor truck or Landrover has brought in a new kind of hunting and nearly led to the extinction of some species. I do not think the Hunt described here existed on the Persian Gulf, for when I asked Amīr Suḥaim of the Āl T̲h̲ānī of Qaṭar about it he knew nothing of the kind, and the mediaeval hunting of the Mameluke type of the anecdotes of Usāmah b. Munqid̲h̲, related with charming simplicity, is quite different altogether.

K̲h̲azrajī speaks, in several places, of the hunting in the Yemen of the wild ass, but this seems to have been purely for sport, and if there are any wild asses left in eastern Yemen or in Ḥaḍramawt I have at least not heard tell of them. In the Ma'rib-Baiḥān region Ibn al-Mujāwir,[4] writing in the latter half of the 7th/13th century, reports that ostriches (naᶜām), lynxes (fuhūd), gazelles (ẓibāʾ) and ibex (ayāyil) abound, but in 1954 in summer-time I only saw gazelle there and not many of them.

The famous Arab king, ᶜĀmir b. ᶜAbd al-Wahhāb, when preparing to attack the Jewish king in Baiḥān, so organised matters that he sent several bodies of soldiers to go to Baiḥān, ostensibly to hunt; they then converged on Baiḥān "from the uninhabited side" and captured the Jewish king.[5] In the summer of 1954 I made enquiries of the Baiḥānīs about this king who, apparently, was still vaguely remembered. It was stated that his headquarters were at Jabal al-S̲h̲iᶜbah, and that he was killed at al-Jidfirah, three-quarters of an hour to the south of Sūq ᶜAbdullāh, and marked on Professor H. von Wissmann's map.[6] The implication is that large-scale hunts on the fringes of Ramlat Saba'tain by tribes not local to the territory were not so uncommon as to excite surprise, but there is no clue as to how they were organised.

In the course of this study it will be seen that pillars or columns were sometimes associated with the Hunt, and it seems appropriate to remark here that when I asked the local people about an isolated column in the ruins of Hajar Kuḥlān of Baiḥān I was told its name was Zik̲h̲k̲h̲aiyirah; it would be interesting to discover its relation to

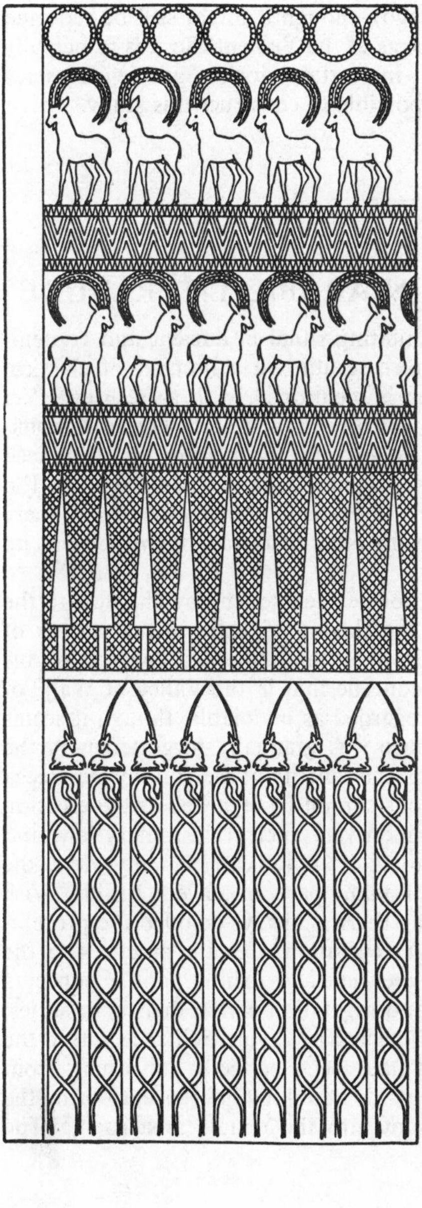

Fig. I
The red granite stets of Qarnāw in Jawf Bin Nāṣir. The seven circles at the top may refer to the star calendar. The two lines of ibexes face opposite directions, probably indicating the zig-zag path the Ibex takes to throw off its pursuers, and the line of patterning below may represent the mountains. The cross hatching below this with spear-like objects should be symbolic representation of the hunting net. A line of pairs of oryx, and below them a panel with decoration possibly representing lassos but the lasso is not known in the region now.

the city as a whole when the American Expedition publishes its account of this part of the site.

At present, however, it is only in Ḥaḍramawt that we know the organised Hunt, a survival of the ancient religion, is still in existence (or was so until a few years ago), though it might still be reported from some of the eastern districts of the Yemen.[7] So it is principally from information garnered in certain towns and villages of Ḥaḍramawt that it has been possible to construct this study.

RITUAL HUNTING IN ARABIC LITERATURE?

Aware of the existence of a hunting ritual in ancient and contemporary Southern Arabia, I have scrutinised a number of classical Arabic texts in which hunting is mentioned, with a fresh eye. Yet though it may be that a thorough review of early literature could reveal a knowledge of this heathen cult, my reading has produced little direct evidence, with the exception of the passage from Ibn Hishām *infra*. However, there are small pointers here and there which, taken in conjunction with other evidence, might be built up into a completer picture.

Many writers and legal authorities devote lengthy chapters to the stringent regulations against the slaying of game in the *ḥarams* of Mecca and Medina.[8] The Prophet himself was obliged, in his negotiations with Thaqīf, to concede that in the Valley of Wajj[9] of al-Ṭā'if the game should be regarded as inviolable, though it seems that the sacredness of the place was gradually forgotten with the march of time and emphasis on the sanctity of the Ḥaramain, Mecca and Medina.[10] These regulations cannot be regarded as the creation of Islām, but must be based upon very ancient customary law, and the great variety of the detail in itself indicates, in my view, the existence of such restrictions in many parts of ancient Arabia. With the prohibition against hunting there is always coupled the prohibition against cutting trees and vegetation. Certain practices in the South Arabian *ḥawṭahs* or sacred enclaves exhibit parallel concepts of the sacredness of animals and vegetation within their boundaries.

While wild animals were protected by divine influence within the *ḥaram* of Mecca, it seems to have been perfectly consistent, from what follows, to go hunting outside it and, by inference, to bring the spoils and trophies of the hunt into the temple area itself.[11] The

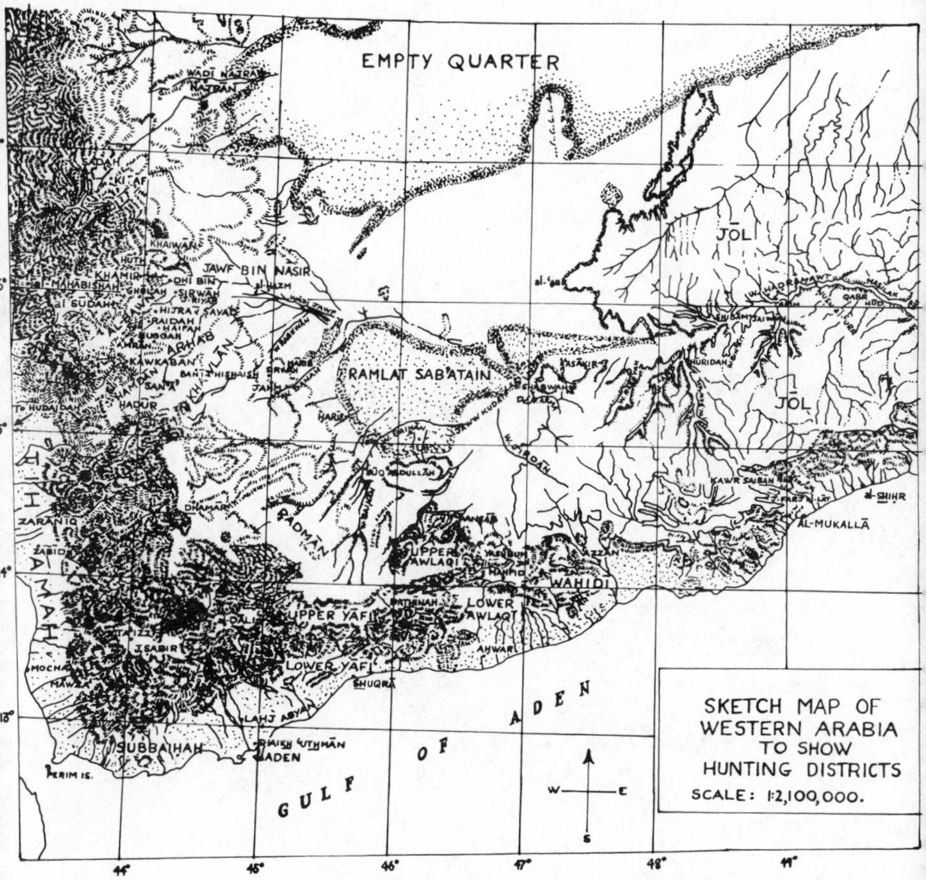

EMPTY QUARTER
WADI NAJRAN
NAJRAN
JAWF BIN NASIR
KHAIWAN
HUTH
KHAMIR
DHI BIN
SIRWAH
al SUDAH
HIJRA
RAIDAH
ARHAB
KAWKABAN
SAN'A
HADUR
KHAWLAN
RAMLAT SAB'ATAIN
JOL
JOL
SHABWAH
W. HADRAMAWT
QABR HUD
HURIDAH
KAWR SAIBAN
al SHIHR
AL-MUKALLA
WAHIDI
AZZAN
UPPER AWLAQI
LOWER AWLAQI
UPPER YAFI
LOWER YAFI
AHWAR
SHUQRA
DHAMAR
RADMAN
ZARANIQ
ZABID
TAIZZ
MOCHA
LAHJ
ABYAN
SUBBAIHAH
ADEN
PERIM IS.
GULF OF ADEN
TO HUDAIDAH
W
E
S
17°
16°
15°
14°
13°
44°
45°
46°
47°
48°
49°
SKETCH MAP OF
WESTERN ARABIA
TO SHOW
HUNTING DISTRICTS
SCALE: 1:2,100,000.

Sīrah[12] tells us that, "it was not long before Ḥamzah b. ᶜAbd al-Muṭṭalib approached with his bow slung over his shoulder, returning from a hunt (*qanaṣ*) of his, for he was keen on game (*ṣāḥib qanaṣ*) which he used to shoot, and which would come out to him (or — to which he would go out). When he returned from his hunt he never joined his family until he had performed the circumambulation of the Kaᶜbah. When he did this, he would not pass by a group of Quraish (sitting at the Kaᶜbah) without stopping to greet them and talk with them, for he was the noblest youth (*fatā*) in Quraish and the most fiery in spirit".

This scene recalls to me at once a group of Saiyids who used to sit in front of the Jawhar mosque in Tarīm in the late afternoon, chatting before performing the Maghrib prayer. Holy places—mosques—have always been resorted to for informal gatherings.

The salient fact here is that the returning hunter circumambulates the Kaᶜbah which has embodied in its walls a sacred stone; this element of the hunting ceremony is precisely the same as that in Dammūn today.[13] Whatever explanation may be given for Ḥamzah's action, I cannot dissociate it from hunting ritual, and it might indicate that there was something closely approaching a ritual hunt in Mecca itself. It may seem slender evidence upon which to base such a contention, but so much has been pruned of the past by the time that *Sīrah* material was compiled that there is hardly anything to show that pagan life which Muslims like Ḥamzah lived before, and even after their conversion. The memory of Muslim heroes could not be desecrated by the ascription of heathen rites to them. Furthermore the *Sīrah* has eliminated all but the principal actors, and we are not told that Ḥamzah had with him parties of townsfolk. He may have hunted alone, though in Ḥaḍramawt, in the organised hunt, the guns rely on beaters, and the guns are always tribesmen. It may possibly have been that in ancient Arabia the bowmen also were tribesmen, but not men of the class of *miskīns* or *ḍaᶜīfs*. Through the accession of Ḥamzah to his cause, Muḥammad's reputation was enhanced,[14] Ḥamzah's name being coupled with that of ᶜUmar. Could Ḥamzah have held an office of some sort in relation to a ritual hunt? To revert to the question of the spoils of the hunt—as the text stands, Ḥamzah went straight to the Kaᶜbah, so he must have taken his trophies of the chase with him, the gazelle, or ibex, or whatever it was he had won. May it not fairly be deduced that he went to thank the protector of the game within the Ḥaram for these trophies which he had slain outside it, and perhaps by analogy with the Hunt in south Arabia, maybe even to offer the portion of meat due to the shrine and its attendants? Philby thought that I go too far here, and he pointed out to me that when he lived in Mecca, any person leaving the town would ordinarily, as he returned, visit the Kaᶜbah, rather perhaps as Ḥaḍramīs, returning to Tarīm, would visit the cemeteries and their ancestors there before going to their own houses. Philby's view is supported by an account in al-Wāqidī[15] of the return of ᶜUrwah b. Masᶜūd to al-Ṭāᶜif, "And his tribe (*qawm*) forbade/disapproved his entering his house before he should go to al-Rabbah" (the Lady—i.e. the goddess al-Lāt).

We learn too, from the Traditions[16] that the Prophet "prayed in the Kaᶜbah, and he saw two horns hung up in the Kaᶜbah and ordered them to be veiled (takh̲mīr), i.e. covered, lest they distract the person praying, through looking at them". Azraqī, who describes them as the horns of a *kabs̲h̲* (a ram, but it might mean simply a male animal), adds that they were painted the significant colour red with *mag̲h̲rah* or *mis̲h̲q*, red clay, perhaps the same substances as used in the rock drawings of southern Arabia.[17] This latter must surely be the same as the dark red *mis̲h̲k* (sic) which, in 1972, I saw being used in S̲h̲ibām Kawkabān to decorate pottery—it was stated to be earth or disintegrated rock and to come from K̲h̲awlān.

Crescents, emblems of the Moon-God, were also hung up in the Kaᶜbah. The authenticity or otherwise of the Tradition is not really a matter of importance, for it is the attitude expressed therein that counts. Horns, trophies of the chase, we may be fairly sure, are tolerated, even though it be with mild disapproval, within the sacred fane itself. The very disapproval of their presence testifies that they were not placed there merely as an ornament, a *zīnah*, as Ḥaḍramīs would say. Professor al-G̲h̲ūl has referred me to al-Bundārī's[18] account of the Saljūq, Maliks̲h̲āh, who, at the end of the 5th century A.H., leaving Kūfah to bid farewell to the pilgrims setting out on the *ḥajj*, busied himself with hunting till, when he reached a place called al-Subaiᶜah, he built a minaret onto which he fixed the horns of the gazelles and hoofs of the wild asses he had killed en route. The place became known as Manārat al-Qurūn. The traveller Ibn Jubair, passing that way about a little less than a century later, puts the place some three days south of Kūfah and says the minaret stood in a wilderness with no buildings around it.[19] It had the form of a conical column with patterns of baked brick, "all of it covered with gazelle horns fixed into it, so that it looks like the back of a hedgehog". There were stories about it which he does not relate, so that it will never be known whether there were religious or superstitious ideas associated with it. Horns have never ceased to be fixed on to buildings not only in southern Arabia but in many other parts of the Islāmic world. In Wādī Jirdān there were horns set in a *mudᶜā* of a saint, Kuwaib, above the side of the *wādī*, and the tomb of ᶜAbd al-Ḥaqq the ancestor of the famous family of hereditary appeal judges (*manqads*) also had ibex horns set in it. In the Wādī Ḥalfā district of the Sudan, our friend Dr. Aḥmad Muḥammad ᶜAlī al-Ḥākim[20] has found bull's horns set on a sort of column crudely representing a man, and somewhat similar to the south Arabian *mudᶜā/midᶜā*. I have also seen in the Balkh district of Afghanistan horns set at the head of a tomb though I cannot recollect whether they were bull's or ram's horns, or those of some other animal, domestic or wild.

We know that, before Islâm, a golden image of a gazelle in the Kaᶜbah was stolen.[21] For the purpose of this study it is not really the gazelle which is significant, but the ibex. Yet we find the term *ẓaby* (gazelle) includes the ibex (*waᶜl*) and that even the word *baqar* or cattle can mean the ibex.[22] It is unnecessary however to press the point as to the exact species of the animal which was portrayed—it is enough that there should have been such an image at all, a votive offering perhaps, and this immediately links the Meccan sanctuary with the cults of Southern Arabia, where the ibex is the commonest motive of decoration. We even find that it is game of the deer family under the general name of *baqar* which come and rub themselves against the gate of the fort of Ukaidir of Dūmat al-Jandal to entice Ukaidir to hunt them and thus fall into the hands of the Muslim raiders.[23] A strange verse is quoted on this event,[24]

تَبارَكَ سائقُ البَقَرَاتِ إنّى   رأيتُ اللهَ يَهْدِي كلَّ هادي

> Blessed is the Driver of the (wild) cows, for I
> saw Allah guiding every leading animal.

Undeniably the epithet "Driver of the Wild Cows" is reminiscent of "Ilmaqah/Ilumqah Lord of Ibexes" (Baᶜl Awᶜāl-an).[25]

It could possibly be that in pre-Islāmic times a ritual hunt was associated with the worship of Allāh in Mecca, Allāh protecting the game in his *ḥaram*, but the game being lawful to the hunter outside it, and the ritual hunt being a special ceremony distinguished from ordinary hunting. In the case of the ritual hunt (it may be suggested perhaps even in ordinary hunting) tribute of the spoils of the game would be presented to Allāh at the Kaᶜbah. The Prophet consistently demanded of Quraish that they should return to the worship of the one God, Allāh, and it does seem quite possible that the Meccan

Pantheon was an accretion, due to the rise of Mecca as a commercial centre frequented by many tribes, perhaps till, indeed, the worship of Allāh, the special diety of Quraish was overlaid by the worship of many other Gods. So it may be speculated that we might look to Southern Arabia for the origins of a cult of a ritual hunt established at pre-Islāmic Mecca in association with a sanctuary primarily that of Allāh, though any evidence is, at best, slender indeed.

Even if it be thought over-bold to argue the existence of a ritual hunt for pre-Islāmic Mecca, there are certain indications that it did not disappear in the South with the advent of Islām. Al-Hamdānī[26] refers to a Ḥāshid section (*baṭn*) of Hamdān known as al-Ṣayad, stemming from Kaᶜb al-Ṣā'id, presumably to be rendered as "Hunters". At a place, which the editor of *Iklīl X*[27] speculates may be Ṣāghir of the Najrān district that lies within the area where the ancient ritual hunt was carried on, al-Hamdānī refers to a group which he describes as "*min aqnaṣ al-ᶜArab*, the most hunting of the Arabs". Yet again, discussing the word *dasara* he gives an example, "*Ṭaᶜana 'l-ṣaid wa-dasara fi 'l-shabakah*, the game thrust and butted in the net".[28] A group of the ᶜUmrīyūn or ᶜAmrīyūn which mixed with the Bal-Ḥārith at al-Raḥbah he describes as "*al-qunnāṣ sayyāḥat-un/an bi-'l-Yaman ᶜala 'l-qanṣ*".[29] Though the interpretation of this phrase is most dubious, it seems to describe itinerant hunters, and further on he says that they are the most hunting of Hamdān (*aqnaṣ Hamdān*).

Yet more curious is what Ibn al-Mujāwir[30] reports of the Arabs of the Tihāmah from Mawzaᶜ to the provinces of Abyan, with all the ᶜAqārib (the modern ᶜAqrabī tribe?). "When one of them finds a gazelle having died of itself (*ghazāl-an maitah*[31]) they take it and wash it, enshroud it, and bury it. For seven days, mourning for the gazelle continues amongst all the tribes, splitting their neck-openings (*juyūb*[32]), cutting their hair, and scattering dust on the partings. When they are asked what they are about, they say, 'We act according to the basis (*aṣl*), and believe in abandoning the branch (*farᶜ*)'." He remarks that they are people who claim to love God and (love) in God (*maḥabbat-an li-'llāh wa-fi 'llāh*), and says that these people are known as the *Banu 'l-Ḥārith*. On this the sole comment I can make is that the Arabs of the area seem ready enough nowadays to kill gazelle, and certain Ṣubaiḥīs even hunt them on camel-back.[33] In the summer of 1940 I recall eating gazelle freshly killed on the Ṣubaiḥī coast, west of Khawr al-ᶜUmairah. A hole was dug in the sand and a drift-wood fire lit in it—when it was reduced to hot coals the gazelle steaks were put on top of them, and the pit covered with palm-mat and earth to form an oven—the meat was delicious!

THE *TALBIYAH* STANZAS OF THE GOD AL-NASR AND THE HUNT

A pre-Islāmic *talbiyah* reported by Ibn Ḥabīb seems to have preserved a reference to hunting or game (*ṣaid/ṣīd*) which, taken in conjunction with other historico-geographical data, would appear to throw some new light on the ritual Hunt in ancient Southern Arabia. It is quite clear to me that, in essence, the *talbiyah* is simply a conventional chant declaimed by tribesmen, doubtless to a traditional jingle, as they approach the sanctuary to perform a pilgrimage or visitation, such as the pieces I have already published in connection with the *ziyārah* to the prophet Hūd. I have now even a recording of the curious and ancient *tahwīd* which is sung on this latter occasion. Although the early antiquarian writers of Islām quote but a few of these *talbiyahs*, all my experience of Arabia leads me to believe that there would be an almost infinite number of *talbiyahs* and variations of them, and the tribesmen might declaim them in their traditional wording or even extemporise new versions en route to the sanctuary —and I cannot accept the antiquarian view that they were so fixed and confined within distinct groups as the writers imply.

The god "Nasr belonged to Ḥimyar", says Ibn Ḥabīb, "And it (Ḥimyar) used to come to him with animals for sacrifice (*tansuku-hu*) and venerate him and worship him (*tadīn lahu*). He (Nasr) was in G͟humdān,[35] the castle of the king (*malik*) of the Yemen." Ibn al-Kalbī[36] however places Nasr in the land of Saba', in a place called Balk͟haᶜ (though it is possible this last name is corrupt), and he adds that Nasr was worshipped by Ḥimyar and their neighbours.

Now, south of Ramlat Saba'tain (The Sand of the two Saba's?)[37] and a few miles north-east of al-ᶜUqlah where some of the hunting inscriptions are found, close to S͟habwah, are two isolated little peaks known as al-Nasr al-Qiblī and al-Nasr al-S͟harqī, i.e. the northern and eastern Nasrs (Eagles). Dr. Brian Doe tells me that as one comes over to S͟habwah from Ḥuṣn al-ᶜAbr these Nasrs stand out as landmarks. I propose that these peaks are so named because they were in some way identified with the god Nasr. There were many more sanctuaries of the pre-Islāmic gods than the one single sanctuary that the early Arab antiquarians might at times lead one to suppose was alone the cult centre of a particular god. There are many cases in which a rock or a small hill is identified or associated with a pre-Islāmic god. Indeed Yāqūt quotes a verse which is attributed to a poet of the *Jāhilīyah* who has the interesting name of ᶜAmr b. ᶜAbd al-Jinn,[38]

> Now, (I swear) by blood flowing in streams which
> you would think (when you see it) on the single
> peak of al-ᶜUzzā and (that of?) al-Nasr, was
> brazil-wood.

This immediately brings to my mind's eye, a rock cliff with caves in its face near the headquarters of Saif al-Islām al-Ḥasan b. Yaḥyā at al-Kitāf—which I passed by in 1964. The flat side of the cliffs below the caves had long streams of blood, dry or fresh, from animals slaughtered at the caves—in this case merely for food—and the blood is a sort of boast of affluence or generosity not uncommon in southern Arabia. The allusion of ᶜAmr, "the son of the Servant of the Jinn", is to the many animals sacrificed on the little peaks that either held the sanctuaries of al-ᶜUzzā and al-Nasr, or which were identified themselves with these divinities; the blood flowing from the slaughtered animals turned the sides of the rock as red as brazil-wood. Another god Saᶜd worshipped by Kinānah, is described as "a rock in a desert" upon which blood is poured.

To this very day Ḥimyar is very close to Shabwah for the neighbouring Wāḥidī tribes claim Ḥimyar descent. For their borders are perhaps only two or three days' march from Shabwah itself. Al-Hamdānī[39] states that Shabwah is a town belonging to Ḥimyar, "and when Ḥimyar and Madḥij (Madhḥij) fought together the inhabitants of Shabwah came out of Shabwah and settled in Ḥaḍramawt, Shibām being named after them". Not even an approximate date is quoted by al-Hamdānī for this event, though one assumes it took place before Islām. Into this context of Shabwah town, one time a centre for the ancient Hunt, if one be permitted to deduce this from inscription Philby 84, held by Ḥimyar at some period presumably more recent than this inscription, then lost to it, with which the name of the Ḥimyar god Nasr is still associated, the *talbiyah* of the god Nasr fits so nearly that it seems almost too good to be true,

لَبَّيْكَ أَللّهُمَّ لَبَّيْكْ
لَبَّيْكَ إِنَّنَا عَبِيدْ
وَكِلْ لَنَا مَيْسَرَةً عَتِيدْ
وَأَنْتَ رَبُّنَا ٱلْحَمِيدْ
أُرْدُدْ لَنَا مُلْكَنَا وَٱلصَّيْدْ

Labbaik, o God, labbaik![40]
Labbaik, for we are worshippers/slaves.
Measure out to us abundance/time of ease, made ready.
You are our Blessed Lord.
Restore to us our rights of possession and our game/hunting.[41]

The stanza, in *rajaz*-metre naturally, has an interesting pattern.[42] I have made one slight alteration to the text in line 2, substituting *wa-kil lanā for wa-kullu-nā* (if it is to be so vocalised), but in fact this does not add a single letter or vowel to the line. Possibly the original collector of the verses even made a slip in transcription. To justify the modification, I must quote a stanza from a poem on the 28 stars of the working year, dictated to me by a tribal poet of the Bā ᶜAwḍah of the ᶜAzzān district in the Wāḥidī sultanate, ᶜAlī b. Ḥamad b. ᶜAwaḍ—the Bā ᶜAwḍah are of course Ḥimyar. This poem he gave me verse by verse during the course of our travels with Sulṭān Nāṣir on his progression through the sulṭanate in December 1947. I cannot now remember whether ᶜAlī b. Ḥamad composed the verses especially for me or not, but in either case they follow rigidly traditional lines, and I seem to remember he was unlettered. On my last visit there in 1964 I heard he was dead, killed some years before, and I could not therefore reconsult him.

لَـكْلِيل لا كال مِيكايِيل وَآمْـسا يِكِيل ْ[43]
يِمْسِي يِسقِّي بِسَيْلَهْ مِن عَشَـاء لا مَقِيل ْ
ولا مُرَوِّحْ ولا سارِحْ بِخَطّ ٱلسَّبِيل ْ
يِذْرَوْن حَبَّ ٱلسُّحَيْبِي جَمّ وِلّا قَلِيل ْ
وَٱلا ٱلطَّهَفْ ذي ضِيَادَهْ يِحْبَلَون حَبِيل ْ
ما تِسْمَع ٱلا حَنِينَ ٱلرَّعْد بِدْقَام سُودْ

(توشيح)

يا رَبّ تَسْتَرْ علَيْنا يا كريمَ ٱلوُجودْ

Al-Iklīl, if Mīkāyīl gives good measure, and at evening pours out (rain).
Watering with his flood from evening until afternoon,
And none pass at night along the highway, nor go out along it in the morning to work,

They sow *suḥaibī*[44] millet grain, much of it or little, or else *ṭahaf*-millet[44] the stalk of which they twine into foddering twists,
Nor can you hear aught but the thunder rumbling on the black mountain crests.
O Lord, protect us (from all harm), O Generous of riches!

In Wāḥidī country the star Kalīl/al-Iklīl was said to be the *abū* of the season *ṣaif*, i.e. the first thirteen days or so in April. Mīkāyīl, Michael the Archangel, described to me as "he who measures out the rain (*alla<u>dh</u>ī yikīl al-maṭar*)", is pictured as dealing out measures of rain as if they were corn or oil, and he is the Islāmic successor to the pagan <u>Sh</u>ams, Lady of Maifaᶜ of the hunting inscription *infra* (p. 35). The floods sweep down from the mountains into the narrow *wādīs* of Wāḥidī country which are also its roads, and so long as they are in full spate, they render them impassable.

I have already translated the late Saiyid ᶜAlawī b. Ṭāhir al-Ḥaddād's account[45] of how the Bedouin, i.e. the tribespeople, circumambulate the tomb of <u>Sh</u>ai<u>kh</u> Saᶜīd in Wādī Dawᶜan chanting *zāmils*, probably quite similar to the pre-Islāmic *talbiyahs*, peremptorily demanding that the saint accord them rain—to these I might add a *zāmil* which I took down from our ᶜAwlaqī soldiers in 1941, addressing the Bā Nāfiᶜ saint of Wādī Ya<u>sh</u>bum. They sang this on a day of floods at Ḍāliᶜ after heavy spring rains.

يا شَيْخَنا يا عُبَيْد آليَوْم شارَهْ   الله يِدِّى لَكَ النُّور فَوْق أَلْمَنارَهْ

O, our <u>Sh</u>ai<u>kh</u>, O ᶜUbaid, a sign be yours today,[46]
Above your minaret, God give you light we pray.

There is a spirit common to that of the tribesmen demanding rains from <u>Sh</u>ai<u>kh</u> Saᶜīd of Dawᶜan, and certain verses quoted by al-Mubarrad[47] from the Umaiyad period. The rude tribesmen (*al-jufāt min al-Aᶜrāb*), he says, use the phrase, "May you have no father", in begging and demanding. Sulaimān b. ᶜAbd al-Malik (Caliph from A.D. 715–17) heard one of them say, in a year of drought,

رَبَّ العِبادِ ما لَنا وما لَكَا   قدْ كُنْتَ تَسْقِينا فما بَدَا لَكَا
أَنْزِلْ علَيْنا الغَيْثَ لا أَبا لَكَا

Lord of worshippers—what *has* gone wrong between us?
What's come over you? You used to send rain to us.
Send down good rains on us—may you be fatherless!

To revert once more to the *talbiyah* stanza of the god Nasr, it could be interpreted as a demand to Nasr by his servants of the Ḥimyar group to restore to them S̲h̲abwah district and the hunting territories there. Since however there is of course no sort of proof that the *talbiyah* expresses Ḥimyar's desire to recover S̲h̲abwah—which is on the main highway from Ḥaḍramawt to the Yemen, nor is there even the slightest chronological indication that these data are linked in point of time, one can go no further.

It would be reasonable to infer that the "hunt" or "game" which Ḥimyar desires the god to restore to it, has also certain ritual implications, and this is more than the mere wish to recover lost hunting territories.

HUNTING IN ḤAḌRAMAWT IN THE EARLY ᶜABBĀSID PERIOD

As the main part of this study is concerned with hunting in Ḥaḍramawt, an incident narrated by Ṭabarī[48] is particularly relevant. The ᶜAbbāsid Caliph al-Manṣūr made a man of the Arabs, perhaps he means tribal Arabs, his governor over Ḥaḍramawt, but his postmaster there wrote to the Caliph accusing the governor that, "He goes out frequently in search of game (*ṣaid*), with hawks (or falcons, *buzāh*) and dogs which he has made ready". So al-Manṣūr deposed him, and wrote to him, "What is this equipage (*ᶜuddah*) which you have prepared to inflict slaughter (*nikāyah*) on wild animals (*waḥs̲h̲*)?" It is of course well known that the postmasters were the spies and information service of the Caliphial government.

There is a tantalising lack of detail. Hawks are not nowadays used for hunting by Ḥaḍramīs, nor have I come across allusions to them in the Ḥaḍramī histories. The most suitable country for hawking however would surely be in western Ḥaḍramawt in the S̲h̲abwah region where the country is open, or in the steppe land north of the Jōls. The pretext for dismissing the man was re-echoed in the sentiment, expressed to me in recent years, of pity for the animals, but I wonder if al-Manṣūr's displeasure could have been partially motivated by some religious attitude.[49]

POPULAR CONCEPTIONS OF THE HUNT

The artisans and petty tradesmen (*masākīn*), said my s̲haik̲h in Tarīm, love hunting, and in former times they were very much given to it. There was, perhaps still is, a saying amongst them, "The Hunt is the sixth Pillar of Islām (*Al-qaniṣ sādis arkān al-Islām*)". S̲haik̲h Hādī b. Ṣāliḥ Bā Ḥātim of Madūdah told me that al-Zubaidī who resides near the village of Maryamah, himself a hunting judge, informed him that, "A Jinnī founded the Hunt (*Jinnī assas al-qanāṣah*)". The following verse also gives expression to the holy nature of the Hunt,

قال بَدّاع القَوَافِي أَلْقَنِيص آلا اعتبارْ   مِنْ تَرَكْ باب القَنَاصَه عِنْد خَلْق الله بارْ

Says the maker of these verses,
The Hunt must be held respected.
He who fails to go a-hunting
By God's creatures is rejected.[50]

Of (doubtless many) popular saws which draw upon the Hunt I have noted, "A halloo on the mountain is better than a chest (of gold, or the like) at home (*Ṣaiḥah fi 'l-Jabal aḥsan min ṣundūq fi 'l-dār*)", and, "The burn in the cloth (affects) one person, but the success (in the Hunt) belongs to the entire Hunt (*Al-ḥurq fi 'l-t̲hawb wāḥid – al-jamīlah li-'l-qaniṣ*)".[51] This latter saying emphasises of course the corporate nature of the institution. Another proverb runs, "If you should seem to have two pressing needs (at the one time), then pay no attention to the need to go hunting (*Id̲hā badat lak ḥājatain, utruk ḥājat al-qanāṣah*)".[52] That is to say, you should concentrate on the important matter and leave aside the less necessary or trivial. They also say, "Get your ibex and then hunt no more (*Wiᶜl-ak wa-lā ᶜād taqnaṣ*)", i.e., "Be content with the good fortune that you already have". Rather similar to this is the proverb cited by the late Saif al-Quᶜaiṭī of Ḥaidarābād, "If you shoot (a lot) at the game it flees and leaves (*Id̲hā ḍarabt al-jull is̲htall*)". An interesting proverb that he included in his collection[54] is, "*Zurbiṭānah taṣīd k̲hair min bunduq yuk̲hṭi*', a blow-pipe (?) that gets (something) is better than a gun which misses". This is explained as meaning that any trifling thing, if it helps you achieve what you want, is better than a great one which does not do so. Or the Ḥaḍrami may be admonished by "*Fī'l-s̲habak akbar min al-ḍabᶜ*, The (hunting) net contains bigger (game) than the hyena", i.e. "Things are much worse than expected". Al-Quᶜaiṭī records a shortened version of the second proverb supra, "*Al-jamālah li-'l-qanis*".[55] This, he considers, means that the successes belong to the hunter, though all people take part in the festivities that follow upon the slaying of an ibex.

Should the huntsmen fail to obtain game, they say, "Our hunting party is tainted (*Al-qanīṣ ḥaqqa-nā mud̲h̲aiyam*)". All the Quarter (*Ḥāfah*) searches to see what wrong action they have committed. Or the people would say to them, "You have a taint (*ᶜInda-kum d̲h̲aim*). You crossed the road which belongs to the Sūq Quarter (those addressed perhaps being of the K̲h̲ulaif Quarter of Tarīm) without any justification (*ḥaqq*) or injury (*g̲h̲alaṭ*) done you by the Sūq Quarter". "So," said my informant, "they seek to clear their hearts (*ṭībat k̲h̲āṭir*) from sin, in order that they may obtain success in their hunting". Yet again another informant told me that if, on the Hunt, you cannot hit any game you lodge a pledge (*ᶜarbūn*) with the headman (*muqaddam*) of the Hunt. If you see game (*ṣaid*) and fire at it but your gun does not go off, you say, "This is the pledge of the Hunt (*hād̲h̲ā ᶜarbūn al-qanīṣ*)". Then, if you have done this and do hit the game when you fire again you realise that it was something of yours that prevented you from hitting the animal previously. Someone will take the article pledged to the *muqaddam*.

In no way is the consecrated nature of the Hunt more clearly in evidence than in this conception of *d̲h̲aim* which I render as "taint". In Tarīm the term *mud̲h̲aiyam* was explained to me by my s̲h̲aik̲h̲ variously as, "*Sāsuh k̲h̲ārib, nāqiṣ, muta'at̲h̲t̲h̲ir, mug̲h̲aiyar, muk̲h̲arbaṭ*", i.e. "His foundation/basis[56] is destroyed, lacking (in honour, virtue, etc.), affected (by some ill), corrupted, disordered". It is deceit, error (*k̲h̲iyānah, g̲h̲alaṭ*), "Taint" can result from an action morally wrong, or from an action formally incorrect—though in all probability the huntsmen make no such distinction. My Tarīmī s̲h̲aik̲h̲ discussing the nature of *d̲h̲aim*, stated that causes of failure to obtain game might be robbing of one's fellow (*nahb ak̲h̲ūh*), someone not having prayed (*ḥadd mā ṣallā*), someone having cheated another over something (*ḥadd tazaiyad ᶜalā ḥadd bi-s̲h̲ī*). The *Abū* or Headman perhaps has cheated the hunters in the matter of the money deposited with him to meet the expenses of the Hunt in the way of food and equipment. Or else two men may have come to hunt while there is still a quarrel between them which has not been composed. "For," he said, "the Hunt has to be prepared for by certain laws (*qawānīn*) rather like the laws (*qawānīn*) of the Prayer". It is also forbidden to eat on the Hunt[57] until the Headman (*Abū*) gives the order, and I am inclined to regard the latter transgression as an action which has a formal incorrectness about it like the Madūdah law-case

No. 3[58], though I suppose that to eat while one's fellows were still unable to do so might be regarded, in some degree, as immoral.

After the huntsmen have sat down together and questioned each other so as to try to discover what is wrong, and they find where the fault lies, they make a judgement (*ḥukm*) over the person or persons at fault—the latter pay for the slaughter of a sheep over the *ṭaw*ᶜ-pole of the net, and the meat is partaken of by all. Cases are judged by the usual procedure of resorting to the oath, where this is necessary. The Hunt judges in the Tarīm area may be the Headman of the Quarters, Mawlā Dammūn, or a tribal judge, Mawlā Tāribah, etc., but much of this procedure will emerge when I can publish a full study of the organisations of the Quarters of the cities of Ḥaḍramawt. For example a Quarter document from Tarīm dated 1204 A.H. (A.D. 1790), of which I have made a translation, contains the following provisio, "Now concerning the decisions on the Hunt (*aḥkām al-qanāṣah*) which have taken place, and the oath-takers of Mawla 'l-Sūq (Quarter)—Mawla 'l-K͟hulaif (Quarter) will approach Mawla 'l-Sūq (Quarter) with two large head of sheep, one to be slaughtered on the pole of the hunting net so as to make good heart for the hunting, on account of the former (disturbance or quarrel), and the other (sheep) by the house of the headmen, to appease the oath-takers (of the Sūq Quarter)". The same document stipulates that their routes to the hunting grounds (in the mountain) through Tarīm city are to keep to the established customary ways.

The Ḥaḍramī poet Rubaiyaᶜ b. Salīm says in a long political poem, though unfortunately I am not quite sure of the latter half of the line,[59]

وَالَ ٱلْقَنِيص ٱلآن مِبْ عادْ ذَيَّمُوه ْ كُلِّ مكانه ْ وَاو فِي مِرْبَاتُه ْ

The hunters no longer now accuse him of *d͟haim* (taint),
Each one is in his place like (the letter) *wāw* in his pass[60] (?) or sangar.

The word *d͟haim* appears in a name cited by al-Hamdānī.[61] "Of the As͟hrāf (s͟harīfs, nobles, evidently *not* descendants of the Prophet) of K͟haiwān b. Zaid, is Zaid D͟hū D͟haim b. Qais." Is it possible that the title D͟hū D͟haim was hereditary in this Yemenite family because it was a group that deal with cases of *d͟haim* or "taint", or others, referred to it by the hunters and tribes? We have no evidence at our disposal, but we can compare the Madūdah Mas͟hāyik͟h and their hunting court. The fifth century (A.H.) writer Abū ᶜUbaid al-Bakrī al-Awnabī[62] gives *d̲haim/d̲hām* the sense of *ᶜaib*, properly "a defect", but it has a great range of tribal technical connotations. The word *ḍaim* also would seem to bear a semantic relation to *d̲haim* in this sense.[63]

According to my friend Saiyid ᶜAlī b. ᶜAqīl,[64] "Every town or tribe has special mountains, it not being permitted to another town, in accordance with hunting law (*s̲h̲irᶜat al-qanṣ*), to hunt in them or to approach them. Often the trespassing over the boundaries in the hunting mountain leads to difficulties and arouses enmities which may end in fighting. The village of Madūdah was considered until recently the centre to which appeal was made to decide the difficulties and differences of the Hunt." Saᶜd al-Suwainī and ᶜAbūd of al-G̲h̲uraf mock at the village of al-Raiḍah for planting stones in order that a mountain may grow from them, in which they may hunt—for it seems that they have no mountain of their own, though they used to hunt in S̲h̲iᶜb al-S̲h̲aik̲h̲ and S̲h̲iᶜb Āl S̲h̲amlān, until prevented by the owners of these areas.[65] They have received a nickname, "*baqqalaw al-ᶜālī*, they planted the pounding-stone", in allusion to this tale.[66] Perhaps there is an echo of this fierce pride of possession of hunting grounds in the note of Jāḥiẓ on Muḥāriq b. S̲h̲ihāb b. Qais al-Tamīmī, according to the modern editor, probably a pre-Islāmic poet. He is asid to have praised certain people as having many ibex in their mountains, but he satirises others as having many coneys or hyrax (*wibār*).

At this point a slightly puzzling passage from *Iklīl X*[68] must be considered. Al-Hamdānī states that a certain Maslamah . . . al-K̲h̲aiwānī told him, "I read a *musnad* (pre-Islāmic inscription) at a hunting-place of gazelles (*maṣād ẓibā'*), at K̲h̲aiwān an ᶜĀdite (hunting-place) being called al-Madār (? the place of circumambulation) (which ran), 'A hunting-place of fat (*m ṣ y d s̲h̲aḥm*) belonging to Ayman b. B t ᶜ b. Hamdān.'[69] He (the narrator) said, 'By fat it means flesh'. Flesh (*laḥm*) is the bait (*ṭuᶜm*) to which hunting (birds) like the hawk (ṣaqar) are directed."[70]

Assuming al-Hamdānī's informant genuinely did read an inscription, and this I see no *prima facie* reason to doubt, we need not necessarily accept his interpretation of this *musnad* which I have translated formally, according to Lane's *Lexicon*. The K̲h̲aiwān he means should be the centre to the east of Ḥūt̲h̲ on the Ṣanᶜā'-Ṣaᶜdah road. The rendering of *s̲h̲aḥm* as *laḥm* is closely paralleled in Ḥaḍramī verse that I have published,[71] "*Mā qāniṣ iddasam*, lit., No hunter has eaten fat". By this meat is intended; Balād̲h̲urī's[72] *ṭāᶜimīna dasam-an* may be compared, and *dihin* is used in this same sense in the Sudan.

Mṣyd could mean a place where nets were set up if one interprets it in the sense of snare or trap, but it might conceivably mean a hunting-ground, and I should infer from the verse that hunting-grounds were owned, just as they are in Ḥaḍramawt today. The proper name al-Madār at once brings to mind the circumambulation ceremony which concludes the Hunt.[73]

Jamme's view that a Sabaean inscription from Riyām in Arḥab[74] contains the designation of specific areas for hunting would accord with what is current at the present time. There is some post-Islāmic evidence that hunting-grounds were owned before Islām, in addition to the passage I have just quoted, for there is a story that Zaid b. ᶜAbdullāh b. Dārim went as an envoy to one of the kings of Ḥimyar, and found him at a hunting-place belonging to him on a high mountain, and he saluted him, and mentioned to him his lineage. Hereupon the king said to him, "*Thib*"; meaning "*ijlis*" (sit). But the man thought it meant "Jump", as in Northern Arabia, and leapt over the mountain side.[75] Now, although the latter part of the story is not to be taken seriously, the scene fits the circumstances of today well, and in the Wāḥidī area which is Ḥimyar one might imagine such an incident taking place on the top of Jabal Kadūr though the story is not, in fact, set in this Ḥimyar area.

ᶜAlī b. ᶜAqīl also states that, "the period set (*maḥdūdah*) for hunting is three days, during which the hunters may obtain success". If they fail to obtain game they are exposed to the ridicule of the neighbouring villages.[76] The Hunt indeed has something of a heroic quality about it; this quality seems to be inherent too, in the ibex.[77]

SAIYID OPPOSITION TO THE HUNT

The Saiyid ulema have long been opposed to the organised Hunt, though many Saiyids do in fact engage in hunting and would no doubt join with the Quarters in this activity. Indeed the hunting poet ᶜAbd al-Ḥaqq in his verses often refers to the Saiyids, *al-ḥabā'ib*, in connection with the Hunt. These Saiyids would probably be criticised by the ulema for assimilating themselves to the tribes, as they indeed criticised the al-Shaikh Bū Bakr Saiyids of ᶜĪnāt, and others, in the past. Their opposition is, I think, attributable to two motives, firstly their instinctive recognition that here lies something pagan and un-Islāmic, secondly their long feud with the Mashāyikh who still seem largely to be associated with the Hunt, and their inveterate enmity toward tribalism which they have combatted or turned to their own account, with not inconspicuous success, over the centuries. The Saiyids are also strongly opposed to the Quarter organisation of the towns of Ḥaḍramawt and in general they strive to weaken it by all means in their power.

A poem in the Leiden MS.[78] collection of Ḥaḍramī verse by ᶜAbdullāh b. ᶜAlī al-Ḥaddād, in Banī Mig͟hrāh style and metre[79], is a direct attack upon the Hunt in colloquial language, as irreligious and sinful, and, in an admonitory treatise to the tribes, *Tad͟hkirat al-ᶜāqil min al-qabā'il*,[80] ᶜAbdullāh Bā ᶜAlawī quotes the following verses from a Saiyid poet who flourished about the end of the 17th century A.D.

فيا عجباً من كون كلّ قبيلة   تشدّد حكم الجاهلية والكفر
ومن كون أرباب القنيص وزمرة العبيـــد لهم حكم يمشّى بلا عـذر
وأحكام شرع الله مطروحة بلا   ملام على من زاغ عنها ولا نكر

Astounding is it indeed that every clan
To Unbelief and Pagan Law is partisan,
The Masters of the Hunt[81] and a mere pack of slaves
Their own Law should sustain—the which no excuse saves,
While the Commandments of God's Law are left aside,
And one who strays from them none doth reproach or chide.[82]

The theoretical legal position has also been stated by a number of the authorities, of which the most accessible is probably the collection known as *Bug͟hyat al-Mustars͟hidīn*[83] which says, "The widely known Hunt (*qanīṣ*) in Ḥaḍramawt is one of the most highly disapproved innovations (*bidaᶜ*) and evil things which bring (Ḥaḍramawt) into disgrace, on account of its transgressing what Islāmic law (*s͟harᶜ*) requires". It is averred that this type of hunt did not exist in the time of the Prophet and his Companions, "Because", continues the author, "a custom (*ᶜādah*) of theirs is that, when the killing of the game (*ṣaid*) is withheld from them, they say, '*Bikum d͟haim*', 'You have a taint in you', and they slaughter a sheep (*rās g͟hanam*) on the *ṭawᶜ*, i.e. the wooden pole by which the net is held up, so as to purify the Hunt (*qanīṣ*) from every doubt and evil prompting (*wiswās*), but slaughtering after this fashion does not expedite the killing of anything whose time is not at hand . . . So to slaughter in such a circumstance as this must fall within (one of) three categories—either one seeks thereby to approach one's God without making any created being partner to Him, being desirous of his pleasure and propinquity—which is a pious act and blameless; or else one seeks thereby to approach some (being) other than God as one seeks to approach Him, magnifying it as one magnifies God, as (in the case of) the (above)-mentioned slaughtering, by virtue of its being something with which he seeks propinquity, and upon which he relies to remove the taint (*dhaim*) upon him—this is Unbelief, and the (flesh of) the slaughtered beast is unlawful carrion (*maitah*); or else he intends neither the one nor the other, but slaughters it on such as the *ṭawᶜ*-pole, believing that slaughtering after this fashion removes the impediment mentioned, but without any other belief—this is not Unbelief, but it is forbidden and the slaughtered beast is unlawful carrion also (*maitah*)."

The slaughtering on the pole, says the author, is practised by the common people, as is *istiqrā'*.[84] He quotes Abū Makhramah,[85] a great legal authority who died in 972 A.H. (A.D. 1564–5), as distinguishing the three categories cited in the previous paragraph as applying to those who slaughter to the Jinn.[86] This is to be distinguished, on the contrary, from what is slaughtered for the Kaᶜbah, the Apostles, or for a scholar, (*ᶜālim*[87]), Sulṭān, or bride (*ᶜarūs*), for joy at their arrival, or to appease their anger, all the latter being lawful.[88] He adds that the Hunt has become "in our land" the medium for many vile actions (*qabā'iḥ*), such as indecency in words and actions (*al-tafāḥush fi 'l-aqwāl wa-'l-afᶜāl*), the forgetfulness of religious duties (*farā'iḍ*), the loss of money, and the mingling of women with men. "Notwithstanding," says the author, "they consider these good deeds (*ḥasanāt*), and not amongst the things forbidden". The actions of which the Saiyid complains take place, I was informed in Tarīm, at the ceremonies after the hunt, but I have already reported something of the sort at the *razīḥ*-dance which I first witnessed in 1947.[89]

Sulṭān Miḥsin (1295 A.H./ A.D. 1878–1343 A.H./A.D. 1924–5) was advised to put a stop to the Hunt, and since that time, said my shaikh, the laws (*qawānīn*) of hunting are disappearing if indeed they have not already disappeared, but it seems to me that his statement applies to Tarīm where Saiyid influence is so strong, and not to Madūdah where the Hunt evidently flourishes in its pristine vigour. The *dawlah*, i.e. the Sulṭān, he said, put a stop to much of the hunting at the instigation of the Sādah because Tarīm is considered a holy city—this sanctity of Tarīm might even be identified with Yāqūt's ᶜAbdalu—"a name of the city of Ḥaḍramawt", the name presumably meaning "servant of God" usually a personal name which is strange to find applied to a place, although Ḥaḍrami cities do have nicknames of diverse kinds.

A poet al-Fāris attacked the Saiyids for stopping the Hunt—a measure which they achieved through the intermediary of the Kat͟hīrī Sulṭāns whom they persuaded to this action, as, incidentally, they persuaded them to prohibit other *raᶜs͟hahs* or ceremonies traditional amongst the *masākīn* of Tarīm.[90] I can only quote the opening hemistich of the poem of al-Fāris which commences with the bitter words, again in Banī Mig͟hrāh metre,

[93] [91] نَصِيف ٱللّٰه في ناس مَلْبَسْهم فرَافِير • [92] ومِنْ كُثْر ٱلتَّحَيَّال يِشْبُون ٱلْعَتَارِير •
وَمَنْ عَطَّلْ قَنَاصتنا [94] يَعِلُّهْ في [95] وَسَطْ بِير •
عَسَى يا رَبّ صَلَّوْا عليه أَرْبَعْ تكابير •

إلى آخر ما قال :

شِوارِ آبْلِيس مَعْهم يِتَبْعُون ٱلتَّماوِير • [96] قَناصه طاهِرَه ما لها دَوْلَه ولا مِير •

God grant us justice on folk wearing white coats (on their backs),[97]
Who, for their very trickery, would climb up mountain tracks.
The man who spoils our hunting—may he fall plumb down a well.
Let them, O Lord, pray over him four *takbīrs* (for a knell).

Till he says at the end:

Devil's counsel in their heads, they pursue their wicked thought.
A hunt pure ours is—where Sulṭān and Emir are as nought.

The Āl Bā Farfārah are those who wear the *jubbah*, the long white coat which is the uniform of the Saiyids and many of the Mas͟hāyik͟h, and I suppose the allusion to climbing up mountain tracks means that they would go to any lengths in their trickery to avoid the simple straight and honest road. The last verse contrasts this scheming and plotting with the honest nature of the Hunt which is independent of such rulers as Sulṭāns and Emirs and is not sinful or wrong. To many Ḥaḍramīs, especially some forty years ago or more, such a poem must have seemed near blasphemy or impious, and I did not succeed in obtaining the whole satire. In the atmosphere of Tarīm as late as 1954 indeed I count it surprisingly broad-minded that the very existence of such a poem should be mentioned, and although it was a Saiyid who dictated the verses to me he excused himself from repeating a verse attacking the Saiyids for writing amulets, which he said he thought I should not hear from his lips, even should it come to me from other sources.[98] The reasons given me for this Saiyid démarche were, firstly because of their pity for the animals, especially in the case of killing females big with young, secondly because the hunters do not pray on the Hunt, there being no water for them to perform their ablutions, etc., and thirdly because of the disturbances and even pitched battles which flared up as the parties of hunters returning home flushed with success, passed through the town. The temptation for the young hot-heads of the party to cross a disputed Quarter boundary in the face of a rival Quarter on the watch for them, must have touched off many a bloody tussle.[99] As will be related *infra*, during the period of Yāfiᶜī tribal rule in Tarīm ᶜAbd al-Qawī G͟harāmah, the ruler of the Sūq Quarter, was satirised by his own *masākīn* when the rival Yāfiᶜī ruler of al-K͟hilaif Quarter prevented them from going forth to the Hunt by way of the ᶜAidīd suburb. ᶜAbd al-Qawī straightway again sent them out to hunt by way of ᶜAidīd headed by a body of his own armed slaves to wipe out the insult offered to his power.

The first of these reasons, the sentiment of compassion for the hunted animals has already been noticed in the curious message sent by the Caliph al-Manṣūr to his governor in Ḥaḍramawt,[100] and, in view of the account of the same sentiment that is to follow, one may speculate that it is somehow linked with the religious or semi-religious notions that have agglomerated around the Hunt.

An article by the Aden historian Ḥamzah ᶜAlī Luqmān, now settled in Ṣan'ā', entitled "Hunters of the sacred animals"[101] which appeared in Aden after the bulk of this study had been written, contributes some additional details from the Kat͟hīrī state. These were derived from ᶜUbaid Surūr al-Jābirī whom he describes as one of the best ibex hunters in Ḥaḍramawt, adding that his grandfather was an ex-slave in the royal palace at Saiwūn. ᶜUbaid knows all the cliffs around Saiwūn and Tarīm. ᶜUbaid stated to Luqmān that the hunters cannot differentiate between the male and female ibex, but they are extremely sorry to kill a female. Once he was about to press the trigger with an ibex in his sights when he felt his finger paralysed, and saw the ibex looking into his eyes. Fearlessly it moved and disappeared behind the rocks. ᶜUbaid climbed up to the rock where he had seen it and, from its tracks, perceived that it was pregnant. "While praising Almighty God about the inspiration," writes Luqmān, "ᶜUbaid heard a sound and looked upwards—to see the shape of a big ibex standing proudly like a fine statue". This ibex he did shoot, as also two others. "He thought it was a gift from God because he did not kill the pregnant ibex."

Luqmān attended hunters' dances at Ḥawṭat Aḥmad b. Zain al-Ḥabs͟hī in Saiwūn town, but he does not state whether the

Ḥabs͟hī Saiyids had any link with the Hunt. He does however remark that, according to custom, the meat of the ibex is distributed amongst all the hunters, and the best part is presented to a Saiyid family in the vicinity of which the ibex was hunted. The hunters, he says, respect the Saiyids as sons of the Prophet, and believe that by surrendering this tribute their next hunt would be blessed. (I suppose he means that the hunters would have "*barakah*" which is more nearly rendered in English as "luck" than "blessing".) No hunter ever dared to ignore the Saiyid family! In view of the detailed information offered in this study, Luqmān's generalisations are somewhat superficial, since it will clearly appear that these gifts of the choicest parts of the meat—the best cuts as we might say, were made before Islām to the temple, and to the Mas͟hāyik͟h, who are a more ancient layer of religious aristocracy than the Saiyids, at Madūdah today, and to the Saiyids also in some places, but in their case as heritors of ancient customary privileges which have persisted in Islām, not simply because they form the uppermost stratum of Islāmic aristocracy.

Luqmān comments also that the ibex today is a rare animal on its way to extinction, and no steps were being taken by the sulṭanates to protect it. Its chances of survival now that those parts of south-west Arabia are armed to the teeth with modern rifles and automatic weapons seem still slimmer. This is to be contrasted with the Wādī ᶜIrmā inscription when a Hunt of "Aḥrār" (tribesmen?) with 200 dogs actually managed to kill 600 ibexes.[102] I should question if there are so many ibex as that today from ᶜIrmā to Qabr Hūd. Luqmān has also dug out the information that before the British occupation of Aden (?) the S͟harīf who was ruling Baiḥān presented a live ibex to the Aden Government as a mark of friendship and co-operation, and that this animal was sent to the London Zoo.

QUARTER HUNTING PROCESSIONS IN MEDIAEVAL BAG͟HDĀD

Although it is when the ibex has been successfully hunted in south-west Arabia that a city ward or quarter marches in ceremonial procession around the quarter displaying the trophies of the chase, this is not confined to Arabia. I am indebted to Professor Claude Cahen who has supplied me with the reference to Ibn al-At͟hīr's *Kāmil*,[103] which includes the following notice under the events of the year 601 A.H. (A.D. 1204–05).

"On the 17th of S͟haᶜbān a quarrel (*fitnah*) took place in Bag͟hdād between the inhabitants (*ahl*) of Bāb al-Azaj[104] and the inhabitants of al-Ma'mūnīyah,[105] its cause being that the inhabitants of Bāb al-Azaj killed a lion (*sabuᶜ*[106]) and wanted to make a procession (*yaṭūfū*) with it, but the inhabitants of al-Ma'mūnīyah prevented them, and a quarrel fell about between them at al-Bustān al-Kabīr in which many persons among them were wounded, and a number slain. The Lord of al-Bāb (The Gate) rode up to quell the riot, but his horse was wounded, so he returned. On the morrow the inhabitants of al-Ma'mūnīyah went to Bāb al-Azaj, and a violent riot took place between them accompanied by fighting with swords and arrows. The state of affairs turned serious, and the houses near-by them were looted."

The Turkish soldiery entered and camped by al-Manẓarah, the rioters were prevented from meeting and subsided, but this was not the end of the troubles.

"On the 20th of S͟haᶜbān a riot came about between the inhabitants of Qaṭuftā and al-Qaryah of the western quarters (*maḥall*) also because of the killing of a lion (*sabuᶜ*), with which the inhabitants of Qaṭuftā wished to collect together and go in procession around (*yaṭūfū*), but the people of al-Qaryah prevented them from running in their quarter with it (*an yajrū bi-hi ᶜinda-hum*), and they fought together, a number on both sides being slain. So the soldiers were sent to them from the Dīwān to repair the matter and prevent the people from rioting, and they were duly restrained."

"On the 9th of Ramaḍān there was a riot among the inhabitants of Sūq al-Sulṭān and al-Jaᶜfarīyah, the original cause of which was that two men of the quarters quarrelled and each threatened the other, and the people of the two quarters gathered and fought in the Jaᶜfarīyah cemetery."

The Dīwān then sent certain persons to settle the disputes, but when many riots broke out an important Emir was stationed there with the Caliphal slaves (*mamālīk al-K͟halīfah*). A number of persons on whom some suspicion lay, were executed and the people quietened down.

In the year 614 A.H. (A.D. 1217–8)[107] in the month of Muḥarram a similar incident occurred between the inhabitants of al-Ma'mūnīyah and Bāb al-Azaj about a lion which had been killed. In the riots some people were killed or wounded, and the lieutenant of the Gate (*nā'ib al-Bāb*) was insulted. To settle matters, the Dīwān despatched an Emir of Mamelukes who sent back the people of each quarter to their own quarter, and thus the riots quietened down.

From the text certain inferences can be drawn. Firstly, the boundaries of each quarter, by analogy with what we know of Ḥaḍramawt, must have been fixed and jealously guarded against the intrusion of other quarters in procession. Secondly, it is in the important month of Shaᶜbān just a few days after Niṣf Shaᶜbān, that the riots began to break out, and they extended into Ramaḍān. In the year 614 A.H. (A.D. 1217–8) the riots took place in Muḥarram, also a month with religious associations, ᶜĀshūrā' day being observed by both Sunnīs and Shīᶜah. By analogy with the Ḥaḍramī hunt, I should certainly deduce that in the Baghdād processions there was an underlying religious element, though it was probably pagan and not Islāmic.

THE HUNT AT TARĪM

On December 3rd, 1953, we crossed over from Wādī ᶜAidīd by the mountain road to Wādī Thibī and there my wife came upon graffiti representing palms and ibex (Fig. No. II) upon a large square rock at the mountain base. This and other rocks in the vicinity bearing similar graffiti may, I think, have been shelter or assembly rocks for parties of hunters, perhaps even stones for circumambulation prior to, or on the return from the hunt. From various indications I am inclined also to think that the palm was an object of veneration, even of worship, in pre-Islāmic Ḥaḍramawt, and we know it was worshipped in Najrān.[108] Again, at the corner of the Wādī a little below Hūd's tomb, just before the entrance to Mahrah country, there is a rock with figures like those in Wādī Thibī nicked in it. These were probably made by hunters for I was told that this is a place by which they go up the mountain, and here the ibex come down to drink from the river. The figures were too indistinct to copy (Fig. No. II). The stone itself lies just a little above the large clay mounds at this corner. Such graffiti are common enough in South Arabia,[109] but their proximity to Tarīm and to the tomb of Hūd is significant. There is also a graffito of an ibex with some lettering above Saiwūn.

One might expect that a hunt with ritual associations would take place at known times and seasons, but on questioning shaikh Raḥaiyam he stoutly maintained that there was no fixed time for the hunt—no particular phase of the moon, and no particular month. It may take place at any time, always during the intense cold (*shiddat al-bard dawām*), but also in the intense heat (*shiddat al-ḥarr*). When

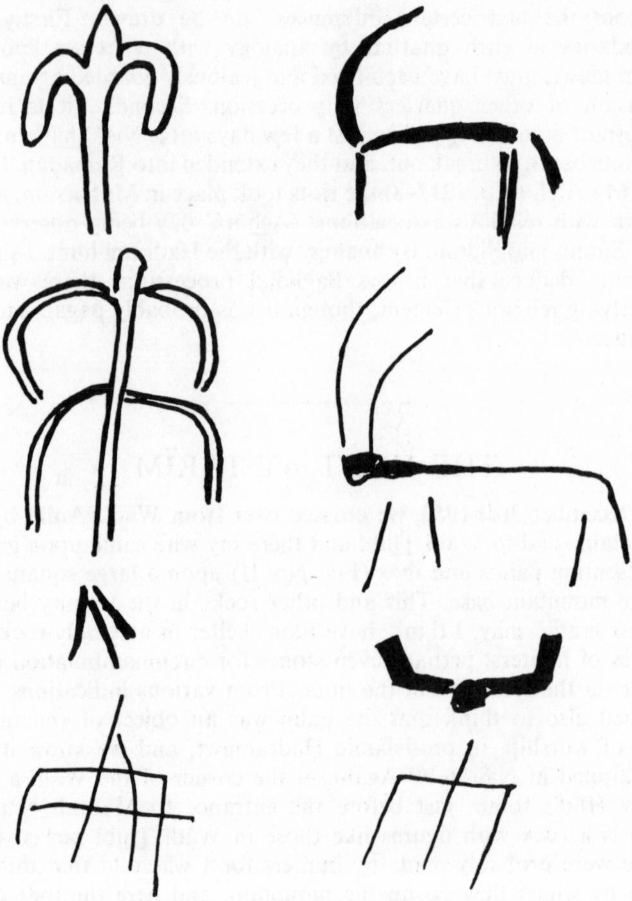

Fig. II

Graffiti from hunters' shelter rock in Wādī Thibī near Tarīm, and bottom right, a graffito associated with ibex country near Qabr Hūd

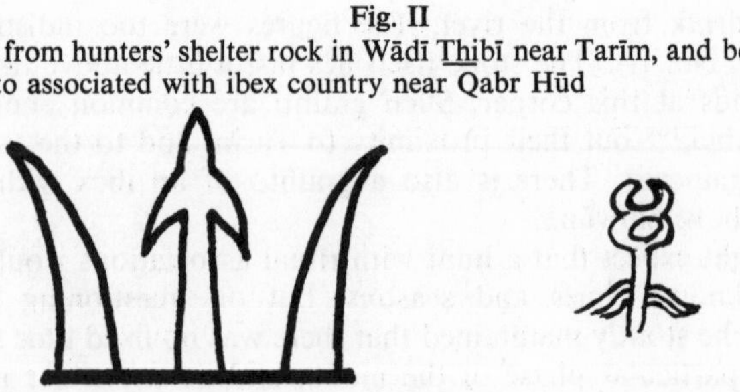

Fig. III

A. Palm decoration in plaster over doors in the Government fort at Najrān.
B. Winged caduceus on coins which also bear the name of the Moon God (cf. footnote 409)

the weather is cold the game hides in caves, but in the heat some people say it is wrong to hunt because the game must go to water to drink, and you have to find it there—which is wrong. However, said my s̲haik̲h, there is no hunting at night and no following of the moon in this way. It is nevertheless to be remembered that in inscription RES.3958, 14, *ṢYD* is the name of a month.

There are three types of hunting distinguished by my Tarīmī s̲haik̲h—firstly *qanīṣ al-g̲hirr*, encountering an animal by chance on the road or elsewhere, and killing it; secondly *qanīṣ al-rumyān*, killing an animal by shooting it from ambush (guns only), and thirdly *qanīṣ rumyān wa-s̲habak*, the Hunt employing both nets and guns.

If someone, perhaps an outsider, were to notice two head of *wiᶜl*[110] or so in a pass (*s̲hiᶜb*) he will bring the good news (*bis̲hārah*) to the *Abū* of, for instance, al-K̲hilaif Quarter. The latter will assemble the men of the Quarter and make plans for taking the ibex. The hunters (*ahl al-qanāṣah*) collect at the house of the *Abū* and *yits̲hāwarūn* (consult together), about the proposals and decide on the general strategy of the hunt. Often they will say to their Manṣab—"*Iduᶜ lanā bi-'l-naṣr wa-'l-ẓafar wa-lak qism*, Pray for victory and success for us and you shall have a share". They make *raᶜs̲hahs*, i.e. ceremonial dances, and go out to hunt.

In the days of the Yāfiᶜī tribal ruler G̲harāmah last century, as we have seen, the Sūq Quarter tried to go up the mountain by way of S̲hiᶜb ᶜAidīd, but they were stopped by a rival group from going by this route, so they turned back and ascended K̲hailah mountain by way of a pass called al-ᶜUraiqah. This is stated to have been a source of trouble between the two Yāfiᶜī groups controlling these parts of Tarīm as G̲harāmah told the Sūq Quarter to go up by S̲hiᶜb ᶜAidīd—and damn the consequences! Bā Hārūn[111] about the mid-10th century A.H. (16th century A.D.) speaks of a man who went up K̲hailah mountain with the hunters (*rāyiḥ maᶜa 'l-qanīṣ*) and the mountain has doubtless been hunted from remote times.

From the Sūq Quarter of Tarīm a party of men perhaps 200 strong, which would be called a *qanīṣ* or hunting-party, would go out taking with it provisions for eight days. Its chief was the *muqaddam* or headman of the *ḥaḍar*, i.e. the craftsmen and small shopkeepers of the quarter. The *qanīṣ* would be composed of a number of *k̲hibrahs*, i.e. parties of about 20 men, each under its own leader known as *abu 'l-k̲hibrah*. A *k̲hibrah* might be a group of *masākīn*, or tribes (*qabā'il*), or even of Saiyids. All these *k̲hibrahs* proceed in a known order of precedence, and one cannot move in front of another. The *ḍaᶜīf* (clay-worker) follows the *ḥaḍarī* as they say—he is subordinate to him. There are four classes of participant in the Hunt, the beaters (*shānn*, pl., *shannānah*), the guns (*rāmī*, pl., *rumyān*)[112] in concealment with their rifles, the *khaddāᶜah* in ambush (*mukbinīn*) with clubs and daggers ready to make the kill, and *ahl al-shabak*, the net-men, hiding at the foot of the mountain. The *wiᶜl* is found on the Jōl plateau and in the caves at its foot, or in mid-mountain; if you find the ibex on the top they go down, but if you find them at the foot they go up the mountain. So sensitive are they to the presence of man that the Arabs say they even smell his breath.

Of a hunting party of thirty, ten beaters (*shanan*),[113] will go to the top of the Jōl escarpment, and with such calls as, "*Yā wulīd ᶜindak al-ṣaid*, Look man, the game's coming your way!" and, waving cloths, they start the game which runs down into the *wādī*, to be shot at by those lying concealed behind rocks, or caught in the nets. Animals in their caves are started by throwing a stone in at them, and then driven to the lower parts of the mountain. The beaters come up behind the game which is thus hemmed in on all sides.

The Headman of the *masākīn* sets up the net-poles (*Abu 'l-ḥaḍar yiḍrib al-ṭawᶜ*), and the men take up their stance behind the net with their knives at the ready, one or more at each stake or pole according to the numbers present. Bā Jarād, the poet, says using this as a metaphor,[114]

قِرْش حَيْدَرْعَبَاد جاب لَهْلَهْ بلاد   قانِص الصَّيْد حصَّل لقُطبه مَلَق [115]

To its owners, the Ḥaidarᶜabād *riyāl* a country has brought.
For his pole the hunter of game found the occasion he sought.[116]

These verses were composed on the taking of al-Ghuraf by the Kathīrīs.

When the hunted animal is caught in the net, the net-men throw the rest of it over him and entangle him within it. As many as fifteen animals may rush the net at a time, but the usual number is one to five. Some succeed in breaking through the net, and get clean away, but those caught they despatch with knives. When the ibex passes by the hunters (guns or net-men) and they fail to kill it, people laugh at them and make derogatory remarks (*yiᶜaiyirū-hum*). These nets were described to me as woven of rope about a man's stature (*qāmah*) in height, but varying in length, perhaps 18 to 20 cubits (*dhirāᶜ*). Palm stakes (*ṭūᶜ/ṭawᶜ*, pl., *aṭwāᶜ*, syn. *jarīdah*), about two *qāmah* in height, support the net, one at each end, and two or three in the middle. These are dug into the ground like posts. I first saw one of these nets at ᶜĪnāt, made of black goat wool. Often three to four nets are used in one day's hunting.

If the hunters are successful in obtaining game they fire four or five shots on the top of the mountain to show the town or village and announce their good fortune. If the Hunt however obtains nothing, they return one by one to their homes, quietly. The people come out of the town to meet the successful hunters up to the fringes of the mountain (*aṭrāf al-jabal*) and all enter with the marching-song (*zāmil*) and ceremonial procession (*zaff*). Entering the village they go round the streets there and shout their rallying cries (*yinaṣṣirūn*),[117] at the end of the Hunt, under the house of the *Abū* or the Manṣab. The villagers will say to the hunters who have made a bag, "*Jibtū bi-'l-jamīlah*, You've done well!" The word *jamīlah* was invariably explained to me as "*al-ẓafar*, victory", and as, "the making of a bag".[118] On the contrary, to those who return empty-handed one exclaims, "*Jibtū bi-'l-qaṣīrah*, You've fallen short!" Or else one would say, "*al-qaṣīrah*!" or "*k͟haibatain!*"[119] The fuller phrase of congratulation is, "*Tahnā-kum al-jamīlah yā qāniṣīn*, Congratulations on your success, O hunters!" Similarly, one says to those returning from a visitation to the Prophet Hūd, "*Tahnā-kum al-jamīlah yā zā'irīn*", or "*Tahnā-kum al-ziyārah*".

The ibex is described by the rings (*ᶜijrah*) on its horns, e.g. "*ᶜAlā k͟hamsīn ᶜijrah*, A fifty-ringer!" ᶜAlī b. ᶜAqīl says[120] that a *zaff*, a ceremonial procession which I have described elsewhere, is made only if the ibex has forty rings on its horns, and he calls it the festival which the village (*baldah*) makes to greet (*istiqbāl*) the men of the Hunt.[121] If the ibex has less than forty rings the ceremonial entry is called a *duk͟hlah*, with the usual songs, the dancers bearing the head and trotters of the ibex. These songs or verses always commence with the phrase, "*Qāl baddāᶜ al-qawāfī*, The maker of these verses said". If the hunters bag an ibex with twenty or more rings[122] on its horns they "*yis͟hᶜarūn bi-'l-ᶜas͟hwī ᶜas͟hīyah*, i.e. they give notice of an evening ceremony in the evening". The herald goes into the centre of the Quarter and proclaims, "*Awwal – ṣallī ᶜalaih*!" To which the the Quarter replies with the chorus of many a deep voice, "*Ṣallī ᶜalaih!*" The herald then proclaims "*T͟hānī – ṣallī ᶜalaih! T͟hālit͟h –ṣallī ᶜalaih!*" "*K͟hair!*" shouts the Quarter. "*Yiqūl al-Abū – 'ᶜas͟hwī ᶜas͟hīyah hād͟hih al-lailah. Man arād yitbārak yaḥḍur*' ". To which the Quarter rejoins, "*Bas͟hs͟har-k Allāh bi-'l-k͟hair!*"

The *Abū* then invites a man with the *madrūf* or flute and two to four poets to perform, while two men carry the head and two make play with their *jambīyahs* (daggers). They sing Banī Mig͟hrāh and other poems and the ceremony goes on till the *mag͟hrib*.

For al-K͟hilaif Quarter of Tarīm, in a document dated October 30th, 1937, dealing with the precedents of the Quarter, it is laid down that, "Firstly, the Hunt (*qanāṣah*) and the like is the right of the *ḥaḍarī*. The Headman of the Ḥaḍar strikes the pole, and the meat is brought to his house for distribution by his hand. As for the going-forth (*misrāḥ*, but it could also mean "precedent") of the Hunt (*qanīṣ*) and its ceremonial procession (*zaff*), *ḥaḍarī* and *ḍaᶜīf* are in a (single) body." By the phrase "strikes the pole" the assigning of sites for each net by lot, as described *infra*, is intended. The artisan and petty merchant group, then, control the Hunt, and the *ḍaᶜīf* or worker in clay is subordinate to their Headman, but in other ways, as described, they act as a corporate body.

DIVISION OF THE MEAT

The carcase of the ibex, probably earlier on, is taken to the house of the Headman (*Abū*), and next day the meat is divided between the hunters. An ᶜĀmirī hunter of Tarīm told me that the man who fires the first shot to hit the animal receives the leg (*rijl*), horns, the portion from the tail downwards (of the haunch), which is called *al-naqar*,[123] the skin, and the skull (*kawr*). The name of the portions given him is called technically *al-qas͟haᶜah*, which is described variously as "*rās al-muqaddamah maᶜa 'l-qurūn, maḥall nas͟hw al-qarnain*, the head of the forepart with the horns, the place where the horns begin to grow", or, the forehead (*jabhah*) and horns.[124] According to Saif b. Ḥusain al-Quᶜaiṭī, one says, "*Qalab al-qas͟hᶜah*, He breathed his last". The metaphor is drawn from the Hunt, for the ibex generally, when shot dead, turns its head and horns upside down. The hunter eats the *kawr*, which can then be used like a camel's skull and placed on a wall against the evil eye—one sees this not infrequently in Tarīm. The horns he sets on his *dār* (Plate No. IV) to show that he is a hunter (*qāniṣ*),[125] so that when people see them they will exclaim, "*Hād͟hā qāniṣ kabīr*, This is a mighty hunter!" The man who first perceives the animal receives a share (*qism*) but I have not recorded whether he actually obtains anything extra. In Quzah of Dawᶜan, the local *qubbah*, I am told, has horns of the ibex set in it.[126] In the then recently excavated site at Ḥaid bin ᶜAqīl in the Wādī Baiḥān I remarked the small figure of an ibex carved at the corner of one of the buildings quite close to the level of the ground. Dr. Walker suggests that bull's horns were used for the same purpose in an alabastar slab containing the representation of a Sabaean temple.[127]

The most significant of all, however, is the share given to the Manṣab. In many places the Manṣab is made a gift of some portion when a sheep is killed, and at Ṣaᶜīd in Wāḥidī country I have myself sent the Manṣab a share as a present. In Tarīm or its environs he receives what is termed *qasmat ᶜajim*, the top half of the back leg or haunch and/or the *jufsh* which is also called *shirqat al-qāṣir*; this consists of the top ribs near the shoulders which have the nicest meat and white fat.[128] I have recorded the dictum from some speaker, probably not from Arabia, that, "*Khair al-laḥm mā jāwar al-ᶜaẓm*, The best part of the meat is what is next the bone". In the Qiblī and ᶜAlwā of Ḥaḍramawt[129] the part in question is called *muqdum*, and these chest ribs are a much esteemed part of the meat in Southern Arabia.

Now one of the inscriptions re-translated by Professor Beeston[130] reads, "Now let him offer to the God a thigh (*fakhidh*) and two *muqdums*, the expiation and offering in order that he may rejoin the tribe". That is to say that the same two portions of the animal are presented to the Manṣab today as were, in one case at least, to be offered to the god in the pre-Islāmic era. This seems to me a very clear indication of how close the functions of the Manṣab are to those of the pre-Islāmic priest. The presentation of this gift of meat to the Manṣab is known as *takhṣīr al-hishmah*, the making of the *khuṣār*[131] of respect.

It has occurred to me to query Professor Beeston's acceptance of the word *sh ᶜ b* as bearing the sense of "tribe", not of course that this does not make very reasonable sense, though al-Hamdānī and other sources define *shaᶜb* as the largest units in Arabia, composed of a number of tribes (*qabīlah*).[132] Muḍar, he says, is a *shaᶜb* and Kinānah is a *qabīlah*. Ḥimyar is also a *shaᶜb*. If understood as *shiᶜb*, in the way it is so often used, for example, in the account of the Hunt at Madūdah (*infra*), meaning the mountain passes where the Hunt takes place, this sense might however be more suitable here. As the inscription in question comes from one of the pillars outside the town of Mirwath, perhaps the hunter or the Hunt made its offering here and returned to the mountains, or, as Professor Beeston has suggested, the offering may have been made to remove some taboo or taint, such indeed as would be considered to fall within the definition of *dhaim* by the Ḥaḍramī hunter today. In the inscription under discussion I am inclined to prefer his derivation from *wathab* which he renders "rejoin", in its sense of "remain", and understand the inscription as "in order that he may remain in the mountain".

THE HUNT AT DAMMŪN

I was unable to contact the Headman of the Dammūn Hunt which, being in Quᶜaiṭī territory and the Qu'aiṭīs to some extent opposed to the strong Saiyid influence of Kat͟hīrī Tarīm, still flourishes. Dammūn has long been famous for its Hunt, and the great exponent of the Banī Mig͟hrāh hunting poetry ᶜAbd al-Ḥaqq was a Dammūnī.[133] I was informed of, and have indeed seen on several occasions, some large rocks there known as Ḥaṣāt al-Ḥadd just outside the walls of Tarīm. The Dammūnīs circumambulate these rocks at festivals (*afrāḥ*) of any sort, at the time of hunting, before the *S͟habwānī* dancing at marriages, etc.[134] For this reason it would seem probable that the rows of columns to be found outside some ancient temples in the eastern Yemen, were not associated solely with hunting which was probably only one of many ceremonies performed at them.

THE HUNT AT ᶜĪNĀT

ᶜĪnāt is famous for its own breed of hunting dog. The people of ᶜĪnāt feed these dogs well, and they eat dates, bread, meat, etc., which is astonishing when one knows how little food forms the staple diet of the people there. They wash their dogs and look after them properly because the dogs are good hunters and of great assistance to them. According to my s͟haik͟h they were not distinguished from the usual "pie-dog" of the country, and were not for instance of the type known as Saluqi, but in 1953 the Manṣab of ᶜĪnāt informed me that the dogs are of Qiṭmīr/Qaṭmīr[135] stock and one other kind; dogs, he said, were still bred there, but they are now few. The dog which has fastened its jaws on the hind leg of the ibex on the pre-Islāmic lamp (Plate No. 1) is probably typical.

When they are setting off on the hunt from ᶜĪnāt the huntsmen cry out, "*Wa-'l-hajīr*", which is said to mean *al-bidār ila 'l-qanāṣah*, hastening to the hunt. In former times they used also to call out in the same way at Tarīm when they moved off, but of course as we have seen, these ancient customs have been suppressed there. On coming to the hunting area a man of ᶜĪnāt will say to his dog, "*Istikbir*, pick out a big one", and along come the dogs wagging their tails. These dogs attack the game, and, seizing hold of it by the testicles so that the animal cannot move, they cling to them until the hunter arrives. While still on the hunt in the mountain, a man will call his dog, tie to its neck a letter describing the hunt and number of animals taken, and tell it to return home. The dog goes off and stops before its master's house; there the note is untied and read. When they see a dog arrive in this way people know that there is good news from the Hunt. The dog too gets his share (*rānī*) of the meat.

Here, the Manṣab acts as the judge in hunting cases, but he had, as he informed me, no documents relating to hunting law or hunting cases. These judgements however are quite normal cases, with recourse to the oath according to the well-known rules of Ḥaḍramawt, usually upon a saint's tomb. The Manṣab compared hunting to a partnership, a partnership in which one of the parties has perhaps deceived the other, and he said that it was to rectify such wrongs that there are hunting rules. One would of course expect a more sympathetic attitude from a Saiyid of the Āl Bū Bakr b. Shaikh, the holy family of ᶜĪnāt, in such questions as hunting, than one anticipates from the Tarīm ulema, as the latter accuse this Saiyid family of assimilating themselves to the Bedouin, i.e. the tribes.

There are several Quarters in ᶜĪnāt, but, as the town is much decayed and its inhabitants reduced to about one-third since the war-time famine, there is now at any rate, no individual Quarter organisation there. In effect there is only one Quarter, the Abū of the Hunt (*Qanāṣah*) acting for the whole village of some 1,300 souls where formerly there were 5,000. The Abū has a small document showing the passes where the nets are set up, etc., and laying down the procedure fairly exactly, but I was not able to return to ᶜĪnāt to see it.

HUNTERS AT QAᶜŪḌAH, ETC.

One of the sections of the Āl ᶜAjjāj, the famous tribal judges of appeal of Ḥaḍramawt, at Qaᶜūḍah, is known as Āl Qāniṣ, the Hunter family, and I had some discussions with Ṣalāḥ b. Ṣāliḥ al-Qāniṣ Bā ᶜAjjāj Āl Qāniṣ of the Nahd, on tribal matters. A topographical feature in the vicinity is marked in Philby's map of 1938 as Khushm al-Qāniṣ—which probably refers to the family name. Bā Rashaid, a companion of this man, informed me that the meat allotted to the hunter who actually kills the game is called *laḥmat al-bunduq*, and it consists of a certain share in specifically known parts of the animal including the *matnah*. Tribal names signifying hunting, or the animals hunted, are probably fairly common in Ḥaḍramawt. The Manāhīl have a Bait al-Qiwainiṣah (diminutive of *qāniṣ*, i.e. little hunter), and there is also Āl Wuᶜail (the little ibex family?) of the ᶜAwāmir. These may be compared with Qanaṣ b. Maᶜadd of Balādhurī,[136] and, perhaps, the enigmatic *rajaz* verse quoted by al-Hamdānī,[137] attributed to Asᶜad Tubbaᶜ

حمير قومي على علا ٘تها　　(و) حضرموت الصّيدُ منها والصُّدُفْ/الصَّدِفْ

> Himyar is my tribe under all circumstances,
> Ḥaḍramawt al-Ṣaid (Ḥaḍramawt of the Game)
> is of it, and the Ṣadif/Ṣuduf.

Al-Hamdānī states that in the wars among the tribes of the Ḥimyar confederation, the tribe called Ḥaḍramawt settled in S̲h̲abwah. Two other groups called Ṣayad/Ṣaid/Ṣīd are known to al-Hamdānī, Ṣāʾid of the tribe al-Ṣaid in Ḥaḍūr, of whom the editor Muḥammad al-Akwaᶜ says that some still remain there to this day, and Ṣayad of Ḥās̲h̲id.[138]

A former slave of the Quᶜaiṭīs told me that all the passes on the present-day East Road from al-Mukallā, before one enters the Wādī Ḥaḍramawt, were well known to him, since he and his fellow slaves had hunted there extensively before the British protectorate.

HUNTING IN WĀḤIDĪ TERRITORY

The Wāḥidī Sulṭanate, like Ḥaḍramawt, has its own mountain hunting grounds. Each one (of various groups) had his own (hunting) territory (*kullin ḥadd-ah lah*), and no group will go near the mountains that are the hunting grounds of another. For example S̲h̲aikh ᶜAbdullāh Bā Qādir, the Manṣab of Ṣaᶜīd, told me that "*Yinbak̲h̲ al-gabal ḥaqq Manṣab al-Ṣaᶜīd*, Yinbak̲h̲ is the mountain of the Manṣab of Ṣaᶜīd". "*Kadūr al-jabal ḥaqq Bā Marḥūl*," i.e. Kadūr belongs to the Bā Marḥūl Mas̲h̲āyik̲h̲ of Lihyah. Landberg describes[139] their Manṣab as prominent and the family as having much influence in the country, and he also avers that Kadūr mountain is a *ḥabaṭ*, i.e. a kind of sacred enclave.[140] Rifles, he says, are not fired in it, and there is complete security. He adds that it is full of ibex, though I cannot say I saw any when I climbed its steep sides in December 1947. They take the ibex with nets (*s̲h̲abak*, pl. *s̲h̲ibāk*) in which the animals entangle themselves *yitᶜas̲h̲bakūn fī-hā*). They are then despatched by dagger thrusts. The two state-

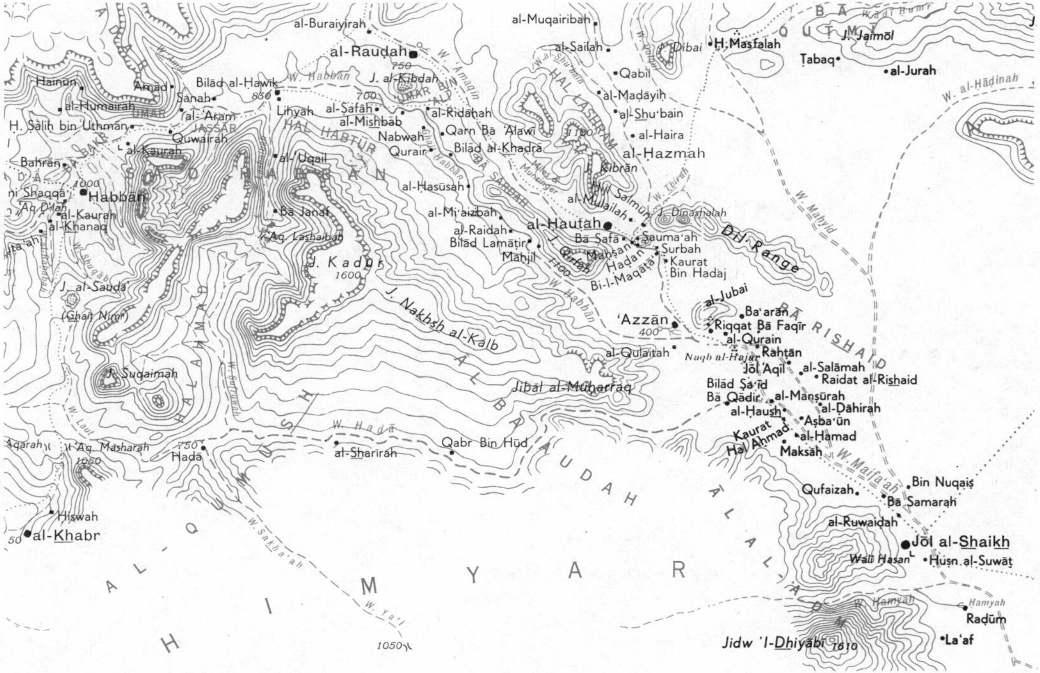

al-Buraiyirah
al-Raudah
al-Muqairibah
al-Sailah
Dibai
H. Masfalah
J. Jaimōl
Ṭabaq
al-Jurah
W. al-Hādinah
Hainūn
al-Humairah
Amad
Sanah
Bilād al-Hawik
W. Habbān
J. al-Kibdah
W. Amaqin
Qabil
al-Madāyiḥ
al-Shu'bain
al-Haira
al-Hazmah
H. Ṣālih bin Uthmān
Quwairah
al-Kaurah
Lihyah
al-Ṣafāh
al-Mishbab
Nabwah
al-Ridahah
Qarn Bā 'Alawi
Qurair
Bilād al-Khadrā
J. Kibrān
Bahrān
Habbān
al-'Uqail
al-Hasūsah
al-Mi'aizbah
al-Mulailah
J. Dinashalah
al-Kaurah
al-Khanaq
Bā Janaf
al-Raidah
Bilād Lamāṭir
Mahjil
al-Hauṭah
Bā Ṣafā
Sauma'ah
Surbah
Kaurat Bin Hadaj
Dil Range
J. Kadur
1600
J. al-Saudā
(Ghait Nimr)
J. Nakhsh al-Kalb
'Azzān
al-Jubai
Ba'arān
Riqqat Bā Faqīr
al-Qurain
Rahṭān
al-Qulaitah
Naqb al-Hajar
Jōl 'Aqīl
al-Salāmah
Raidat al-Rishaid
J. Suqaimah
Jibal al-Muharraq
Bilād Ṣa'īd
Bā Qādir
al-Manṣūrah
al-Haush
al-Ḍāhirah
Aṣba'ūn
Kaurat Hal Ahmad
al-Hamad
Maksah
W. Hadā
Qabr Bin Hūd
al-Sharīrah
Hadā
'Aq. Masharah
Aqarah
1050
Hiswah
al-Khabr
W. Maifa'ah
Bin Nuqaiṣ
Qufaizah
Bā Samarah
al-Ruwaidah
Jōl al-Shaikh
Wali Hasan
Huṣn al-Suwāṭ
AL-QUMUSH
HIMYAR
AL BA'AUDAH
BĀ RISHAID
W. Sakha'ah
W. Ya'l
1050
W. Hamyah
Hamyah
Radūm
La'af
Jidw 'l-Dhiyābi 1610

ments that Kadūr is a *ḥabaṭ* and that the ibex is hunted there, are not altogether easy to reconcile. Al-Muḥarriq[141] is the mountain of the Bā Raḥmah Mashāyikh who have a *ḥawṭah* or sacred enclave in Lamāṭir where there is a splendid waterfall which I saw after descending Kadūr. In Landberg's day the Wāḥidī Sulṭān of Ḥabbān had no power over it. *Raḥmah* of course means rain, and the name of this Mashāyikh family may contain some allusion to the waterfall, or it could possibly be to their power to make rain. Muḥarriq is the name of a pre-Islāmic god, but not, apparently, a god worshipped in Southern Arabia. Qirfah, al-Saqāh and Madbī[142] were described as Gabal Bal-Faqīh ᶜAlī, the mountains of the Mashāyikh of Ḥawṭat al-Faqīh ᶜAlī. Kibrān is *al-gabal ḥaqq Bin Sarayīl*, i.e. the hunting mountain of the Hal Isrā'īl Mashāyikh of al-Rawḍah. They are also associated with the supply of water to the country since their ancestor is believed to have miraculously brought a well into existence by striking the ground with his spear.[143]

We know already from the inscriptions that in Maifaᶜ, about three days' march from Ḥawṭat al-Faqīh ᶜAlī to the east, Shams, Lady (*Baᶜlat*) of Maifaᶜ ordered her slave/worshipper Sh r ḥ ' l B t ᶜ to set up some kind of song ritual, though we are unsure as to what this sharḥ so rendered as proposed by Professor Beeston, actually meant.[144] Yet his hypothesis seems to be supported by the account (*infra*) of the festival at al-Ḥawṭah where *sharḥ* was danced, and in Ḥaḍramawt the *sharḥ* is accompanied by drums and pipes. It might be more than a coincidence that *sharḥ* forms part of the name of Sh r ḥ ' l which might mean, if we apply senses existing today in South Arabia, God is pleased, or watches, or rejoices. It might be understood also in the optative. The name *Sharāḥil* figures in Arabic sources as an Arabian name, its normally accepted meaning in South Arabian being "God protects" or "Protected by God".

The inscription (CIH 571) gives Sh r ḥ ' l to expect only *niᶜmah* for having performed the hunt, though as all *niᶜmah* or well-being is dependent on rain, it might be interpreted in that way. CIH 547 however goes further, and in Professor Beeston's rendering, the god refrains from blessing the Ahl ᶜAthtar with rain because they had not duly performed for him the hunt at a certain time. This latter inscription comes from Ḥaram in the Jawf district of the Yemen, not from the Wāḥidī Sulṭanate, but the belief that the god would punish neglect of the hunt was paralleled in the strangest of ways by what the Manṣab ᶜAbdullāh Bā Qādir told me in 1964. There is no special season for hunting, he said, and the Wāḥidīs do not hunt if they have work to do. There used to be a belief in the country, though, he commented, it is probably not much held now, that

"*In kān mā qanaṣnā al-maṭar mā yigī-nā - bā yikūn al-quḥb fi 'l-bilād —al-shiḥḥ fi 'l-ṭaᶜām*, If we did not hunt the rain would not come to us, and there would be drought (?)[145] in the country—scarcity (?) in grain (*dhurah?*)". If they do hunt, then four days (or so?) after the hunt, rain will come. "*Yishūfūn al-rakhā' min Allāh gā, yawm qanaṣnā*, They will see that well-being has come from Allāh when we hunted".[146] *Rakhā'* is in effect synonymous with the *niᶜmah* of the inscription. This is to be compared with the pronouncement alleged to have been made by the Prophet Muḥammad himself, that, "No tribe (*qawm*) refuses (to pay) the *zakāt*-(tax), but Allāh withholds from them the rain of heaven (*qaṭr al-samā'*)".[147] In Southern Arabia the *zakāt* or *ᶜushūr* is the tithe of the crops which, in the Zaidī state, was paid to the Imām, and in certain other districts of the south it would be paid to the Manṣab of the shrine of the local saint. In the Wāḥidī district the Mashāyikh function as rain-makers, and the Manṣab ᶜAbdullāh Bā Qādir himself gave me a revealing account of how tribes would repair to him in time of drought to ask his aid to bring them rain. That the peculiar quality or virtue of rain-making was believed to reside in the person of the Zaidī Imām by the Zaidī tribes of the northern highlands is to be deduced from the words of the famous Yemeni poet of the Liberals (*al-Aḥrār*), al-Zubairī, in his polemic against the imāmate,[148] "When the sky rains it is said to it (Upper Yemen), 'These are the Imām's blessings'. When it is a year of dearth it is told, 'This is through the invocation of the Imām against the recalcitrant rebels' ". The Imām's great ancestor, the Prophet Muḥammad too, was successful in prayers for rain—yet even he came in a long line of tradition, for when the tribe of ᶜĀd came to Mecca to beseech for rain (*yastasqūn*), then repaired to the Kaᶜbah, Abū Saᶜd said to them, 'You will not have rain till you believe in Hūd, God bless him' (*tu'minū bi-Hūd, ṣalla 'llāh 'alaih*)."

If, in the Maifaᶜ inscription (CIH 571), Shams is to be understood as the name of the goddess of the district, then it would appear that the Hunt was associated with a Sun cult in this instance, and not with ᶜAthtar.

In 1958 the Aden newspaper *al-Janūb al-ᶜArabī*,[149] already defunct before the British withdrawal from Aden, reported "The custom in al-Ḥawṭah (Ḥawṭat al-Faqīh ᶜAlī) is to set up two large parties to hunt the ibex (*li-qanāṣat al-ṣaid al-waᶜl*) in the mountains. The second party (*farīq*)[150] is called the Farīq b. Ḥalfūṣ (the winning party being al-Jāfān). On Friday the Farīq al-Jāfān hunted three ibex, the age of one of which was 42 years. The *farīq* on this occasion fired off shots and set up a *sharḥ*[151] for the period of two days."

The present shaikh (1964) of al-Ḥawṭah is called Shaikh b. Muḥammad Jazal al-ᶜAzzānī, one of the Mashāyikh Āl al-Faqīh ᶜAlī of al-Ḥawṭah. The various houses or families of the Āl al-Faqīh ᶜAlī are ᶜAqīl, Muḥammad, Jazal, and Yā-Sīn, in the last-named of which the office of Manṣab lies, but all the four houses elect to it. Ḥalfūṣ was said to be the name of a shaikh of the Āl ᶜAqīl branch of the Āl al-Faqīh ᶜAlī who founded the Farīq Bin Ḥalfūṣ which was called after him. The two *farīqs* of al-Ḥawṭah were known as the Aṣḥāb Bin Ḥalfūṣ and the Aṣḥāb Bin Hādī. One informant told me that these *farīqs* were a mixture of the four houses (*diyār*) which make up the Mashāyikh Āl al-Faqīh ᶜAlī, and another said that people joined these *farīqs* as they wished, and hunted in al-Saqāh and Gibāl Ḥimyar, Wāḥidī territory being Ḥimyar. Father and son might belong to different *farīqs*, and it is to be pointed out that these *farīqs* had no connection with the quarters (*ḥuwaif*) of the town; in this they diverge from Tarīm and, it may be, other Ḥaḍramī towns. These hunting parties do not go forth with a *zaff* festivity of any sort, but in groups (*jamāᶜat/gamāᶜat*), and they have a boundary (*ḥadd*) outside al-Ḥawṭah where they assemble, before making for the particular mountain where they intend to hunt. They hunt the ibex with the net.

My most recent information (February 1964) is that the *farīq* hunting has been abolished as it gave rise to disputes. Two years ago (from 1964) the State Secretary, Muḥammad b. Saᶜīd al-Wāḥidī (who in the last days of Aden was blown up in a plane in which a bomb had been planted, not by terrorists, but, it seems, at the instigation of the Sulṭān, Nāṣir, or his brother), forbade the Hunt because of rivalry between the two *farīqs* at al-Ḥawṭah, and their *raᶜāyā* or *ḥawīk*, i.e. non-tribal class who were the net-men (*aṣḥāb al-shabak*). This was told me by my old friend from 1947, the Manṣab ᶜAbdullāh Bā Qādīr, and he said of them, "*Al-ḥawīk mā shī bās fī-him*, There is no harm in the weaver (class)".[152] The Mashāyikh even give the *ḥawīk* class money to go a-hunting if they have insufficient to provide for themselves. The Bin Hādī *farīq*, which is called al-Qadīmah, numbers about 200, and the Aṣḥāb Bin Ḥalfūṣ about 80 men.

Besides Mawla 'l-Ḥawṭah, Mawla 'l-Rawḍah also has a hunting group. Of Mawla 'l-Ḥawṭah I was informed that there are two *ḥāfahs* of *ḥawīk* who follow the Mashāyikh of the Ḥalfūṣ and Hādī *ḥāfahs*, while Mawla 'l-Rawḍah has two hunting groups (*ḥāfah*), the Hal Sifālah and the Hal ᶜAlāhah[153]—as already stated *ḥāfah* does not appear to mean a town-ward or quarter as the hunt here is organised in *farīqs*. What is remarkable is that the organisation of the hunt in the *Wāḥidī* Sulṭanate is in the hands of, and promoted by the Mashāyikh who, as a class,[154] constitute the ancient pre-Islāmic aristocracy of religion, and who, at any rate in two cases *supra*, appear to have some link with rain-making. Mawlā in these titles may be rendered as "Lord" of al-Ḥawṭah or al-Rawḍah. The Ḥaḍramīs of Tarīm, as we have seen, refer to the quarters of the town in some of their documents as, e.g. Mawla 'l-Sūq. It might be that Tarīm had, in pre-Saiyid days, a hunt controlled by the Mashāyikh families, but the patron saints of the Tarīm quarters seem to be mainly Saiyids nowadays, though the Khilaif Quarter still has Shaikh ᶜAlī al-Khaṭīb, "He of the Ibex", and their *tanṣūrah* or rallying cry is "We have hunted the game in its lairs (or mountain sides). Our shaikh is ᶜAlī bin Miḥimmid".[155] The ancient saint buried near Kōr Saibān is known as Mawlā Maṭar, Lord of Rain, and another unknown saint whose tomb I came across at al-Khabar on the Wāḥidī–ᶜAwlaqī border was called either al-Shaikh mi-'l-Qubbah, or as others say, Mawla 'l-Qubbah, with a *ziyārah* on the second Friday in the month of Rajab.

There is rivalry, said the Manṣab Bā Qādir to me in 1964, over the hunt (*ḥanaq wa-shiḥnah ᶜala 'l-qanāṣah*). One hunting party will go out and succeed in bagging so many head of game, so then another group will sally forth to hunt in its mountain and try to out-do the first party by making a larger bag of game. Then yet another party would come out to vie with them, or perhaps the original hunting party would come out a second time to compete with their successful rivals. An expression they use is "*Anā anmar minn-ak*, I am more courageous than you are". Literally it means "More of a leopard", for the *nimir*, says Landberg,[156] means a brave man, a warrior, as well as its basic sense of leopard. Leopards are found in the Wāḥidī Sulṭanate, and when I went for a walk unarmed up a steep narrow gulley just north of Burūm I saw a leopard's spoor leading into a cave and beat a hasty retreat. In 1947 also, a child herding animals upon whom we chanced at Naqab al-Hajar told us that a *nimr* had once killed thirty camels there!

The Wāḥidī hunters follow the rule that the provisions (*zawād*) are deposited in one place and that they refrain from eating on the hunt —this, alleged the Manṣab Bā Qādīr, is so as not to scare the game, but I incline to see in it the vestige of some ritual practice. Nor, on the hunt, must they use any deceit (*khiyānah*) or evil words (*kalām baṭṭāl*).[157]

When an ibex is slain by the hunters they appoint a messenger to take back the good news to the village, who should go first to the victorious hunter's own house. They say to the messenger, "*Bashshir ahl-ah anna filān ādamī baddā*[158] *waᶜl,* Tell his family that such and such a man has killed an ibex". The messenger takes the trotter (*kurāᶜ*) of the ibex to the village, and he would say, "*Waᶜl ᶜind al-shaikh ᶜAbdullāh,* Shaikh ᶜAbdullāh (for example) has got an ibex". For bringing back the good news he is given *shuqur fī rās-ah*—sweet basil to put in his turban, and he receives a *bishārah*—gift of anything from six to eight *riyāls.* All the people of the house of the slayer of the ibex give the messenger money, i.e. all the adult males, the paternal and maternal uncles, the relation by marriage (*aᶜmām, akhwāl, ṣahīrah*), and the *ahl al-ribāᶜah wa-'l-nisābah, les hommes de la même tribu ou de la même localité.*[159] The house entertains him to a meal and sprinkles him with scent.

The returning hunters make a *maḥaffah,*[160] which is a procession in line, back to the village with the ibex head carried in the hands raised above the bearer's head or shoulders, to the accompaniment of the popping of rifle-shots and declaiming of *zāmils.* When they have entered the town or village they go up to the open space in the centre of it and circle round it. They do not go to the *dār* of the Manṣab, but to the house of the man who slew the game (*ṣaid*).[161] It appears that in this district there is no need for a headman or chief (*ra'īs*) to accompany the Hunt (*qanīṣ*).

The people take the skin and head (*al-dīm wa-'l-rās*) and stuff it with any sort of grass or leaves (*shigar*)—perhaps, I imagine, with the *rā,*[162] used still for stuffing leather pillows, and set it up on the little ornamental stepped projections (*bāshūrah,* pl. *bawāshīr*) at the corners of the wall of the *raim* roof-top, i.e. the roof battlements if one can so call them. They then make a *sharḥ,* a dance to the music of pipe and drums, lasting from three to four days, feasting and talking into the night (*yismurūn*), slaughtering, of course, other (domestic) animals to feast upon as well as the ibex, just as the king of Ḥaḍramawt of the Philby 84 inscription did, long before Islām. The man who actually slew the ibex gets nothing—indeed he has to spend (*yikhsar*), since he is obliged to make an entertainment (*ḍiyāfah*) for the hunters and the like.

HUNTING POEMS

Elsewhere, I have spoken of the poems of the Hunt at greater length, proposing for them a high antiquity on account of their conventionalised form and metre.[163] The characteristic hunting poem of Ḥaḍramawt is that known as Banī Mighrāh which I suppose may be derived from such a phrase as that quoted by Lane, "*Aghraitu 'l-kalb bi-'l-ṣaid*, I set the dog on the object of the chase".[164] The following example by the great master, ʿAbd al-Ḥaqq, is typical.[165]

1 Banī Mighrāh! Halloo[166]—even be it with sad heart or dismay.
2 And of thy daily bread despair not—the Lord will provide—
but say,
3 "O Soverain Lord, relief for a poor hard-done by fellow, pray!"
4 For so you see me, troubled for my friends, stricken sorely of
heart.
5 What they do I know not nor am aware. How distance doth
us part!
6 Yet hunting is my passion. To wound my eyes the tears bitter
start.

* * *

7 This night to Dammūn Pass from the lower valley came a
message.
8 Says he, "Your comrades have been hunting. There's dancing
in the village.
9 Two ibexes they've taken, all you could wish, without a blemish,
so,
10 Glossy one of them, his skin like cloth newly dyed with indigo.[167]
11 His shank, man, I'm telling you, a whole pound it was, weighed
on the scale.
12 Both of them the men skilled in hunting took—but that's not
the whole tale!
13 Those I mean who 're the good shots, and the excited young lads
as well.
14 Yet another thing—ʿAbdūn—to him they say the biggest ones
fell!
15 Bū Mubārak had a fine kill. With him a special net he brings,
16 Indigo-dyed, by clever thumbs woven, with strong poles and
stout rings.
17 Al-Khishash, God bless it with good floods, there the largest
ibex rove.
18 Ḥamduh's the place for fine fellows too, lying hid like treasure
trove!"

* * *

19 Enough, enough! Up now and take my letter with its *kāf* and *nūn*.

20 Be off with it to Qasam, and give it to the sons of ᶜAbdūn.

21 Say, 'Your news has reached me. Let it put all jealous folk to shame.

22 Felicitations on the kill, and yet still more luck of the same.'

23 Off now with you to ᶜIjiz! Falter not, nor in your purpose fail,

24 Seek out Muḥammad my old comrade, God keep him both well and hale.

25 But I, alas, with you who go tonight, were I but going too!

26 When you are a-passing by S̲h̲ajᶜūn's peaks—there shall I be with you.

27 The very hour you're off tonight, my sandals ahead you shall be,

28 But poor ᶜAbd al-Ḥaqq, comrades mine, at the dancing you'll never see.

* * *

29 Oft times as they recite the Book, let us close with the Prophet's name.

The conventional opening, addressing the hunting dogs, is followed by the no less conventional *d̲h̲ikr Allāh*, and the poem concludes as usual with a reference to the Prophet. The poet's plaint that he is unable to join his comrades in the hunt is, I think, yet another convention, like the lament of Bū S̲h̲aik̲h̲ that old age has put an end to his hunting days.[168] Verse 17 seems to associate the largest ibex (which the hunter hopes to bag) with the invocation to God to bless with rain the place where they are to be found.

HUNTING AT MADŪDAH

Madūdah might seem to have been a more important place in the early centuries of Islām than it is now, for al-Hamdānī[169] refers to it along with four other towns in the area called al-Sarīr, of Wādī Ḥaḍramawt; these include Tarīm, Tarīs and Ḥabūḍah, but not Saiwūn which perhaps only outstripped near-by Ḥabūḍah (no longer an important place), about a couple of centuries later. Madūdah was inhabited by Āl Kulaib and Āl Nājiyah. A tribe Kulaib is still fouud in Wādī Ḥaḍramawt, and I have wondered if Āl Nājiyah is a corruption for Āl Bā Jaray who live some miles to the east of Madūdah.

The Ḥaḍramī chronicler Shanbal only occasionally mentions Madūdah.

Through the good offices of Amīn ᶜAbd al-Mājid, then (1954) Assistant State Secretary to the Kathīrī Government, and Shaikh Hādī b. Ṣāliḥ b. Ḥātim of Madūdah village, who entertained us and assisted me in numerous ways, I was able to visit this important hunting village at last. In Shaikh Hādī's reception room we met an entire *majlis* of those villagers associated in one way or another with the Hunt. I explained to the *majlis* that, on my previous visit, I had heard of Madūdah's fame not only as a hunting centre but for its traditional authority in settling hunting disputes. I was seated next to one of the Manṣabs, both of the Bā Ḥumaid Mashāyikh, of the village, his name, if I am correct, being Ṭāhā Muḥammad, who lives in Madūdah, but when I tried to engage him in conversation and induce him to tell me about the Hunt he refused to do so, averring that he had nothing to do with hunting and had never judged in hunting disputes. Though the *majlis* would not openly contradict their Manṣab, a charming and venerable personage in every respect, there was a certain amount of merriment as he made these declarations, and I was told later that they were, in point of fact, mere excuses. I suppose that the Manṣab was apprehensive that his name be associated, perhaps in print, with the Hunt, which as I have indicated, is strongly disapproved of in religious circles. Possibly too the Manṣab may have disliked meeting a Naṣrānī, though this is less likely, but certain scholars refuse not only to meet Naṣrānīs, but men whom they stigmatise in traditional Ṣūfī style as "evil persons" or "tyrants"—by which terms they often allude the tribal rulers of the country.

On our arrival the net (Plate No. 2) had already been set up across the main street of the village and the place buzzed with excitement. While we partook of tea and cake a poet at the *majlis* was produced, to sing a Banī Mighrāh song or two, and the time was whiled away pleasantly until an increase in the noise of the crowd outside the house indicated that the show, the mock Hunt[170] a local custom, was ready. We descended to the street to find that one of the peasants had twisted his *rādī* into a long horn which he held with his hand above his head. Going to the top of the street he impersonated the ibex and, though we could not see him, a couple of crackers were let off—soon he came in sight, making swift zigzag runs from one piece of cover to another, pausing to look out from each rock as it were, to see where his enemies lay. Whenever he moved the villagers flung a cracker or two at him; these went off with a bang simulating the crack of a rifle, nearly frightening the poor "ibex" out of his wits, till finally, in his confusion, he rushed straight into the net which the net-men at once threw on top of him, all rushing in to put an end to him with their knives. Straightway the women in the street and on the house-tops or at the windows broke into the ululation for joyous occasions, and the whole village which had been following the play with enthusiasm, burst into a welter of shouting and laughter.

Jāḥiẓ[171] quotes a very strange report indeed which conceivably may have some bearing on the mock hunt at Madūdah. "Al-Makkī told of (slave)-girls in the Yemen who have plaited horns (*qurūn maḍfūrah*) of the hair of their heads, and that one of them will dance and handclap (*talᶜab wa-tarquṣ*[172]) in metrical harmony (*iyqāᶜ mawzūn*), then she raises (*tushkhiṣ*) one of those horns, then she dances and handclaps, then she raises one after another of these plaits woven together (*al-ḍafā'ir al-muraṣṣaᶜah*) until they stand up on her head as if they were the horns of wild animals."

There are, for reasons which I did not explore, two Manṣabs at Madūdah, but one lives at Ḥawṭah Ṭuyūrah. It was the young shaikh ᶜUmar b. Ḥasan Bā Ḥumaid, son of the Manṣab of Ṭuyūrah, the chief speaker at the *majlis* in Madūdah who, with another young man Shaikh Aḥmad b. Saᶜīd Bakhḍar (i.e. Bā Akhḍar) who provided me with the "Hunting Customs of the Villagers of Madūdah" *infra*. Madūdah is a village, it seems, without Saiyid inhabitants; I gathered that there was a certain amount of antipathy to them in Madūdah and the remark was made that they did not find that the village suited them. It would seem that the Mashāyikh then have still not been displaced here by Saiyid influence.

I had heard that the Madūdah people had a book of hunting law—probably a case-book, for when I investigated the supposed book of tribal law, said to be in the possession of Bin Yamānī of Tamīm at Qasam, through the kindness of the late Saiyid Sir Bū Bakr b. Shaikh Āl-Kāf, it turned out that this book was in fact a series of cases without any order or rationalisation. My informants had also heard of this hunting law book but when they came to examine it they found that it had been almost entirely consumed by the white ant.[173] They had notwithstanding, assembled three typical cases which appear in the Appendix (p. 57 *seq.*).

THE MADŪDAH DOCUMENT, METHODS AND TEXT

It is urgent to record every aspect of the unique ancient culture of Ḥaḍramawt for, owing to the startling rate of emigration, the country is being rapidly stripped (1954) of its adult male population. It is impossible to investigate every process by observation and questioning for lack of time, and I therefore in certain cases adopted a new method of making inquiries of qualified informants, and having them write, or alternatively dictate, their own accounts to a clerk, emphasising always that I wish the material to be written in colloquial Arabic and local technical terms to be employed. The resultant text I then use as a basis of discussion and have it fully explained and commented, observing the process itself if possible, as opportunity offers. This method has at least the merit of preserving the memory of certain institutions from decay. I have also applied it to the sardine fishing.

With the text *infra* my informants supplied me with additional Banī Mig͟hrāh poems. The text itself is in a sort of written colloquial Arabic with a semi-literary content; in style it is loose, straightforward, careless to some extent, all of which characteristics I have tried to show by rendering it in English, semi-classical semi-colloquial, but the translation is fairly literal. The actual text is not of great linguistic interest but all significant words and phrases have been given in transliteration.

THE HUNTING CUSTOMS OF THE VILLAGERS OF MADŪDAH

When the inhabitants of the village (*baldah*) of Madūdah want to hunt the passes (*s͟hiᶜāb*) of the Wādī Juᶜaimah, namely the passes of al-K͟hutt, Hus͟haimah, al-K͟hiṭmah al-Qiblīyah, and al-K͟hiṭmah al-S͟harqīyah,[174] first of all the members of the Hunt (*qanāṣah*), that is to say—five persons,[175] meet together at the house of the Headman of the Hunt (*muqaddam*), known as Headmen of the Hunting Party and of the Quarter (*Abwā al-Qanīṣ wa-'l-Ḥāfah*). They assemble in the Headman's house to discuss the matter of the Hunt, and decide upon an appointed time for their going forth to the Ḥawṭah (sacred enclave) of Ṭuyūrah to seek permission of the Manṣab[176] of the Āl Ṭuyūrah to hunt.

Once they have set the time appointed for going forth to Ṭuyūrah they tell the poets (*s͟huᶜᶜār*), the flute-players (*mudarrif*) and anyone of a mind to go,[177] of the night appointed for attending the granting of leave to hunt, and they despatch the messenger (*al-ᶜānī*) to the house of the Manṣab of Ṭuyūrah. The messenger sent by the Headman would say, for example, "The Headman of the Hunting Party and the Five Members (*Ahālī Lak͟hmās*)[178] will come forth on the Monday evening[179] by night, after the evening prayer". To which the Manṣab will make reply, "Welcome (*ahl-an wa-sahl-an*)".

THE GRANTING OF PERMISSION TO HUNT

On the night appointed they will come forth, bringing a small sheep, a male goat (*māᶜiz*), and, producing a *ṭawᶜah*, i.e. the pole by which the net is held up; they slaughter the sheep on the *ṭawᶜah*[180] in front of the house of the Manṣab, i.e. under it.[181] When they have slaughtered the sheep, those with him (the Headman) will chant out the rallying-song (*yiṣalliqūn*, syn. *yinaṣṣirūn*[182]) saying,

Many a wide net,[183]	كَمَّنْ وَشْر ضافى
The killing of the game	دَمار أَلصَّيْدْ
In al-Aḥqāf.	في الأحقافى
Wā—Lamsak—Wīk!	وا لَمْسَكْ وِيكْ

To these others will make reply, saying,

The keenest joy,	خَيْر الزَّهِيَّهْ
The killing of the game	دمار أَلصَّيْدْ
In the ibex of large horns.[184]	في المَرْبَعِيَّهْ
Wā—Lamsak—Wīk!	وا لمسك ويك

Then they go up to the Manṣab's reception room (*maḥḍarah*) in Ṭuyūrah. As they enter the Manṣab's reception room they bring him coffee, coffee-berry (*jifil*), ginger, and sugar, to the value of about half a shilling, and they (the household) prepare coffee for them,[185] for all those who come.

Those who attend the first soirée (*al-samrah al-ūlā*) number about 150 persons, and, when the company is all seated and settled down in the reception room of Ṭuyūrah, they ask permission of the Manṣab for their going to the passes of al-K͟hutt in Juᶜaimah as I have mentioned above. But if the Manṣab thinks that the inhabitants are in difficult circumstances and in straitened means[186] he will not grant them permission to hunt, for hunting involves them in heavy expense (*maṣārīf*), and a great many guests come to the village people —on this account therefore, the Manṣab will not grant them permission at all.

But if the Manṣab sees that the village people are in easy (*razīnah*[187]) and comfortable circumstances he will grant them permission and pray for favour (*samāḥah*) for them[188] but enjoin them to keep assiduously to the five prayers,[189] to truth, consideration for each other, and assistance of the poor (*ḍaᶜfā* or *ḍuᶜafā'*). He then performs a *Fātiḥah* for them in the reception room of Ṭuyūrah at the cup-boards of the old men, the ancients of the people of Ṭuyūrah (*ᶜammāri 'l-S͟hībān al-Qudamā'*), the saints of times gone by.[190] When he concludes the *Fātiḥah* to the Presence of the Prophet, God bless and honour him (*k͟hatam al-Fātiḥah bi-ḥaḍrat al-Nabī*[191]) all present recite the *Fātiḥah* of the Book.[191] Then after that, the flute-player blows (*nafak͟h*) on his pipe (*qaṣabah*), the poet sings a certain number of odes (*kam quṣud*) of Banī Mig͟hrāh,[193] and a third beats (*faqaᶜ*) the *hājir*-drum, and yet another two beat *marāwīs*-drums,[194] while four persons get up and dance (*zafan*). These odes fortify the resolution of the tribes for the Hunt; and the net-man[195] and every person wishing to enjoy (*sālī*),[196] and desirous of the Hunt, for the odes recall to their minds the Hunt in the time of the s͟haik͟hs, tribes, and petty tradesmen (*masākīn*) of long ago (*al-awwalīn*).

After the poet ends his odes, the Manṣab, the Head of the Quarter (*Abu 'l-Ḥāfah*),[197] and the Five Members get up and go into another reception room by themselves, while the rest of those there remain, they and the poets, singing and dancing. When those first mentioned are met together in the other reception room before the Manṣab, they enter into discussion on all matters affecting the affairs of the Hunt. They lay a contribution (*yifarriqūn*)[198] on the Five Members, each Member being followed by about fifty persons, and ascertain how much money, dates, and grain which they take in the form of date-baskets of shredded bread (*k͟hubar fattah*)[199] will be sufficient for them. They decide that each Member shall attend, bringing with him the money for which he is responsible, under the house of the Manṣab of Ṭuyūrah who lives in Madūdah.

Then on the Wednesday (*Rabūᶜ*) morning, they send so many of the Members' sons to go out and take coffee to the tribes and Mas͟hāyik͟h and inform them of the time appointed for the Hunt. To each of those mentioned (below) who has a customary right to receive coffee from the Hunting Party (*Qanīṣ*) the amount of coffee given is an eighth of a pound of sugar (*sunkar*) and a weighed ounce (*ūqīyah mīzān*)[200] of coffee-berry only.

List (*bayān*) of those who are given coffee:

A *dair* (pl. *duyūr*, i.e. two ounces of sugar and a little coffee) goes to the Mas͟hāyik͟h Āl Bā Ḥumaid of the tribe of Āl ᶜAwaḍ. A second *dair* goes to the Mas͟hāyik͟h Āl Nādir, and a third *dair* to the Mas͟hāyik͟h Āl Faraj—they live in the village of Madūdah.

The coffee due to the tribes bearing arms, goes to the Āl Munaibārī, i.e. four *dairs* of coffee for four tribes of Āl Munaibārī[201]:

(1) The tribe of Āl Saᶜīd b. ᶜĀmir
(2) Āl Sālimīn b. ᶜAlī
(3) Āl Faraj b. ᶜAlī
(4) Āl ᶜUbaid b. Badr

The coffee due to the tribes of Āl Jaᶜfar b. Badr[202] goes to three tribes:

(1) To Āl ᶜAbūd am-Badr[203]
(2) To Āl ᶜAwn b. Badr
(3) To Āl ᶜAzīz b. Badr

One (*dair* of) coffee goes to the tribes of Āl Ḥuṣn, and a *dair* of coffee to Bin ᶜAlī b. Saᶜīd, Mawlā Nuṣairah (at Ḥawīr), and to the tribe of Āl al-Ṣiqair[204], three coffees[205]:

(1) To the Āl Saᶜīd ᶜĀmir b. al-Ṣiqair
(2) To the tribe of Āl Muᶜaikim
(3) To the Āl ᶜAwaḍ b. ᶜAbdullāh who are called al-Badū

One *dair* goes to the Āl ᶜAlī b. Saᶜīd.[206]
So also one *dair* of coffee goes to Āl S͟hamlān.[207]

All this is laid down, along with the designation of the persons who will actually take the coffee and the specification of the merchant (*al-tijārī*) from whom they will purchase it, in accordance with the customs (*bi-mūjib al-ᶜawā'id*), neither more nor less (*bi-lā ziyādah wa-lā nuqṣān*).

After this decision and allotment of duties they fix a time for the great soirée (*al-samr al-kabīr*) under the house of the S͟haik͟h Muḥammad b. Bū Bakr Bā Ḥumaid, the Manṣab of the Āl Ṭuyūrah who lives (*ᶜāmid*) in Madūdah village. They appoint, for example, the Friday[208] evening for the soirée after dusk, from about three o'clock, Arab time, till six, Arab time.[209] Then they announce [210] the decision by the broker (*dallāl*),[211] rising to proclaim to those in the Manṣab of Ṭuyūrah's reception room, after the Manṣab, the Headman, and the Five Members have rejoined those attending the soirée (*summār*).

They instruct the broker to make the proclamation in these words of his which follow[212]:

"Oyez, all ye present. Whereas the people of the village have agreed in the presence of the Manṣab upon a Hunt, and the great soirée will take place on the Friday[213] evening under the house of the S̲h̲aik̲h̲ Muḥammad b. Abī Bakr Bā Ḥumaid. Let him who is present tell him who is absent."

The poets then recite a poem by way of ending the meeting (qaṣīdat k̲h̲itām). They now bring the meat of the sheep which they slaughtered at the beginning of the soirée and set it down—after it has been boiled in a large vessel. Someone puts it (the vessel) on his head, and, taking in his hand whatsoever piece he grasps, divides it amongst those present, one after another.[214] After this they bring coffee to them, and after the coffee the Manṣab performs the Fātiḥah for them. At the conclusion of the Fātiḥah the petty tradesmen (masākīn) shout (yahūkūn) diverting words (kilmah musliyah) and beat the drum, i.e. the hājir and marāwīs, and all shout at the tops of their voices:

شيخنا مَوْلى طيوره لي يبيّنها جهار

والوعل ضربوه في المِبَدًا والظّهار

Our S̲h̲aik̲h̲ is the Lord of Ṭuyūrah who manifests it[215] clearly
The ibex they struck in the first net and the second.[216]

This they repeat some thirty times, marching round the house of the Manṣab of Ḥawṭat Ṭuyūrah the while.[217] They then depart to the strains of a song by one of the poets and the others to the village of Madūdah until they come under the house of the S̲h̲aik̲h̲ Muḥammad b. Abī Bakr Bā Ḥumaid, then they go to the house of the Headman of the Quarter. The soirée continues until it ends at six o'clock at night, Arab time.[218] When morning comes those whom they have ordered to take coffee (yiqahwūn) to the Mas̲h̲āyik̲h̲ and Tribes go forth as I have mentioned (supra), taking up a poet like ᶜAskūl[219] or Sulmān (b. ᶜAbdūn) of Tarīs[220] for the entertainment of those attending the great soirée.

THE GREAT SOIRÉE

On the Friday night people meet under the house of the S̲h̲aik̲h̲, the Manṣab Muḥammad b. Abī Bakr Bā Ḥumaid for the soirée, those attending numbering about 1,500 persons (including men, women, and children).

First of all the petty tradesmen (*masākīn*), the people of the Quarter bring their Headman accompanied by a squad (*marzaḥah*)[221] chanting new poems, to the place I have mentioned. Then they return, bringing the Members of the Hunt, tribe by tribe (*ᶜalā qabīlah qabīlah*), each Member of the Five preceding the squad (*marzaḥah*), in front of his men, until they arrive under the Manṣab's house, making three rounds,[222] and then seating themselves for the soirée.

When their processions (*marāziḥ*) are over, the poet sings Bani Mighrāh so as to entertain those there and fortify the resolution of the Hunting Party. About the middle of the soirée the Headman of the Quarter rises and goes up into the (afore-mentioned) Manṣab's house and is summoned[223] by the above-mentioned Manṣab, and the Manṣab of Ḥawṭah Ṭuyūrah, and their people of the Mashāyikh of Āl Ṭuyūrah; and he summons the above-mentioned Members of the petty tradesmen (*masākīn*) inside the house. Talk then goes around amongst them on their going forth to the Hunt.

Firstly he says, "Which of you, o Manṣabs, is going to go with the Hunting Party?" And they inform him of the individual who is to go with them. Then he receives the money from the Members—which they require by way of expenses for the Bedouin, camel-men (*jammālah*), poets, and each person to whom they customarily owe outgoings (*kharaj*). Thirdly they decide upon the camel-men who are to convey the provisions (*zawād*) to the Wādī Juᶜaimah, that is to say, the food of the Hunting Party. Fourthly (they decide) how many nets it is they are going to take with them for the Hunt, the least number being seven, the usual number eight, and the limit nine nets.

They decide that the departure (*mirwāḥ*) of the Hunting Party to Juᶜaimah will be at the Midday Prayer[224] at eight o'clock, Arab time, on the Sunday evening, in order that their return from the Hunt may be on the Friday morning so that they can join the Friday Prayer in Madūdah. The Hunt will then be four days, i.e. from Monday, Tuesday, Wednesday, the morning and evening of each day.

When the final decisions have been made, they summon the broker, ordering him to proclaim at the top of his voice before those attending the soirée, the words[225]:

"The first—bless him! The second—bless him! The third—bless him! May ye hear nought but good! The people of Madūdah village proclaim that their mind is resolved (*iᶜtaṣab ra'y-hum*) upon hunting in the direction of Juᶜaimah. They will depart on Sunday evening in the early afternoon (*awwal al-ẓuhr*) at eight o'clock.[226] The camels will march (*dabbar*[227]) at the meridian of the sun at six o'clock[228] to Juᶜaimah. The Hunting Party's journey on the first evening[229] will be to al-Jidfirah. On the early morning of the Monday there will be a hunt in al-Khiṭmah al-Sharqīyah. Concerning the tribes, let each man look to his bullet (*yaḥzur bunduqīyat-ah*), for he of whose bullet there is no sign has nothing.[230] Whosoever has provisions, let him bring them on the early morning of the Saturday up to early Sunday morning. Let him who is present inform him who is absent."

The poets then recite two odes for entertainment, and they stay dancing the *razīḥ*-dance[231] with four persons in the circle (*madārah*[232]) in front of the poets, flute-player, and drummers (*faqqāᶜ*), until six o'clock, Arab time, when the soirée ends. The Manṣab performs a *Fātiḥah*, and they depart from under the house of the said Manṣab with their dancing squads (*marzaḥah*) until they reach the house of the Headman of the Quarter where they stop.

THE HUNTING EXPEDITION

When Sunday comes, at six o'clock, Arab time, the camel men load up the camels with the provisions, nets, etc. (*yiḥammilūn al-jammālah ᶜala 'l-rikāb min zād wa-shibāk*) required by the Hunting Party, moving by way of the mountain edge (*bi-ṭarīq al-ṭaraf*[233]), while the Hunting Party which is going, sets off by night at eight o'clock, Arab time, as I have pointed out *supra*. As they march (*dabbar*) by, under the Headman's house, they form ranks for dancing and singing (*yishillūn marzaḥah*) up to the house of the Manṣab, and pass through the village up to the open space (*sāḥah*[234]). Then they go up to visit the Dome of the Shaikh ᶜAbdullāh b. Yā Sīn, then the Dome of Āl Ṭuyūrah which is called al-ᶜArshah, singing *rajaz* verses (*yartajizūn min al-shiᶜr*), all of them in a body, singing,

وَآهْل الخَنَبْ[235] ساروا بنيّه[236]
وَآدْعوا لهم يا الصالحين
وَآدْعوا لهم بأَلْجماله
من عند مولانا الكريم

With good intent the Huntsmen forth are set.
Pray for them O Holy Ones.
Pray ye that by good fortune they be met,
From our Beneficent Lord.

After the conclusion of the visitation, they ascend (*yilqafūn*[237]) by way of al-ᶜIrqah, i.e. the mountain which lies above Madūdah to the north, and after descending the mountain they cross a place in Juᶜaimah called Ruḍaimah, which is the first place in the Wādī Juᶜaimah below al-ᶜIrqah. They then pass by another place called Mithwā Ḥūṣī (or Ḥawṣī), and here one or two persons take coffee to Āl Zīmah Umbārak Āl Jaᶜfar b. Badr, and a *dair* of coffee to Āl Ḥuṣn at Ḥuṣn b. Qairān, and a *dair* of coffee to Āl Zīmah at Tawakhkharī. Then the young men arrive in the evening at al-Jidfirah about 11 o'clock, and some at 12 o'clock.[238]

As for the camel-men who have the provisions with them, they arrive at three o'clock,[239] Arab time, at night, and spend the evening in al-Jidfirah. After taking their supper they hold a soirée (*yilqūn samrah*) under Murabbaᶜah[240] Muḥammad Kūfān, all the Hunting Party assembling together, while the people of the Wādī Juᶜaimah come to attend the soirée. They inquire of one another concerning the departure (*misrāḥ*) of the Hunt early on the Monday morning. The soirée comes to an end at four o'clock, Arab time, at night,[241] and everyone goes to sleep somewhere in al-Jidfirah.

When the morning of the Monday comes all the Hunting Party wakes with the appearance of the morning light, and, as soon as they have performed the duty of the Morning Prayer, a servant by order of the Headman heats (*awqad, sic*) coffee in a large copper pot for the entire Hunting Party, and they take the coffee round to everyone. Whosoever drinks one single cup is forbidden to eat once he has drunk the coffee of the Hunt.

They now assemble together to cast lots (*li-'l-rawᶜ*) for the nets. From each net they put down one pole (*ṭawᶜah*, pl. *ṭawᶜ*), each one of course knowing his own pole, and they summon the Manṣab or one of his company (*jamāᶜah*, family), who takes the poles as a single bundle (*ḥizmah*), and turns to the Qiblah, rotating the poles round each other (*maᶜa dawr al-ṭawᶜ*). Then he addresses himself to the Headman, and says, "Take out a pole", for example, "for the Pass of al-ᶜAnkūb; the next is for al-Rajjāl Pass. Take out two for Shiᶜb al-Ghanam, a *mibaddā* and a *ẓuhār*,[242] and one pole for a pass, one for the Pass of al-Ḥisī, and one for Bā Ḥabl." Each one whose pole has been taken out receives it, and when he recognises it, along with the information with which it supplies him as to the pass which has fallen to his share (*kharaj ᶜinduh*), he takes his pole and net and sets out that morning towards the mountain. This is how the net-men do.

As for the guns (*rumyān*) and beaters (*shannānah*) they disperse, one of them will go up along al-Kutur Pass, and another will go up along the pass (*ᶜaqabah*) of Ba-'l-Khashab, but they do not ascend by the paths used by the net-men.

As the net-men reach their positions they set up their nets by inserting hooks (*kullāb*, pl. *kalālīb*[243]) of iron in crevices of the rock, an iron hook for each side of the net, while the poles they place at intervals in the net, five or six men settling down at each net. This is how they do.

As for the guns, when they reach the Jōl (flat plateau-like mountain top), each sits down in a *taqdūm*, a *mirbāh* (both words meaning a sangar[224]), i.e. they arrange a certain number of stones like a building, sitting down behind (*fī ṣadaf*[245]) the stones, so that the animals of the chase may not see them when they approach.

As for the beaters, i.e. the young men who drive the game up to the guns, they go to the farthest end of the pass, in the eastern area most remote from that pass, and go up on top of (*ẓahar ᶜalā*) the Jōl, they being about fifteen persons in number, or more. On top of the Jōl they shout at the pitch of their voices (*ṣallaq*),[246] crying "*Wō habūh!*" If they chance upon game they shout out, "Death! O men of the Pass of al-Ghanam!" (*Wa-'l-mawt yahl Shiᶜb al-Ghanam*) or "the Pass of al-Rajjāl", or "Ba-'l-Khashab". One, or two, of the beaters stands at al-Ḥājib,[247] i.e. al-Qārah which is on the Jōl, looking for the game to see down into which pass it will go (*saqaṭ*) so that they can shout out the words, "*Wa-'l-mawt*, Death!" (*yimawwit*) to those guns expecting (*mutaqaddimīn*) the game (i.e. those) to whom it is coming down (*saqaṭ*).

The position of the guns is at the top of the pass, at al-Qarīn, above the net-men. As the game reaches them they fire bullets at it—whatever is hit (*iṣṭāb*) by the guns they despatch (*yadhukkūn-ah*), but anything that is not hit comes along the pass, and, the nets being set up on the paths along which it makes its way, it falls into the net. If there be any game with them in the net, or with any of the guns, those who are there shout out (*yihūkūn*), and one of them shows himself (*ẓahar*) to the people of the *wādī* lying beneath these passes, crying at the top of his voice, "The old man is killed (*Wa-'l-shaibah maqtūl*)!"[248] This he repeats until the people of the *wādī* hear—all those who hear, women or men, shout out rallying-cries (*yiṣalliqūn*, syn. *yinaṣṣirūn*), and everybody's joy and delight increases.

When they have seized the head of game (*rās al-ṣaid*), and at the time of despatching it, the executioner says to it, "Your neck, o Bin Ḥumr (*ᶜUnuq yā Bin Ḥumr*[249])!" and raises the head of the ibex so that his neck, the place for execution, may show, and the executioner despatches him. This is how the game is despatched.

Now the Hunting Party, when they have finished hunting the pass I have mentioned, and wish to come out of it—one of the petty tradesmen (*masākīn*) goes up to the Jōl and shouts at the top of his voice, the words "Tonight, o Hunting Party, *Al-lail yā Qanīṣ*!"[250] repeating this until the whole Hunting Party hears it. Everyone who hears it comes from the mountain to its foot, all assembling together beneath the mountain. Then they form ranks for dancing and singing (*yisuwwūn marzaḥah*) and a poet gives them verses of *rajaz* till they arrive at the place in which they spend the heat of day (*yibridūn*), namely al-Jidfirah. In the course of the marching-song (*zāmil*) the tribes hunting the game fire off bullets, one after another, for joy at this, and by established custom.[251] On reaching the place where they pass the day (*maḥall al-muẓillīn fīh*)[252] they march round in a circle there with the head of the ibex (lit. *ṣaid*) in front of them, making and singing extempore verses on it (*yitzammalūn*).[253]

After this they stop, resting until eight o'clock,[254] Arab time, on the evening of that day, when the guns and beaters set out at night to hunt without nets in the western pass known as Khiṭmah Bā ᶜAbbād,[255] above Hushaimah to the west, and above Tawakhkharī, al-ᶜUqaiyiqah, al-Shāghī, and the passes which they hunt, i.e. the passes of al-Dawm and the pass of al-Bīr, al-Himih, Juwwat Āl ᶜAwaḍ b. ᶜAzzān, al-Ghubairah, and Shiᶜb Luthail.[256] When the Hunting Party get any game they do as on the morning hunt.

Arriving in the camp (*maḥaṭṭ*) which is the place called al-Juruf they spend the night there, and if they have any game they send a messenger with a letter from the Manṣab and the Headman to the other Manṣab of Āl Ṭuyūrah to inform him that the Hunting Party has a head or two head, notifying him whether it be ibex or game[257] and of the size of the ibex and number of rings (*ᶜijar*) which the horn bears. From the time that the messenger leaves (*min yawm yidabbir al-ᶜānī*) the camp of the Hunting Party he cries out in a loud voice, the words, "The old man is killed, *Wa-'l-shaibah maqtūl!*" until he reaches the mountain above the pass of Madūdah, and again when he appears before the village of Madūdah, with those words at the very top of his voice. The people of the village are in a state of eager expectation, and when they hear the sound of his voice a large number of the inhabitants there comes out to meet that man who brings the good news of the success (*jamīlah*) of the Hunt, until they come face to face with him. He tells them what the Hunting Party has got, and the messenger we have mentioned goes to the Manṣab's house and hands him the letter from the Hunting Party, and they give the messenger his reward (*bishārah*) for good news under the eyes of the Manṣab. This is what happens about the messenger.

Where the Hunting Party is concerned, they spend the Monday evening in al-Juruf, and, after supper, they hold a soirée in this place during the early part of the evening from one o'clock, Arab time, till two.[258] Then up they go with marching songs (*zāmil*) to Ḥawṭah Hishaimah, the place of the Mashāyikh Āl Bā Wazīr, and hold a soirée under the house of the Shaikh Saᶜīd ᶜUmār Bā Wazīr,[259] until five o'clock,[260] Arab time, at night, and then go to sleep.

As soon as it is light they wake up and all drink coffee together and cast lots (*rawwaᶜ*) and the Hunt goes forth (*saraḥ*), guns, net-men and beaters, to the northern (Najdī) passes called Hishaimah, Shiᶜb al-Rāk, Shiᶜb al-Ṣafāh, Maqṭaᶜ al-Duqum,[261] Bā Ṣifyāh, and Bā Ṭarfāh. Thus they hunt these passes, guns and net-men, in the same fashion as the hunting and its dispositions (*tarātīb*) on the first day. This is how the Hunt which ascends the mountain pass operates.

As for the Headman, the Manṣab and the rest who remain in the camp at al-Juruf, they order the camel-men, when the sun is up and the hour is about one o'clock, Arab time, to load up the provisions on their beasts and go by morning to al-Himih and off-load (*ḥaṭṭ*) by the pool (*qilt*) which is by al-Himih. The Manṣab and his companions sit on stones known as Ḥaṣāt ᶜUmar b. ᶜAbd al-Kabīr, Mawlā Ṭuyūrah.[262] One year this same day, the Hunt got four head, and, passing the heat of the day (*bardaw*) in al-Himih, they made an entry (*dukhlah*)[263] at which the smoke from the firing of rifle-bullets from joy and pleasure in the success (*jamīlah*), nearly covered everyone there with shade.

At eight o'clock[264] of the afternoon they go forth to hunt in Shiᶜb al-Ṣaiᶜar and al-Khuraibah al-Aᶜlīyah. The order of the Hunt is as before. On the third day, which is the Wednesday, they issue forth in the morning to hunt al-Khurbah, Marḥabā,[265] and Rūḥī maᶜa 'llāh (Go (fem.) with God).[266] On the afternoon of that day they come back to al-Himih. On the fourth day they return, hunting[267] al-Khiṭmah al-Sharqīyah, spending the heat of the day at Tawakhkharī, returning in the afternoon to go and make an entry (*dukhlah*) to *Maṭāriḥ*[268] and spend the night at Ḥūṣī. In the morning of the Friday they go to al-ᶜIrqah,[269] assembling under al-ᶜIrqah until the Manṣab and the Headman arrive, and make a formal entry (*dukhlah*).[270] All those in the village and its neighbourhood come out to meet them. The formal entry continues until about four o'clock in the morning, Arab time,[271] on the Friday, and in the afternoon following it (*ᶜuqbuh*) and at night, they hold a great soirée under the house of the Manṣab of Ṭuyūrah. They bring forth the game from the Headman's house to beneath the Shaikh's, the

Manṣab's, house, and hold a soirée at the end of which (_ghalāq al-samr_) they take back the game to the Headman's (_abū_) house.

On the Saturday morning they form into a great ceremonial procession with dancing and singing (_zaff_)[272] first thing in the morning, about one o'clock,[273] going forth to under al-ᶜIrqah and performing what resembles a marriage of bridegrooms (_al-ḥarāwah ḥaqq al-maᶜārīs_).[274] Afterwards they return to north of the village and make a sangar (_mirbāh_, syn. _mitrās_) inside which five persons make sham play (_huqlah_, syn. _liᶜb_[275]) to amuse the people. They now enter the open space (_sāḥah_) of the S̲h̲aik̲h̲ ᶜAbdullāh b. Yā-Sīn, those who are making the play (_mutahaqqilīn_)[276] carrying matchlocks (_Al Bā Fatīlah_), and, to make a tamasha (_tamās̲h̲ah_),[277] they set off about twenty boxes of squibs (_qarṭūs_, pl. _qarāṭīs_), after all of which they enter the village, and the morning procession (_zaff-al-bukrah_) finishes about six o'clock midday.[278] After the Noon Prayer they go to Ḥawṭat Ṭuyūrah with the game they have taken, and in ranks for singing and dancing (_marzaḥah_), they then return to the village to the open space, singing odes about the game and performing the _razīḥ_-dance. The _zaff_ concludes before sunset at half-past-eleven, Arab time,[279] and everybody goes his way.

AFTER THE HUNT

The next day after the _zaff_ the Headman invites all the Members to his house to make a reckoning (_muḥāsabah_) and divide (_taᶜdīl_) the meat.

First comes the division of the meat; the largest leg (_al-līd al-kabīrah_) of the three head[280] goes to the Manṣab of Ḥawṭah Ṭuyūrah and a share (_rānī_, syn. _qism_) to him as well.[281] Secondly, the _qaṣmah_ (i.e. a piece from the knee down to the middle of the leg[282]) of the big(gest) ibex goes to the Master of the Coffee-Pot (_Mawla 'l-Ṭuss_)[283] in which is made (_ṣallaḥ_) the coffee for the Hunt, they being Āl ᶜĀmir Muḥammad. Thirdly the large _fiqrah_ (top part of the neck (_raqabah_)) of the throat (_mad̲h̲bah_) (i.e. after the head has been cut off), goes to the man who prepares the coffee, and the coffee of the people of the circle (_ahl al-ḥilqah_).[284] Fourthly, meat called _al-k̲h̲immah_[285] they divide into eight shares, one share for the Mas̲h̲āyik̲h̲, Āl Ṭuyūrah, for (each of) the two Manṣabs, and six (shares) for the Headman and the Five (Members, syn. _Abū_). The gun (_rāmī_) who gets the game has the head, skin (_dīm_) and the _mayassah_ (syn. _d̲h̲ail_ or _ᶜajz_, rump and tail piece), while the net-man (_mawla 'l-s̲h̲abak_) receives the same.[286]

When all this is over the Headman and his Members make a reckoning together of the expenses (*makhāsīr*) and anything over- or underspent. The Headman will spend about 500 shillings. He refers them (the expenses) back to the Five Members, and each Member in turn refers back the expenses that fall to him to his men (*awlād*, lit. children[287]) and the rest of the Hunting Party. Each person may spend about 3 shillings. Those who go to the Pass (*shi*ᶜ*b*) number about 350 persons. They pay the camel-men who carry the food their hire, each one 30 shillings hire (*kirā*)[288] for his camel and the poets to the number of three, each one 10 shillings. The disbursement (*khasārah*) is the duty of the Headman and he refers it back to the Members.

This is what came to my mind of the customs of the Hunt, and God directs us to what is correct.

* * *

Concerning the individual who eats after he has drunk of the coffee of the Hunt (*qahwat al-Qanīṣ*), or after the casting of lots (*raw*ᶜ), thereby becoming "attainted (*mudhaiyam*)", so that when he foots it with the Hunting Party they get no game until he purifies himself by slaughtering a sheep, even just a small one, a goat (*mā*ᶜ*iz*) which they divide amongst only the Hunting Party as a group—if he does not perform the sacrifice (*dhabḥ*) incumbent upon him the Hunt will not allow him to accompany them until he purifies himself with a sacrifice (*fidū*[289])—if he is a villager (*ḥaḍarī*[290]), i.e. not a gun (*rāmī*). If however he be no less than a gun, i.e. one who bears arms, then he "attaints" (*yudhaiyim*) himself and his gun only, nor can he hunt himself until he pays ransom (*yufaddī*) of a sheep for his rifle, which is divided amongst the hunters as I have indicated above.[291]

LAWS IN USAGE RELATING TO THE KILLING OF THE GAME

Firstly, amongst the net-men, when one head of game is struck in the *mibaddā*-net—which comes first, but extricates itself from it, a link (*ḥalqah*) of the net remaining on its horn—be it even a single thread, and it is then struck in the second net, i.e. the *ẓuhār*, and killed there, it is adjudicated by customary usage to the man at the first net.

Concerning the killing of the game (*qitāl al-ṣaid*) by those who bear arms,[292] the head of game belongs to the man whose bullet hit it first, even if it draw little blood and the least blood appear.[293] The gun in question gives notice of (*aᶜlam ᶜalā*) his shot, and produces fair proof before the Manṣab and the Headman.[294] In the case of the animal hit and felled (*ṣaqqaṭ*) by the others (i.e. after the initial wounding), the latter receive nothing apart from a share in the meat.

If a dispute should break out between those who bear arms so that each (party) says, "I hit the head of game which has been shot, and my shot was the first", it is then up to the one who claims that his bullet hit first, to produce two fair proofs attesting that his bullet first struck the animal in question. The proof is substantiated before the Manṣab who adjudicates it to him (*yaḥkum buh luh*), but if the proof be not established, judgement of the matter is up to the circle (*al-ḥilqah*), namely the entire Hunting Party. This is how judgement in the killing of the game takes place between those who bear arms.

If any misdemeanour or abuse (*zalal aw sabb*)[295] proceed from one of the members of the Hunt (*awlād al-Qanīṣ*) against one of the Hunt the matter lies in the Manṣab's hands. If it be substantiated by a proof, or by his own admission (*iqrār*) the matter lies in the Manṣab's hands to pronounce sentence against him by way of rebuke and of restraint upon the rest, either by fining him (*k͟hasārah*) or by punishment with the net-pole (*ta'dīb bi-'l-ṭawᶜ*)[296] in the circle, under supervision of the Manṣab.

HUNTING CASE (No. 1)

A dispute once took place between Sālimīn b. Saᶜīd b. Minaibārī (sic) and Mirᶜī b. Birik b. Saᶜīd concerning the killing of the game.

The former claimed that his bullet had struck an ibex, i.e. one bearing forty rings (*ᶜijar*)[297] in S͟hiᶜb al-Rāk, the wound being in its leg, and Sālimīn went up to the mountain top and shouted, "I've got the ibex!"

The other, he being Mirᶜī b. Birik, replied that his bullet hit it first, the animal containing five of his bullets, that the man who felled it was ᶜAwaḍ b. ᶜAbd al-Ḥabīb b. Saᶜīd,[298] and that (one of) the beaters despatched it, he being ᶜAbdullāh b. Sālim Bak͟hḍar[299] and his companions there with him.

The first, Sālimīn, however, again repeated (*zād al-tikrār min Sālimīn*) his assertion with lengthy dispute, and wanted to bear the head of the animal in his hands, but the beaters would not allow him to take it; so they came forth from the mountain quarrelling until they reached the camp (*maḥaṭṭ*) at al-Himih—to the Manṣab and the

Headman at al-Himih, where the beaters delivered the animal's head in front of the Manṣab and the Headman. After the end of the lunch of the Hunt of that day the Manṣab convened the disputants when he had studied the plaint and the counter-plaint, charging the first plaintiff to produce just proof testifying to his claim.

Sālimīn produced two witnesses, Sālim b. ᶜAlī b. Firaij and Musaibilī b. Saᶜīd b. ᶜUbaidullāh,[300] and each gave evidence on his own account with the words, "I bear witness, I, Sālim b. ᶜAlī b. Firaij, that the ibex was (hit by) Sālimīn b. Saᶜīd b. Munaibārī, and that he hit it in S̲h̲iᶜb al-Rāk in the tail of the pass (near the nets) where it comes into the main valley (*al-qirih*)[301] above the fissure (*al-ṣudᶜ*[302]), and that the first bullet to hit it came from Sālimīn, and that the ibex gave a jump (*hamaz*) at it". The other gave similar evidence.

Then the Manṣab and the Headman asked for particulars (*istafṣal*), saying, "Is it this ibex here now that Sālimīn hit?" To which they answered, "We do not know whether it was this or another one". Thus their evidence fell to the ground for lack of confirmation.

The other then produced two witnesses, ᶜAlī b. Umbārak Bā Miftāḥ and Umbārak ᶜUmar His̲h̲mān, each stating, "I bear witness that this ibex here was (hit by) Mirᶜī b. Birik b. Saᶜīd, and that it came up to Mirᶜī unwounded (*ṣāḥī*) before a bullet from anyone else hit it, and that Mirᶜī first of all hit it with his first bullet, and put five bullets into it (in all) while ᶜAwaḍ b. ᶜAbd al-Ḥabīb felled it with a sixth bullet, and the beaters despatched it".

The decision, after the studying of the plea and counter-plea and acceptance (*istilām*) of the witnesses, was that the ibex was confirmed to Mirᶜī b. Birik. This is what the Manṣab and the Headman adjudicated, and in God is success.

HUNTING CASE (No. 2)

A case between (those) of the Hunting Party (*Qanīṣ*) of the brokers (*dalal*)[303] of S̲h̲ibām was brought up, and they referred it to the Headman of the Quarter (*Ḥāfah*) at Madūdah, it being as follows (*infra*).

It is that the people of S̲h̲ibām took a small ibex (*ṣaidah ṣag̲h̲īrah*),[304] and, sparing its life (*baqqaw-hā*), brought it into S̲h̲ibām, making a ceremonial for it (*zaffū bihā*) while it was still alive; for there were already six head with them, despatched by the guns (*rumyān*), and they made a ceremonial procession (*zaff*) for the lot. As for the live ibex, they kept it, alive, after the end of the *zaff*, in the house of the Headman of the Quarter of S͟hibām. Then, a few days later, the ibex died of itself a natural death (*faitah*).

They then went forth to the pass to hunt again (*ᶜazamū ᶜalā qanāṣah t͟hāniyan ila 'l-s͟hiᶜb*). Six days they remained hunting and finding game, but they got nothing at all until the Headman came out, and, making the Hunt stop in the pass, he went off to Madūdah with his question to the Headman of the Quarter of Madūdah about the above-mentioned ibex. The latter answered him that the Hunt had "attainted itself (*tad͟haiyam*)", and that the cause was the live ibex for which they had performed a *zaff* on the first hunt while it was still alive, because everyone who sees it has a share in its meat, but by its dying they had deprived the Hunt of its meat since it had died a natural death, i.e. without legal slaughtering (*d͟hakāt s͟harᶜīyah*).

The judgement in this (case) and purification of the Hunt (*qanāṣah*) from "attaintedness (*d͟haim*)" is (as follows).

First the judgement was that the game (*ṣaid*) be weighed against incense (*duk͟hūn*)[305] instead of[306] its meat, but since the body of the ibex was no longer in being, the cost of the incense would be 300 French (*Frānṣah*) *riyāls*.[307] Then the Headman of the Quarter of S͟hibām asked for mitigation (*tak͟hfīf*) from the Headman at Madūdah and his Five Members. So they deducted 200 French *riyāls* but compelled the Headman to pay (*taslīm*) 100 French *riyāls* and to pay them towards the rebuilding of the dome of al-Qadīm ᶜAbdullāh b. Muḥ. Bā ᶜAbbād, he being named al-Qadīm,[308] buried to the west of the town of S͟hibām. The Headman of S͟hibām undertook to pay this to the overseer of the alms (*nāẓir ṣadaqah*) of Qubbat al-Qadīm.

Following his acceptance of the judgement by the Headman of Madūdah, he returned to S͟hibām, and paid over what had been awarded against him. He then went to his companions who had remained in the mountain, and after the arrival of their Headman they went forth to hunt in the morning, succeeding in taking four head of game. This is what the Headman of the Quarter of Madūdah decided between the above; and the people of S͟hibām made a ceremonial procession (*zaff*) for their game.

HUNTING CASE (No. 3)

As also a dispute broke out between (those) of the Hunt of the Quarter (*Ḥāfah*[309]) of the people of Wādī Bin ᶜAlī,[310] between the persons mentioned below, they being the former Headman, Ṣamīl by name,[311] and the Āl Bā Qalāqil.[312]

The Āl Bā Qalāqil referred a plea to their *ḥabīb*,[313] al-Ḥāmidī[314] against (*ᶜind*) their Headman, Ṣamīl, namely they pleaded that the Headman of the Quarter eats after the casting lots by the Hunt, without regard for the laws (*qawānīn*) of the Hunt, and that he thereby deprived them of success (*ẓafar*), so that their efforts took them to the mountains on many occasions (uselessly), without their catching anything, large or small.

He replied by admission of the case before their Manṣab, Ibn al-Ḥāmid Ḥasan.[315]

After the plea and counter-plea had been made before Ibn al-Ḥāmid, he did not know (what) declaration (*taṣrīḥ*) to make between the aforementioned, so he directed them to go to the Headman of the Quarter of the village of Madūdah, and to follow whatever decision was made between the two parties, sending them off accompanied by a messenger from himself with a letter concerning what had befallen between those mentioned therein. After their arrival in Madūdah, and when the Headman of Madūdah had studied the plea and counter-plea, along with the order of the Saiyid Bin al-Ḥāmid, the judgement (of Mawlā Madūdah) was as follows:

Firstly, judgement is given that the former Headman, namely Ṣamīl, be expelled from the office of Headman (*al-buwwah*) for lack of observation (of the law of the Hunt).

Secondly, he must deliver a sheep to the Quarter, thereby to purify himself, and he will be an ordinary member (*walad*) like the rest. Let him appoint (*ṭallaᶜ*) for them a Headman (*abū*) from Āl Bā Qalāqil in whom he perceives earnest of uprightness (*wijh al-ṣalāḥ*[316]) and to whose headship (*taqdimah*) all the members of the Quarter assent.

They agreed and they delivered over what had been judged (i.e. the sheep). The Headman of the Quarter of Madūdah and the Manṣab sent the judgement they made on the Quarter of the people of Wādī Bin ᶜAlī, in a letter to Bin al-Ḥāmid concerning what was said in the judgement, and they followed it. Only two days after this they went forth to hunt the pass (*s͟hiᶜb*) of Wādī Bin ᶜAlī, and on the first day they were successful in obtaining two head of game, so they came out of the pass and made a ceremonial procession (*zaff*) with them. This is what was resolved by those we have mentioned, and they followed it so that their Hunt was purified.[317]

COMMENTARY

The most striking feature of the Madūdah Hunt is the all-important role played by the Manṣab in controlling the Hunt in which he partakes at all stages except the actual slaying of the game. The Mashāyikh are of course not armed; apart from any other consideration the Manṣab, or his representative, could not act as an impartial judge if he partook in the Hunt, but there must have been other considerations which remount to the more ancient hunting ceremony. In pre-Islāmic South Arabia it may be that success in the Hunt was a sign of the favour of the God and in inscription CIH 547[318] it is evident that this favour had to be sought by performing the hunt for him at the appointed time for it, and that the favour most required of the Divinity was, as is to be expected in an agricultural community, rains for the crops. The authors of the description of the Madūdah Hunt are almost propagandist in their insistence that, following on the decisions in cases of disputes or "taint" and the purification, game is immediately found. This implies to some extent that the Manṣab and Headman have the power to interpret the Divine will. It is interesting, on the contrary, to discover that the Manṣab is sufficiently islāmised to insist on the performance of the prayer, but the Ḥāmidī Saiyid of case No. 3 claims that he has no knowledge of hunting laws, and perhaps, were the truth known, he may have refused to have anything to do with the case at all.

One may perhaps detect in inscription CIH 547, a sense of rivalry between the god ḤLFN and the god ḏSMWY, in that the former was neglected for the latter. Amends had to be made by giving, as one would say nowadays, a *nidhr* or votive gift, to pacify ḤLFN, and no doubt to restore the prestige of his sanctuary. This is similar to the rivalries that exist between some saints' shrines in present-day southern Arabia, or more precisely between the hereditary keepers of these shrines.

The matter of purification and ritual chastity of heart is always to the fore. It is required in hunting case No. 2 that the purification be made by expending money on incense. The incense is to be used for the tribal requirement of whitening face after it had been blackened—elaborate theories should not be built on its function in this special connection for it is also used for such mundane purposes as chewing-gum and sweetening the air of the *ṭahārah*. In the *Kitāb al-Manᶜah*,[319] the individual or tribe which has committed *al-ᶜaib al-adgham* is insulted by others by *tadkhīn*, censing, and in Dathīnah this was at last made clear to me, for it seems that there dung would be burned in the thurible in the presence of the traitor.

The treaty in ancient Mecca known as Ḥilf al-Muṭaiyabīn, rendered by Lane as "the Covenant of the Perfumed Men",[320] appears to be, in reality, a species of lustration, for the parties to the

Covenant mixed perfumes into which they dipped their hands—the common method of perfuming oneself in South Arabia is of course to burn incense and allow the fumes to permeate one's clothing. The symbolic act of censing with sweet odours as opposed to burning dung, is like so many terms in this kind of Arabic, partially a play upon words. The perfume at the Meccan Covenant was brought in a large bowl (*jafnah*),[321] containing charcoal it may be, as it would in an Arab house today, and the Covenant was concluded in the house of a celebrated Saiyid, ᶜAbdullāh b. Judᶜān. In Arabia of the present day the verb *ṭaiyab* means *versöhnen*, conciliate, become reconciled, and *ṭībah* reconciliation, expiation.[322] It will be recalled that the Prophet Muḥammad, as Tradition avers, gave the name Ṭaibah/Ṭābah to Madīnat Rasūl Allāh.[323] Yāqūt connects the name with *ṭīb*, perfume, and a variant of the name, al-Muṭaiyabah, would support this sense; he further cites a 4th-century A.H. traditionist, al-K͟haṭṭābī, as stating that, it is so-called, "On account of its excellence/perfume (*ṭīb*) for its inhabitants, and their security (*amn*) and their freedom from trouble/easy circumstances (*daᶜah*) in it". Medina was pre-eminently a centre of conciliation where the Prophet composed the differences between the Aws and K͟hazraj tribes, as in the years following he re-built around his *ḥaram* in Medina, or, rather, re-aligned the great series of alliances constructed by his Qurais͟h forbears over much of Arabia. *Ṭīb*, perfume, can readily be linked to the ideas of goodness of heart, good faith, purity of intention, akin somewhat, to the words *barī'*, *naqī*, and the like.

Perfumes were employed in religious ceremonies at the Kaᶜbah before Islām. Al-Nuᶜmān of al-Ḥīrah is known to have sent perfumes to be sold at ᶜUkāẓ where, in return, he bought cloth,[324] and there is quite a body of Tradition of the *taṭyīb al-Kaᶜbah.*[325] These Traditions include, "*Ṭaiyibu 'l-Bait fa-inna d͟hālika min taṭhīri-hi*, Perfume the Temple (*Kaᶜbah*) for that pertains to its purification". The Kaᶜbah was censed (*yujammar*) each day with one *riṭl* of *mijmar*, and each Friday with two *riṭls*. *Mijmar* is said to be the substance with which the censing was effected, i.e. good aloes (*ᶜūd*)[326] whereas the *mujmar* was the vessel in which the censing was performed (*mā yutajammar fī-hi*). In Mecca the well of Zamzam was also known as *Ṭībah*.

In hunting case No. 2, the tomb which is to be restored lies outside S͟hibām, in the cemetery. It is of course no uncommon thing for tombs to lie outside a town, as for instance west of Anṣāb in ᶜAwlaqī territory; these shrines may become the centre of important cults. Perhaps therefore the fact that temples connected with hunting seem sometimes to have lain outside the walls of pre-Islāmic cities should not be over-emphasised. Where temple pillars are named it has occurred to me that they may have been identified with the poles of the hunting net, especially where there are rows of pillars as at Maḥram Bilqīs[327] and that mock hunts may have been staged before the temples, or the hunt re-enacted there. At present such a hypothesis is purely speculative.

The strange way in which the meat is divided at the soirée upon which permission to hunt is sought may have some ritual significance, as, I think, has the ceremonial coffee-drinking, and also the insistence that while the hunt is in progress and the ritual coffee has passed their lips, the hunters must eat nothing till all eat together. Thomas[328] says of his Bedouin, "It was their code after a thirsty day's march that when we arrived at a water-hole no drop of water should pass the lips of the advance party until those in the rear had come up, nor would any man eat a crust with me unless his companions were there to share it". We have here a Bedouin custom, founded on their peculiar conditions of life, become a point of religion among the hunters, settled people though they are.

Al-Nūr al-sāfir[329] shows that the more or less chance division of meat, as opposed to the careful allotment of each piece which I have found customary and is also reported by Thesiger,[330] was widely current in Ḥaḍramawt some centuries ago. Ibn al-ᶜAidarūs speaks of the *maẓbī* made by Ḥaḍramīs, i.e. meat broiled on hot stones, and quotes a poem on *habārīsh* not dissimilar to a poem I have published.[331] "The *Ḥaḍramīs* call what is roasted of the *sawād al-baṭn* (offal?) and the like, *al-habārīsh* . . . When they sit at a meal it is a custom of theirs that one of them begins to cut the meat and go round with it to the party, giving to each one a piece, and doing the same with the next until the turn of the first comes round again and he gives (some) to him. This continues till they have finished eating, and they call eating after this fashion *al-waqṣah*.[332] They find in this a great delight which no other delight can equal." In late 1966, when we returned from Qāsim Munaṣṣar's H.Q. in the Banī Ḥishaish district near Ṣanᶜā' to a Jahmī encampment west of Ṣirwāḥ, we were entertained in one of their tents in much this way. A Jahmī brought round a tray or large bowl of meat cooked and cut into pieces, holding it above his head in such fashion that neither he, nor any of us sitting on the ground, could see what it contained. As he went round each guest he put his hand up to the tray, and picking out a piece at random, handed it to the recipient. In this instance at least I think the intention can only have been to avoid making any distinction between guests which might have led to quarrelling since, as the main meat meal followed later, these were probably to be regarded as titbits only.

At Madūdah they told me that you can, if you wish, send part of your share in the meat of the Hunt over to your friends in Saiwūn on the south side of the Wādī, or even abroad to friends in, say, Java or Malaya. You cut it into small pieces and set them on a string or thread and put them in a *ṭuss*. I have seen meat dried and made into a sort of biltong on the pilgrimage to Hūd, and it is curious to see that Yūsuf . . . b. ᶜAbd al-Barr of Cordova[333] in the early 5th/11th century gives, in a list of presents that would be expected from the returning pilgrim who has made the *ḥajj* to the Holy Cities of Arabia, the item "strips of sun-dried gazelle-meat (*qadīd al-ẓibā'*)". Meat is still sent about rather more freely than one might imagine, for our Somali *ayah* in the late forties used regularly to receive meat from Somaliland. It was dried on a line in the sun, cut with the line of the grain, and immersed in a can of ghee.[334] The custom as observed in Ḥaḍramawt struck me as rather similar to the European practice of token gifts of wedding cake sent to friends.

RECENT ARCHAEOLOGICAL EVIDENCE OF THE RITUAL HUNT

Attention has been drawn by W. E. N. Kensdale[335] to the significant red[336] granite stele at ancient Qarnāw, published by M. Tawfik,[337] this city lying on the north-eastern edge of the Yemen,[338] and to the jambs of a temple at K͟haribat Āl ᶜAlī also in the Jawf area, published by Professor Ahmed Fakhry.[339] His attempt at the interpretation of these sculptures must, I think, be modified by what we now know of the Ḥaḍramī Hunt.

The Qarnāw stele is headed by a row of seven circles, each containing 28 markings. Following M. Tawfik, Kensdale suggests that these markings correspond to the 28 days of the lunar month, and sees here symbols of the Moon God. If anything is to be read into these markings, as one may well be justified in doing, it seems to me possible to connect them with the 28 stars of the agricultural year.[340] Then again, the number 7 is equivalent to the number of stars in one of the four agricultural seasons in *certain* parts of South Arabia. Perhaps one-quarter of the year is indicated as the season appropriate for the Hunt, perhaps the seventh star of the year, perhaps it indicates the opening of the hunting season in October with the star *al-Sābiᶜ*, the time when the *Sābiᶜī* millet is sown. The season October–December in Ḥaḍramawt is the most suitable time for hunting, for there is not then, I think, any pressing agricultural operation, the weather is cool but not cold as it is later on, and much hunting does in actual fact take place at this time; but it might continue till the end of March, maybe even later. It may be that the circles are intended to represent the full moon. At Madūdah the hunters do go out to hunt at night, which would imply that they hunt by moonlight, but on the other hand no informant mentioned that the fullness of the moon is taken into consideration when setting the date for the Hunt.

The bands of zigzag design beneath the ibexes must surely represent conventionalised mountain; perhaps the fact that the upper row of ibexes faces left, and the lower faces right, is to indicate the irregular way in which the ibex moves, as demonstrated by the Madūdah hunters. The fine mesh below the ibexes, must, as Kensdale surmises, be netting—the hunting net, for the mesh runs exactly the same way as in my Madūdah photograph (see Plate No. 2), presumably to allow the net to stretch. The interpretation of these nets as temporary fences for holding the live ibex preparatory to sacrificing it at the altar must be abandoned in view of the animal's reputation for spirit, and the fact that no trace of this exists today. The ibex led into Shibām was after all a small animal, probably a kid. Against this I must set the story of the Āl Khaṭīb shaikh in Tarīm to whom an ibex presented itself when he had no animal to slaughter for the feast, the saint known as Ṣāḥib al-Wiᶜl.[341]

If the blade-like objects superimposed on the net are to be interpreted as spears they certainly do not conform to the type of spear I have seen in South Arabia (see Fig. No. IV). Though spears were not mentioned to me as used in the Hunt this is not surprising in view of the virtual disappearance of the spear during the last fifty years. From a practical point of view to attempt to despatch the entangled ibex with a spear seems to me clumsy, perhaps dangerous. I should prefer to suggest that these objects are ornamental heads to the hunting-net poles.[342] Professor Beeston suggests javelins for throwing at the game.

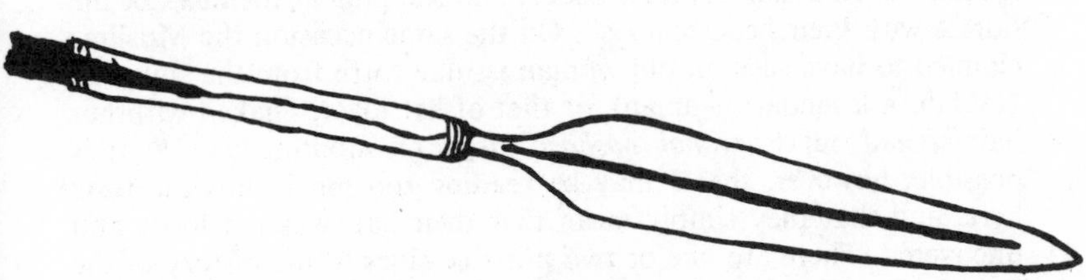

Fig. IV
Sketch of South Arabian Spear

The lower section of the stele still puzzles me, but by analogy with the upper section it must, I think, be assumed that it is a formal representation of the hunting of the oryx which, to the best of my knowledge, is not netted in the open plains fringing the Empty Quarter, though it is true that the Qaṭarī expedition of 1965 did use lassoos to take the oryx alive. In answer to my inquiry Major I. Snell informs me that he knows of no type of lassoo which might be used for this purpose there.

Regarding the actual use to which the Qarnāw stone was put, apart from being used for circumambulation as at Dammūn, trophies of the chase may have been formally deposited there, or perhaps the meat was divided in front of it. In all events I do not think it necessary that the animal should be slaughtered at the stone for the practical reasons which I have indicated.

The K̲haribat Āl ᶜAlī jamb[343] (Fig. No. IX) shows what may be a type of net, similar to the curious decoration under the oryxes of the Qarnāw stele. However, the most significant feature is the dancer. Kensdale proposes that this is the figure of a man as against Professor Fakhry's suggestion that the figure represents a woman. It will be sufficient to compare my photograph (Plate No. 3) of the *ḍaᶜfā*, performing at the picnic of the Tarīm Baqqārah or Cattle-men, with their curved sticks, *not* throwing sticks, to realise exactly what the stele does represent. Incidentally the Baqqārah consider it necessary for their continued weal, and that of their beasts, to hold this picnic annually. The dancing man of the stele is performing what, in Ḥaḍramawt, is known as the *razīḥ*,[344] in the course of which the Baqqārah weave their loosely hanging bobbed hair. Weaving of the hair by moving the head from side to side, since it is so widespread in Arabic-speaking countries, must be esteemed an ancient custom.[345] Even in the time of the Prophet, if one is to interpret certain passages in al-Wāqidī[346] in this way, it may be that we have it recorded. As the Prophet made his triumphal entry into Mecca and approached the Kaᶜbah, the Meccan women issued forth to meet him, "having spread out (the hair of) their heads, and slapping at the faces of the horses with their head-scarves". On the same occasion the Muslims claimed to have seen an old woman issuing forth from the statue of Nā'ilah (a legendary woman), or that of her lover, "naked with her hair spread out (*ᶜuryānah nās̲hirat al-s̲haᶜr*), shouting 'woe'!" It is possible, however, that I may be reading too much into the texts here, and that they simply mean that their hair was left loose and uncovered. There are one or two possible clues to the history of the Baqqārah and their picnic. Al-Hamdānī[347] discusses a tribe ᶜAbd al-Baqar, well to the west of the Yemen, "and it is said they agreed to worship an idol of theirs in the form of a bull". This could be linked with D̲h̲ū Samay, Lord of Baqar-um, the latter epithet being considered by Professor Ryckmans[348] as the name of a sanctuary, but I see no reason why it should not be rendered as "Lord of Cattle". In another connection we have seen Allāh described as Sā'iq al-Baqar, driver of (wild) cows.[349]

I cannot forbear here to quote the strange tale of the 10th/16th-century hagiologist Bā Hārūn,[350] which, though they are not expressly referred to by this name, relates to the Baqqārah. "With the s̲h̲aik̲h̲, S̲h̲aik̲h̲ b. ᶜAbdullāh, son of the s̲h̲aik̲h̲ ᶜAlī there were yokes of oxen (*hujūj baqar*) working for him at Bait Jubair, breaking up the ground, and when they had finished they asked him for their wages, and he said to them, 'Walk with me to Tarīm'. 'We shall work (*s̲h̲ā nas̲h̲tag̲h̲il*) here for someone else,' they said, 'for it is a trouble for us to go back to Tarīm'. So he said to Bā Ziyain, 'Take this stone (*ḥijārah*), strike another stone against it, and thence will come forth what is owing to you'. So he struck it with another stone, and from it came forth silver coins (*darāhim bīḍ*). 'Count them,' he said to them, 'and take your due'. A *buqs̲h̲ah* (small coin) was lacking, so the s̲h̲aik̲h̲ said, 'Do you want it from your horn (crown of the head), or from your ox's horn (*turīd-hā min qarn-ak aw min qarn t̲h̲awr-ak*)?' 'No,' he replied, 'from my ox's horn'. So he said, 'Strike your ox's horn, and it will come forth from it'. So he struck it, and it came forth from it." The association of this miracle, performed by a holy man, with oxen may be more than coincidence.

On the 4th September, 1954, I saw the Baqqārah picnic return from ᶜAidīd to Tarīm, through the ᶜAidīd gate. First came the slaves dancing with a bridegroom (*kulān*) at their head, later followed the Baqqārah in circles, weaving round, they in turn were followed by the massed ranks of the townsmen of the K̲h̲ulaif Quarter. Some carried sprigs of the ᶜ*ilb* tree. Women in their bright red dresses were watching, and the Saiyids come on foot or in cars; the women as it were, draped on the cemetery walls. At one time all used to carry clubs, i.e. all those in the procession. There were great clouds of dust raised by the dancing and shouting, amid which I distinguished the name of the patron saint ᶜUmar al-Miḥḍār. From the picnic place in ᶜAidīd they went up to the Quarter boundaries at the tombs, then up past the Jabbānah (cemetery with a mosque)—where they made a complete circle, and past it, and up into the town. It is evidently, I noted, an ancient ceremony, and most awe-inspiring. The Baqqārah picnic bears certain resemblances to the excursion to mount ᶜArafat which constitutes one of the ceremonies of the *ḥajj*. The Meccan excursion seems to have been in association with Jabal al-Raḥmah which could have been understood in the sense of Mountain of the Rain. I have not recorded that it is to ensure good rains that the Baqqārah go on their annual picnic, and have come across no evidence to show that the ᶜArafāt excursion had originally this purpose either, but it is not impossible that both, like the Hunt, were associated with rain-making.

On reflecting over the date of the picnic I see that it took place early in the sign of the Zodiac, al-Thawr, Taurus, which in Wāḥidī country falls in the last month of Kharīf, i.e. September, so that the picnic would, as it were, fall about the beginning of this zodiacal sign. Again this is reminiscent of the pre-Islāmic month Dhū Thawr.[351] There is an ancient saw current in Ḥaḍramawt which runs in the back of my mind, "*Al-thawr mā yadkhul fi 'l-Thawr*, the bull (presumably for ploughing) does not enter (sc. enter the field) in al-Thawr". That is to say during the period of the star al-Thawr, presumably the sign of the Zodiac.

I inclined to Professor Fakhry's view that the globular objects above the dancers are wine-bottles, resembling, it may be, the hard leather translucent bottles known in Ḥaḍramawt as *baṭṭah*, employed for holding ghee. The coffee drinking ritual of today may have replaced a wine-drinking ceremony of the past, though a long interval has elapsed between the prohibition of wine and the discovery of coffee—perhaps the toddy-palm still used in ᶜAwlaqī country may have filled the gap! However, in 1972, after visiting many *samsarahs*, i.e. hostelries, in Ṣanᶜā' where I saw rows of red pottery water-jars hanging from the rafters, presumably to cool, I am now completely of the opinion that this is what these objects represent. I should even be so bold as to suggest that the waist-wrapper worn by the dancing figure is an ikated Yemenite tissue of a type known from before Islām, during Islām, and still perhaps to be found[352]; imitations still come from Indonesia.

A tiny detail of each of the ibex horns in both stelae remains to be noticed. Each horn contains over twenty rings. Evidently each ibex depicted is one which has qualified the hunters to make a ceremonial procession *dukhlah* or *zaff*, as the case may be, with its head on a pole. The ibexes too, it will be remarked, are all males.

Other fragments found on the Kharibat Āl ᶜAlī site contain representations of ostriches. Philby[353] has already found fragments of ostrich eggs and I have myself seen shells in the hands of the locust patrols. With the extinction of the bird in South Arabia it may be that an entire lore has been lost. In Northern Arabia, on the other hand, Doughty[354] and more recent writers have recorded the hunting of ostriches. F. M. Hunter[355] describes the Somali method of hunting, the hunter concealing himself beneath the wing of a tame bird and shooting his prey with a poisoned arrow, but, although he mentions the import of ostrich feathers from Somaliland to Aden and al-Mukallā, he in no way implies that any came from Arabia itself. In a Yemenite almanac from Milan which I have not as yet fully analysed, it is noted under the 22nd of Ailūl (September) that the cold begins, and, laconically, "*awwal baiḍ al-naᶜām*, the first of the ostrich eggs". The Ambrosiana almanac seems to bear a close correspondence with the British Museum MS. Or.3737 (*Jadwal al-yawāqīt fī maᶜrifat al-mawāqīt*) though the two are not identical. There is internal evidence that both almanacs are at least pre-Portuguese as the seasonal movements of the Hurmuzī are recorded, and of al-Kārim.[356] Fischel[357] believes that the activities of the Kārimī merchants ended about the 9th century A.H. (15th century A.D.). I do not recall any reference to ostrich hunting in Arabic sources on mediaeval South Arabia, but this almanac entry would seem to indicate their existence there at that time.

On the basis of a small corpus of inscriptions Professor Beeston has succeeded in producing a sketch of the ancient Ritual Hunt, remarkably accurate if it be conceded that the contemporary Ḥaḍramī Hunt is essentially the same ceremony. The huntsman is of high religious standing, either the priest-king himself, or the religious collegium such as the "community" of ᶜAthtar. The Mukarrib I have long believed to be in many respects similar to the Manṣab of a Ḥawṭah, but the community of ᶜAthtar might conceivably be interpreted as a name for the members of the Hunt considered collectively[358]—though I am inclined to think of the community as the tribes and *masākīn* associated with a shrine, a temple or a *ḥaram/ḥawṭah*. In Tarīm the terms Mawla 'l-Khilaif and Mawla 'l-Sūq are used as expressions denoting the Quarter organisation of the Sūq or of al-Khilaif. *Mawlā* is the title commonly given to a saint, and in the inter-Quarter agreements Mawla 'l-Sūq treats with Mawla 'l-Khilaif as if they were two individuals. A patron saint is associated with each of these Quarters.[359] In the case of al-Khilaif the patron saint is Shaikh ᶜAlī al-Khaṭīb Ṣāḥib al-Wiᶜl, as already stated, and his mosque is known as Masjid al-Wiᶜl.[360] To consider the people of the Quarter as belonging to the community of the saint is not difficult, indeed their collective personality seems in some way identified with that of the saint.

In the inscription Gl.621 where the ritual hunter is required to offer portions of the animal taken in the chase I have suggested that there need be no blood-guilt but some form of "taint (*dhaim*)", some infringement of a taboo or law. The term *tanadhdhar* in one inscription rendered as "did penance" is today commonly used of vowing a sheep (though other offerings can be made) and is a word frequently to be seen in the hagiologies. So in CIH 547, when the community of ᶜAt͟htar confessed and did penance to Ḥ LFN I suggest that this simply took the form of sacrificing a number of sheep and/or oxen.

The hunting inscription at al-ᶜUqlah, Philby 84, first examined by Beeston,[361] was re-copied more recently by Jamme and published.[362] One assumes that the Jamme reading is superior to that of Philby, though, with worn rock and in different lights, such readings may sometimes be a matter of opinion. Jamme's rendering of the inscription does not, however, appear to improve on that of Beeston.

In brief the inscription speaks of a tribal "king" of Ḥaḍramawt who came to S͟habwah,[363] undertook certain building operations and slaughtered 35 oxen, 82 sheep, 25 gazelles and 8 leopards. It is with the building and slaughtering that this study is concerned, since these actions may be interpreted rather differently from the renderings of either Beeston or Jamme, though the views of both A. S. Tritton and Beeston that it is a hunting inscription seem incontrovertible.

The relevant portion of the inscription relates that the "king" *wḍrs/br'* (*Jamme*) *bytn šqr ṣll bgndln*[364] *mt ṯbrw bn ṣydmn whrgw kh͟mst wšlty bqrm*[364]*/wṯty wṯmnhy ḥwrw*[365] *wkh͟mst wᶜšry ṣbym wṯmnwt 'fhd bgndln 'nwdm.* For this I should like to suggest a rendering, "And (the 'king') crenellated (*ḍrs*[366])/built (*br'*) the temple of S͟haqr at Jandal with *ṣalīl*-stone[367] when they were withheld/frustrated from hunting, and they slew 35 ibex, 82 wild cow, 25 gazelle, and 8 lynx at the Jandal/*jandal* 'NWDM". The interpretation would then be that, when the Hunt had failed to take game, the "king" embellished the temple of the Moon God S͟haqr with ornamental battlements/or/ good roofing, and they were then successful in hunting and made a bag (which probably was so outstandingly notable as to exceed anything previously known). This inscription would then closely resemble the actions taken to remove *d͟haim* set forth in hunting case No. 2 *supra*.

In a *ḥuṣn* at Jinainah[368] in the Wādī Jirdān, only 16 miles from S͟habwah as the crow flies, *ṣalīl*-stone was used to strengthen the roof in places, and on the battlements, houses being built of mud in this locality; it is therefore most unlikely it was used for casing a temple, especially as it is described as neither quite mud or stone. Professor Beeston considers however that I go too far in rendering *ḍrs* as "crenellated". The emblem of S͟haqr shown on the coins published by the late Dr. John Walker is the eagle, and this is reminiscent of the two Nasrs, or "eagles" the small hills outside S͟habwah.[369] With regard to Jandal, I can only say, without comment, that ᶜAlawī b. Ṭāhir[370] speaks of a place called Jarandal which is marked on von Wissmann's map as a hill, some five miles to the east of Shabwah, up the Wadi ᶜIrmā on the route to the *jōl* of Bal-ᶜUbaid over which the "king" may well have hunted. The verb *ṯbrw*, to fit the meaning I should like to assign it, must be read in the passive, which Professor Beeston assures me, is attested from ancient South Arabian, but it is from the Arabic sense I propose to take it—the word in the passive is applied to Pharaoh in the Koran.[371] *Baqar* can mean ibex—this is a suitable sense at this point—since one assumes the ibex would come first in the list. I take *ḥwrw* in the sense of the Arabic *ḥawrāʾ* as in al-Ānisī's[372] *al-rashā al-aḥwarī* applied to a gazelle and a young girl, or to a wild cow. These last two interpretations are conjectural. As regards the lynx (*fahd*), Professor Beeston considers this to be the caracal lynx, a native of the Arabian Peninsula, but apart from the *nimr* spoor already mentioned, I was shown at Ṭawr al-Bāḥah in 1941 a black and white skin flecked with yellow, if my memory be correct of a feline of some sort. Of the difficulty over *ṣydmn*, Professor Beeston writes, "I would concur with your rendering of *ṣydmn* as 'hunt', but one has to admit that this poses very difficult problems. There is no reliable evidence in the Semitic languages for a noun-stem *fᶜlm*; and I am obliged to fall back on the *pis aller* of supposing an engraver's mistake. This can have happened in one of two ways. The simplest is just that *ṣydmn* is a mistake for *ṣydhn* (which would be the normal *Ḥaḍramī* form). The other is that he first engraved *ṣydm* which would be equally acceptable) and then wanted to change it to the emphatic form and did so by adding the emphatic *n* to what he had already engraved. This is, I fear, a desperate expedient!"

Jaww al-Kudaif immediately west of Shabwah[373] has many gazelle, and the locust officer in 1954 shot a couple when we went over to Baiḥān. As regards offering animals of the chase in sacrifice, it must be recalled that according to Islāmic Tradition, a game cannot be offered in lieu of a domestic animal at ᶜĪd al-Aḍḥā. This conceivably might be, in effect, a prohibition of some aspect of ritual hunting, but, if so, the original reason for the prohibition has long been forgotten.

If Beeston's original translation be preferred, and the first two categories of animals immolated be understood as 35 oxen and 82 sheep, these must be regarded as sacrifices connected with the temple.[374] In Wādī Jirdān where houses are built for secular purposes the final sacrifice would be on the roof, or even the battlements themselves, but as the purpose is to ward off evil spirits this might not be observed in building an ancient temple or an Islāmic mosque.[375]

An unresolved problem of the hunting inscriptions is the word *krw* which recurs. In the texts quoted by Professor Beeston it appears twice, *ṣd ṣyd krwm*, and *ywm ṣd ṣyd ᶜṯtr wkrwm*. The latter formula is also found in the inscription from Naqīl Shujāᶜ, published by Ryckmans,[376] this place being on the way to Wādī Ḥarīb, near Baiḥān. As all previous attempts at interpretation of this word have been speculative there can be little harm in adding yet further guesses at its true sense!

One suggestion is that *ṣyd krwm* may be the hunt of the game-bird known as the *karawān* which I shall not attempt to identify, though from the verse which follows it should be something like a bustard.[377] Al-Qāsim b. Aḥmad al-Rassī (ob. 246 A.H.(A.D. 860–1), a Zaidī, one of the Rassid Imāms of Ṣanᶜā' and Ṣaᶜdah, says,[378]

When the *karawān* cries on the Sands (al-Rimāl)
And the new moon comes round to the *burj*[379] of perfection
Ḥubārā (bustard) is the maternal aunt (*khālah*) of the *karawān*.[380]

Al-Rimāl very probably means the "Sands" of the Empty Quarter, and the allusion might be to a hawking expedition with falcons which, as seen above, were employed during the early ᶜAbbāsid period in Ḥaḍramawt.

As an alternative, difficult as it appears to me to fit in to the context syntactically, the following suggestion as to the sense of *krwm* is proposed.

The root *krw* in Arabic can mean, when applied to a she-camel, to make her two legs revolve in running (*al-nāqah bi-rijlai-hā qalabat-hā fi 'l-ᶜadw*). This immediately brought to my mind the *maḥāff*, or riding in circles of camels, that I had seen at Shaikh ᶜUthmān in 1947 at the *ziyārah*, and I seem to recollect that if a riding camel is held on a tight rein it may lift its forelegs up something like a horse. Part of the Thibī *ziyārah* in Ḥaḍramawt consists in the Manṣab riding round in circles, seemingly at some danger to life and limb, and from certain indications it seems that it is important to all that he should achieve this successfully. I have only heard of this by report, however. Might then *krw* not refer to "festal" riding in circles, whether a *ṭawāf* or otherwise? It is related to *karr* which has such senses as "*fair un tour*", etc. This would make the *krw* approximate to the Ḥaḍramī *zaff*, perhaps, when an ibex of truly noble proportions was taken.

Discussing Ingrams I, an al-ᶜUqlah inscription, with Raḥaiyam in 1957, he said that *imtall* means *istaᶜadd* in present-day Tarīm, i.e. to prepare. This roused a new train of thought and again I am prepared to hazard a speculation as to the sense of this inscription, based on the Madūdah practice. Professor Beeston's rendering runs,[381]

YDᶜ'L BYN king of Ḥaḍramawt son of RB ŠMS of the free-men of YHB'R (performed certain actions) (*mtll* [*wṣll*]) at the fortress ᶜRMW (? ᶜIrmā); and they hunted for twenty days and slew four panthers and one (?) . . . and [eighty-six] ibexes.

The Madūdah hunters, of course, prepare, and they proclaim a hunt. The proclamation opens with the formula—*awwal ṣallī ᶜalā Muḥammad*, a phrase which is used to make people stop and pay attention—for instance I have heard it used by tribesmen in the court at Mūdiyah when they wish to break into the flow of talk of one of the litigants. Beeston himself has suggested that it might mean "to proclaim", from the root *ṣall*, but might it not equally well be derived from the word *ṣallī* of the herald, in some such phrase as "ṣallī 'alaih" and be a verb *ṣallal* of the type *basmal* and *ḥamdal?* It may be objected that this is an Islāmic formula but I think it not impossible that the essential word *ṣallī* may have been used in the pre-Islāmic period.

It would be rash to venture further, but the picture that comes to my mind is of the king of ᶜIrmā in which S̲h̲abwah lies, coming out to the open steppe to hunt with the tribesmen of YHB'R and returning via or to al-ᶜUqlah, which stands out as a great landmark in the desert here.

I concur with Professor Beeston that the Hunt was not practised primarily to obtain food, but, although it is a religious act in one sense, it is also an extremely pleasurable occasion. The exclamation uttered by the hunter on hitting the game, given me by the ex-Quᶜaiṭī slave as, *k̲h̲us̲h̲s̲h̲-hā wit̲h̲lāt̲h̲ī*,[382] I had at first thought might have some hidden import and be an oath by the Trinity or by ᶜAt̲h̲tar. I now know better, for Professor Saiyid Yaᶜqūb Bakr pointed out what should have been obvious to me, that it would be an oath by the triple divorce; it resembles very closely the phrase uttered by the archer in firing an arrow at the *naqīb* Saᶜd b. Muᶜād̲h̲, "*K̲h̲ud̲h̲-hā minnī wa-anā Ibn al-ᶜAriqah*, Take it from me, and I am Ibn al-ᶜAriqah!" This is a common formula of ancient Arabia,[383] but *wit̲h̲lāt̲h̲ī* is probably Islāmic.

Finally, Professor Beeston has remarked that the ritual hunt inscriptions are all reported from the Sabaean, Ḥaramī, and Ḥaḍramī areas, i.e. places lying on the fringes of the Empty Quarter (al-Rubᶜ al-K̲h̲alī) or the great open *jōls*. Only on these upland plateaux and vast steppes or sands was there room for those civilised peoples to organise a hunt; nor would they be so likely, inadvertently to cross a tribal frontier as further west where in any case the mountains are often extremely broken. In Dathīnah I did see, south of Mūdiyah, drawings of animals done in red under overhanging rocks, possibly in similar material to the red and white scribbles reported by W. H. Ingrams[385] from Mahrah country, but my inquiries as to organised hunting elicited only a denial that anything of the sort was known there. Landberg[386] too seems to have drawn a blank. I was however told there at Mūdiyah of an oath which runs, "*Bainī wa-bainak dhī yiqaiyid al-ṣaid*, Between thee and me is He who fetters the game". This calls to mind such phrases as "Lord of ibexes". Hunting was probably never an organised affair there. When I asked Mubārak ᶜAbdullāh al-Ṭawsilī about the distribution of the hunt with the net, he said it was a question of the mountain terrain—if the ways by which an animal could move were known and limited by the formation of the mountains, then you could hunt with nets as in Ḥaḍramawt, but in his own country, Upper ᶜAwlaqī, there was no hunting with nets because the terrain simply did not lend itself to that. In Oman there is some hunting with nets (though it looks as if it only referred to birds not animals of the deer type), for *al-iṣṭiyād bi-'l-shabak* is mentioned in the Ibāḍī work *Jawhar al-Niẓām*.[387]

THE GOD TA'LAB

With the complex problems of the South Arabian Pantheon this study is not greatly concerned, but it will be noted that the god Ilmaqah/Ilumqah had, as symbolic animals, the bull, ibex, lion, and sphinx, while ᶜAthtar had the "antilope et taureau". Ta'lab is a god-name already well attested from the pre-Islāmic inscriptions, and, in its sense of an animal, the word is already identified by Ibn Sīdah[388] with the *waᶜl* or ibex.

Professor Beeston, in discussing the meaning of Glaser 1142, renders the epithet *bᶜl mkhlym* which is applied to the god Ta'lab, as "Lord of Pastures".[389] A *khalā'* in the spoken Arabic of Southern Arabia today means open country rather than pastures specifically, and I take it in this way. Of course the *khalā'* would include country grazed over as well as the haunts of wild animals and hunting country. The word occurs in the traditional and very significant ditty sung at the fertilisation of the palm-trees in the Ḥaḍramī town of Saiwūn[390]:

Plate 1
Bronze lamp from Matara, Eritrea, a type also found in Yemen, in the form of a hunting dog seizing a male ibex. The curved horns are broken off, but the beard shows clearly. The lamp is housed in Addis Ababa University Museum.
(Courtesy of F. Anfray)

Plate 2
The hunting net set up in Madūdah village for the mock ibex hunt

Plate 3
The picnic of the Baggārah in Tarīm. The Baggārah are wearing their hair loose in the dancing and procession as they return to Tarīm City. The other groups are dancing and carrying curved sticks which also figure in the stele from Kharibat Āl ʻAlī in Maʻīn. See fig. 9

Plate 4
Decorated door flanked by ibex horns from the Wāḥidī Sultanate

Plate 5
Frieze of bulls' heads from Shabwah similar to the debased formalised decoration in plaster in Yemeni houses at the present time. See fig. 3.
(Courtesy of Miss Caton Thompson)

Plate 6
Winged figure from south Arabia in alabaster. Probably from Ma'rib
(*Courtesy of Bini Moss*)

Plate 7
Tomb of Sa'īd b. Sālim Bā Buraik with ibex horns set on top and a niche on the N. or N.W. side near Shabwah. There are also Bā Buraik in 'Iyādh and Jirdān

Plate 8
This winged figure in bronze was brought to Dathīnah over 20 years ago. It is now probably in India

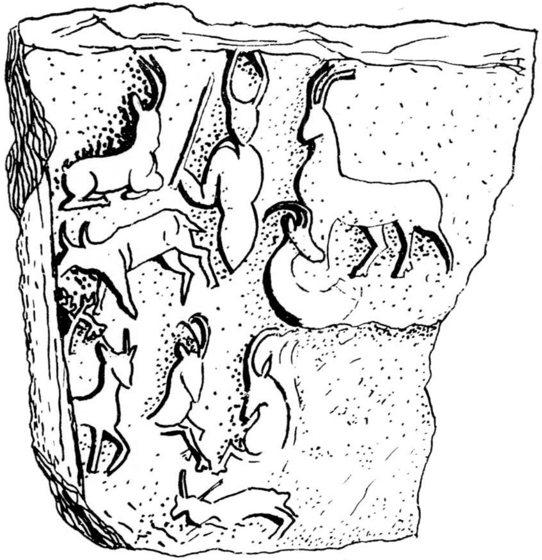

Plate 9

Capital of column from Ḥusn al-'Urr showing ibex in various positions, with, possibly, the triumphant hunter among them, an ibex head on or in front of his own head, and a stick in his hand.

(*Courtesy of Hermann von Wissmann and Dr H. Norris*)

a Plate 10

b Plate 11

a. Door jamb from Ḥuṣn al-ʿUrr of Ḥaḍramawt. Man, ibex and birds in vine-tendril decoration. Front side.
(*Courtesy of Hermann von Wissmann*)

b. Door jamb, side view. Hunter with cross-bow shooting ibex with calf. According to Pirenne about late 2nd or 3rd century A.D.
(*Courtesy of Hermann von Wissmann*)

Plate 12

Ibex hunters at Tarīm triumphantly returning from the hunt with a bag of three head. Across the horns of the best head on the left they have strung some sort of ornament. Some hunters bear the curved sticks which also figure in the stele from fig. IX.
(Courtesy of Mrs. Doreen Ingrams)

Plate 13
Ibex family in Saiyid Sir Bū Bakr b. Shaikh's courtyard in his country house at Ḥabūẓah near Saiwūn.
(Courtesy of Hermann von Wissmann)

Plate 14
Ibex horns set in a dome above a siqāyah or tank for drinking water at the 'Aṭṭās tomb at Mashhad, Wādī Daw'an, a centre of pilgrimage, Ḥaḍramawt.
(Courtesy of Miss Gert.ude Caton Thompson)

Plate 15
Bait Madagher in Ḥārat al-Maidān, a large house in Ṣa'dah in the adobe construction typical of N.E. Yemen and Najrān.
(*Courtesy of Hugh Leach Esq*)

Plate 16

The oryx, wuḍaiḥī or baqar al-waḥsh, from the herd of Shaikh Qāsim/Jāsim b. Ḥamad of the Āl Thānī

Plate 17

Exterior wall of a house in Wādī Rijām E. of Ṣan‘ā’ destroyed during the Egyptian occupation of Yemen.

Plate 18

Shield, doubtless Indian in origin, from Upper Yāfiʿ of leather, lacquered in red and gold with four convex bosses and a single flat central boss, in possession of Stephen Day Esq.

Yā ṭuyūr al-khalā wa-'l-ṣaid wa-'l-nūb
Yā khair maṭlūb.
O birds of the open country, game and bees,
O what an excellent thing to ask.

Al-Hamdānī[391] tells us that a certain Riyām or Dhū Riyām, had attributed to him, the *maḥfad* (castle or fort, a word still to be found in the name of Maḥfid in Lower ᶜAwlaqī territory) on the top of the mountain of Dhaibān b. ᶜAliyān b. Arḥab, where there was a temple (*bait*) to which pilgrims used to make pilgrimage in the ancient days before Islām, and of which, he says, marvellous ruins still remain. A nephew of Dhū Riyām was called Ta'lab Rīm/Ri'm, and al-Hamdānī says he is mentioned in the pre-Islāmic inscriptions of Nāᶜiṭ—to this latter is ascribed Maḥmā (vocalisation uncertain) Ta'lab, i.e. "the interdicted grazing land of Ta'lab" at Ghūlah of al-Bawn.[392] Both these eponyms belonged to the Arḥab tribe. *Ri'm* means an antelope, and *Riyām* might be a plural, but no such plural is given by Lane's *Lexicon*. Ta'lab is associated with this place Riyām, and with the sanctuary of Ṣaid.[393]

At the beginning of December 1966 I crossed the tongue of Republican territory between Jabal ᶜAyāl Yazīd, stretching northwards through the flat Qāᶜ al-Bawn, and Royalist ᶜAyāl Siraiḥ country, and on to Shākir. On December 6th, escorted by Muḥammad al-ᶜUbaidī, son of the *naqīb* ᶜAlī b. Ḥusain al-ᶜUbaidī and Arḥabī tribesmen, I passed under Jabal al-Riyām where he pointed out the ruins to me from the road on top of this fairly low hill. Ṣirwāḥ (not the Ṣirwāḥ of Jahm) and Nāᶜiṭ were also pointed out to me. Although the Arḥabīs are split into two groups, the Dhaibānī and Zuhairī, I have not recorded in my field-book that they mentioned Jabal Dhaibān. The territory to the west of al-Riyām, through part of which I had passed, lying parallel to Qāᶜ al-Bawn is called Ẓāhir al-Ṣayad, the Uplands of the Ṣayad (tribe), by al-Hamdānī,[394] and the Turkish map of 1323 A.H./A.D. 1905–6[395] marks what may be approximately the same area, or the part of it lying in the flat Qāᶜ al-Bawn plain, as Qāᶜ al-Ṣaiyād; if the name has altered thus over a thousand years it would not be very astonishing, but the Turks often misspelled Yemeni names in maps and other documents, and Glaser marks Hijrat Ṣayad in just this area. As I have suggested earlier, the name Ṣayad would, on the face of it, seem to be connected with hunting, but whether this be so or not, the ᶜUdhar b. Saᶜd of Hamdān, who inhabited the valleys draining into the Wādi 'l-Khārid somewhere in the vicinity of al-Riyām, are described by al-Hamdānī[396] as "*aḥadd al-ᶜArab wa-aqnaṣu-hu*, the keenest in eloquence of the Arabs and those of them most given to hunting". Beyond Hijrat al-Ṣayad on the Ḏhī Bīn road is ᶜAththār which we were told had a Jewish settlement—the name looks like the ancient ᶜAthtar.

In this fairly extensive district west of al-Riyām there was apparently then both hunting and an area of interdicted grazing.

From the proper names in the inscription, Glaser 1142, it may be inferred that the inscription relates to a district south of Ṣaᶜdah, quite possibly the very district under discussion, if the ḏḎBᶜNN of the inscription is to be identified with al-Hamdānī's al-Ḍabbāᶜin.[397] In the preamble the names of Saᶜd and YḤM'L are associated with Ta'lab, both being of the Banū Sukhaim. YḤM'L might be read in Arabic as Yaḥmī Ill, i.e. "God protects, guards, defends, interdicts", or, though very unlikely, "He protects a protected person", since ill can mean jār. The root is the same as that in Maḥmā Ta'lab, the interdicted grazing land of Ta'lab. It would be over-bold, at our present state of knowledge or ignorance of the actual and historical geography of this region, to go so far as to suggest that the grazing ground interdicted to ḏḎBᶜNN was that known to al-Hamdānī as Maḥmā Ta'lab in al-Bawn territory.

In the other text, Glaser 1143, quoted by Professor Beeston,[398] it is stated that Ta'lab lord of pastures/open country "has the right to take grtn from all flocks" (pasturing in a locality uncertain). The interpretations of grtn offered both by Höfner and Beeston seem difficult to accept, and I suggest that Ta'lab took jīrah in the sense of protection-money,[399] very probably for the protection afforded by the sanctity of the god Ta'lab's property.

Al-Hamdānī considers Ḏhū Riyām and Ta'lab Rīm as eponyms, though they look much more like god-names. To the north of Jabal al-Riyām we passed by the tomb of the Prophet Ṣāliḥ just beyond Sūdah, but had not time to go up the hill to look at it— perhaps it may have become the focus of local pilgrimage after the destruction of the temple on Jabal al-Riyām.

Now the verb alaba can mean "to hunt or chase", and alabat al-samā' means "it rained". In more than one case, we have seen that the performance of the hunt is necessary to ensure an adequate fall of rain to irrigate the crops.[400] Ta'lab could then mean, "It (al-samā', the heavens, feminine in Arabic) rains". In the hunting poems I have published, including that translated above, there is mention of rain or floods in four out of the five poems, and the one poem in which there is no such allusion is a modern sophisticated composition.[401] In ᶜAbd al-Ḥaqq's dīwān[402] one poem seems to imply that if no game is taken there will be lack of rains, high prices, and already his dates have become dried up; another seems to expect and rejoice in hoped for rains because 19 kills were made by the Hunt; yet another says that the tribes and net-men if they see a kill consider it like ᶜĪd al-Fiṭr. The whole tenor of the Banī Mighrāh poems in ᶜAbd al-Ḥaqq's *dīwān* seems to link rains with the Hunt.

Perhaps all the horned animals mentioned above were associated with that aspect of a god or goddess which blessed with or withheld rain—for the present I avoid the question of the lion and the sphinx.[403] It might be that we are wrong in regarding all the various names of the ancient Arabian dieties as separate gods of a Pantheon, and perhaps one should rather distinguish the various qualities, aspects or attributes which are expressed in the names of these deities as different aspects of Allāh.

To quote Jamme[404] again, on ᶜAthtar with the variant ᶜAstar, "Certains aspects stellaires de cette divinité sont indiqués par trois epithètes: *s̲h̲rqn* 'l'oriental', *ghrbn* 'l'occidental', marquant les deux stades opposés de Venus, et *nwfn* 'l'élevé' celui qui . . . caractérise l'astre à son zenith". He remarks also that two texts show that ᶜAthtar has the character of a divinity of irrigation. This is evidenced in two inscriptions examined by Jacques Ryckmans,[405] *wsqy* ᶜ*ṯtr sb' khrf wdṯ'*. ᶜAṯtar a abreuvé Saba en automne et au printemps.

ṢIRWĀḤ AND NORTHERN YEMEN

Landberg[406] quotes Glaser for a line in an inscription which he (Landberg) proposes to read Maḥram Baᶜl Awᶜāl Ṣirwāḥ—this I would understand as, "The sacred enclave of the Lord of the Ibexes of Ṣirwāḥ". In pre-Islāmic Arabia it seems generally agreed that *maḥram* must mean more than merely a temple and would include the whole sacred enclave in which it stands. When I visited Ṣirwāḥ in late 1966 I noticed, at points on two of the tracks leading into it, what appeared to me to be single pillars—I should have liked to enquire whether these demarcated the limits of a sacred enclave, but, travelling by truck with tribesmen not of the district, circumstances prevented me. Such enclaves cannot but be ancient, and I was surprised to find that as far away as the Sudan a *masīd*—which is certainly to be linked with *masjid*, is a space around a tomb or *khalwah*, *qubbah* of a saint, or mosque, to which a certain degree of sanctity attaches; it is a little raised, covered with sand usually, and surrounded by a low wall or bushes; one puts off one's shoes on entering it. This is to be compared with the *ḥaram* and *maḥram*. On the other hand I did question the local Jahm tribesmen of the Ṣirwāḥ district on the ritual type of hunt as it obtains in Ḥaḍramawt and satisfied myself that they were not aware of the existence of it there. In the ruins of Ṣirwāḥ representations of the ibex are prominent —at the gate of the temple there is a lovely ibex frieze still in position, and a piece representing a pair of confronted ibex has been built into the structure of a mosque at the back of the town. The Islāmic town was deliberately wrecked and utterly destroyed by the Egyptians when they fell back earlier in that year on Ṣanᶜā', with the exception of the temple and mosque, and the site could be excavated though it has been sadly mauled during the occupation, when ancient masonry was pulled out from anywhere to make sangars against Royalist fire.

The tradition of decoration with friezes of ibex heads appears to me to have survived in a rather debased way to the present day in much of the Upper Yemen. For example in al-Maḥābis͟hah in the high western mountains there is, in the Ḥukūmah building, a room with a plaster frieze in low relief around the upper part of the wall, consisting of what looks remarkably like a series of formalised ibex heads. In this district on the black stone (*ḥabas͟h*)[407] of the outside walls of the houses are formalised geometric designs in whitewash which look like friezes of ibex or deer heads. In Sūdah of the western region (not Sūdah already mentioned) I saw what was presumably a formalised head applied to the corner of a room, and again, in Arḥab, on the outside of a house about the first floor, a formalised frieze of the same kind. If my sketches are compared with the frieze from S͟habwah (Plate No. V) of Philby's photograph, though this is a pattern of bulls' heads,[408] I think the proposition I advance is conclusively established. In Wādī Rijām in 1972 we found an ibex in russet-coloured stone built into the buff-coloured masonry face of a *dār*, one of two on the left-hand side of the wādī as one ascends it, unfortunately shelled badly during the Egyptian occupation. We also saw an ibex similarly built in russet stone into light-coloured stone of a house on the Kawkabān escarpment. I do not recall seeing anything similar in other parts of northern Yemen. At the top of the new road up Wādī Sirr next to Rijām I found a rock graffito with a hunting scene in al-Qaḥalah area with two bowmen shooting at an ibex, accompanied by another man on a horse.

The ornamentation of the battlements on the adobe constructed houses of Najrān, just north of the Yemen border, also looks to me as if it were based on a horned head pattern (see Fig. No. VI). One may be permitted to speculate that perhaps the reconstruction of the pre-Islāmic temple of S͟haqr at S͟habwah included battlements of this style.

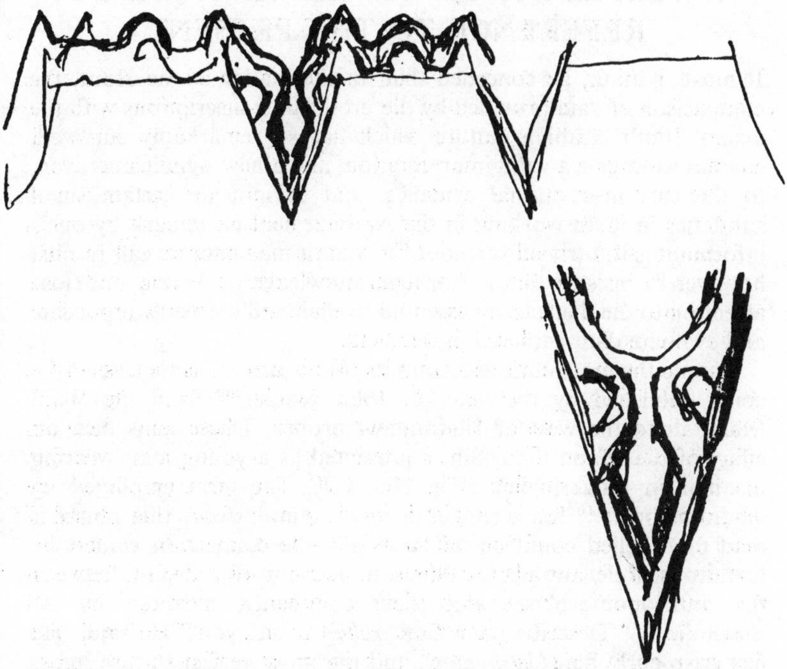

Fig. V
Sketch of a frieze of ibex heads from plaster decoration in the Ḥukūmah building at al-Maḥābis͟hah

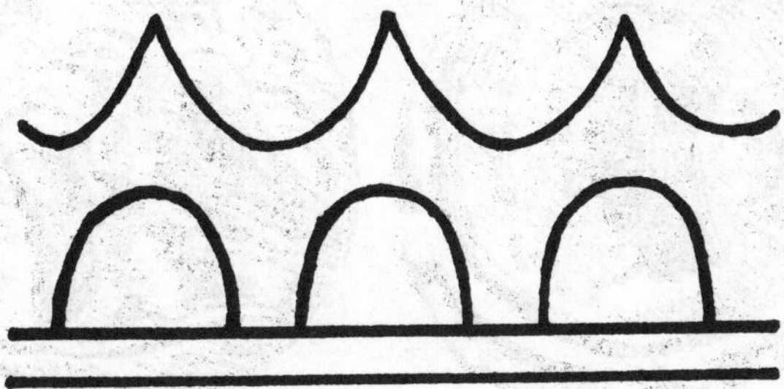

Fig. VI
Ornamentation of the battlements on the adobe constructed houses of Najrān

INTERPRETATION OF THE ANTIQUE BY REFERENCE TO THE PRESENT

It must, I think, be conceded that, in the matter of the Hunt, the comparison of data provided by the pre-Islâmic inscriptions with the extant South Arabian culture which has so remarkably survived, enables us to give a valid interpretation, and a new significance even, to the curt inscriptional evidence, and to indicate certain small subtleties in it. In working in the Arabian field no remark by one's informant is too trivial to record for what it may later reveal. It must however be insisted that a thorough knowledge of Arabic and close attention to the dialects are essential to elicit and correctly appreciate and evaluate data gathered in the field.

Among the more curious examples of this process is the case of the coins published by the late Dr. John Walker[409] from the Wādī Maifaᶜah to the west of Ḥaḍramawt proper. These coins bear an effigy of the Moon God, Sīn, represented as a young man wearing his hair in long ringlets (Fig. No. VII). The term employed by Ḥaḍramī poets[410] for a ringlet is *sīnah*, plural *siyan*; this plural if read unvowelled could be taken as *sīn*—the connection cannot be fortuitous. Relevant also to this is an account of a dispute between the anthropomorphists and their opponents, narrated by al-Tawḥīdī,[411] " 'Describe your God (*rabb*) to me, you!' He said, 'He has crisp curly hair (*jaᶜd qaṭaṭ*), and the most perfect stature, most beautiful appearance and proportion'."

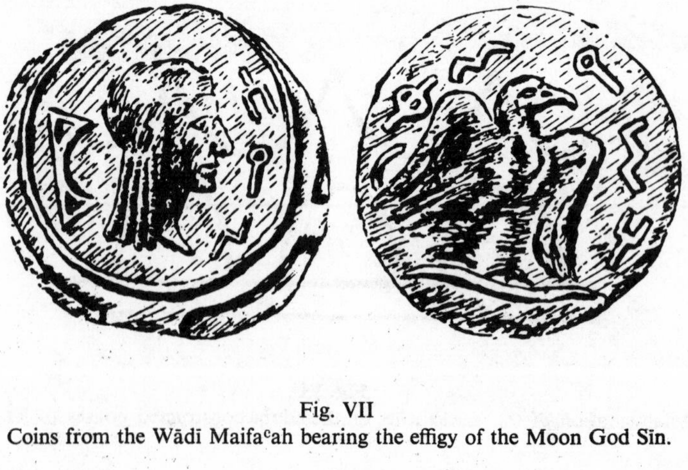

Fig. VII
Coins from the Wādī Maifaᶜah bearing the effigy of the Moon God Sīn.

Nor can I forbear to cite the strange name of a mountain in the Kawr Saibān region to the north-west of al-Mukallā, written by von Wissmann as Fardjalāt on his 1931 map, and spelled by ᶜAlawī b. Ṭāhir[412] as a single word and without vocalisation or commentary on its entymology. Rash though it be to make pronouncements on etymologies of Ḥaḍramī place-names without careful enquiries on the spot, I cannot but conclude that this must be understood as Jabal Farj al-Lāt, embodying the name of the pre-Islāmic goddess, as I have proposed in the case of two al-Nasr hills at S̲h̲abwah. Tribes such as the Saibān and Ḥumūm are often very superficially Islāmised and the significance of the name al-Lāt has probably been forgotten. The phallic names of al-Zibb or al-Zubb, etc., are not uncommon in Arabia, applied to certain shapes of mountain features, and I have already recorded the famous Jabal S̲h̲ummat al-ᶜĀs̲h̲iq on the pilgrim route to the Prophet Hūd.[413]

APPENDIX

Comparisons with the Hunt of the Baggārah Ḥumr Tribe of South-west Kordofan

In certain respects the giraffe hunting of the Ḥumr tribe of the Baggārah/Baqqārah in Kordofan, as reported and described by Ian Cunnison,[414] displays resemblances to the ibex hunt in south-west Arabia, and, were the notions of the Ḥumr to be explored more thoroughly, it is conceivable that more parallels might emerge. It would hardly be possible, I surmise, to suggest whether the Kordofan Arabs brought these ideas from Arabia in some past age or not, though I should not regard this as impossible.

Discussing failure at the Hunt, Cunnison says,[415] "It is not always clear to Ḥumr whether the primary cause of failure comes from human or divine agency. Ultimately all fortune or misfortune derives from Allāh but the presence of an intermediary human agency may be recognised. The fact that human agency may be present allows the Ḥumr to take precautions or counter-action against it." This human agency may cause failure in horses hunting the giraffe in three main ways. There is *hukr*[416] which, in brief, may be said to be induced by magic, Koranic texts being used by *fuqarā'* (*fekkis*) along with roots to bewitch the horse, or its rider, or both, and prevent them from making a kill. This would seem to have an African colour to it, and I have at least not heard that anything of the sort is practised with the South Arabian Hunt; it is not at all impossible though it seems to me unlikely. Another cause is *ᶜain* or *khashm al-ᶜArab*, the eye or mouth of the Arabs, i.e. people praising a fine horse—which is sufficient in itself to make the horse fail. This would correspond to what is widely known in the Arab world as *ḥasad*, enviousness, the evil eye.[417]

To guard against these causes of failure a *faqīh* will be employed to write out a Koranic charm to be tied to the horse's brow, and it can be given the infused ink of certain Koranic texts to drink. In South Arabia amulets in silver cases are often hung round a horse's neck for its preservation from ills in general, and everywhere Koranic infusions are drunk.

Of much greater significance than this ordinary enough stuff is the Ḥumr belief that success in a giraffe hunting expedition largely depends on the behaviour of its members. As the *rizq*[418] or provision which they seek comes from God they should comport themselves with piety. Women accompany these expeditions (which they do not seem to do in southern Arabia), but sexual intercourse is to be avoided even between husband and wife. The Hunt in southern Arabia would seem to be more sophisticated in a formal ritualistic sense than that of Cunnison's Ḥumr tribe, but widely as circumstances differ between the two, they share in the conception that moral conduct must be maintained by the members of the Hunt, and that success may be denied the hunters if this is not observed.

SUMMARY

This essay has taken a rambling course, with many an excursus into topics pertinent, or allied to the central theme of the South Arabian Hunt—in consequence of which it appears desirable to recapitulate its main outlines.

The existence of a "Ritual Hunt" in ancient pre-Islāmic Arabian inscriptions, as first proposed by Professor A. F. L. Beeston, is supported and confirmed by the survival of a type of formal hunt among the settled population of Ḥaḍramawt and possibly, were the area fully explored, in parts of eastern Yemen. In the light of the popular lore on the Hunt presented here it is attempted to re-examine the pre-Islāmic inscriptions in Professor Beeston's original study to see whether they can be more precisely interpreted. Some data from classical Arabic sources with a possible bearing on the "Ritual Hunt" are also presented, but these remain inconclusive.

This Hunt has a strong religious colour which is recognised, and opposed, as un-Islāmic by the Ḥaḍramī *ulema*. Both the ancient and contemporary Hunt are associated with rain-making.[419] In Ḥaḍramawt it is necessary that the hunters prepare themselves by moral behaviour and that they observe a lofty moral code during the course of the Hunt itself. The whole affair is governed by an elaborate procedure, almost a ritual, in such matters even as eating and drinking, and there is a formal ritual of rejoicing following a successful Hunt.

The relevant pre-Islāmic inscriptions seem to indicate that it is necessary to propitiate divinities or supernatural agencies through the Hunt or by other means. In Ḥaḍramawt it is reckoned a disgrace to fail at the Hunt, and in such cases the hunters to not succeed in bagging any game they make scrupulous enquiry to discover into what moral turpitude, or into what purely formal sins of omission or commission, they have fallen.

The actual huntsmen are the tribes, the *ḥaḍar*, and even the slaves, though members of the groups of religious aristocracy may actively participate. The *Mas̲h̲āyik̲h̲* and Saiyids who form this religious aristocracy are often associated with the Hunt in certain supervisory capacities which might almost (in the case of the Madūdah Mas̲h̲āyik̲h̲) be characterised as priestly, though in view of their other functions this comparison should not be pushed too far, and, as stated, the *ulema* of these groups oppose it.

At the present day, the Hunt concentrates upon the ibex which has a certain heroic quality about it, and with which a sort of respect or awe is associated in the minds of the Ḥaḍramī hunters—

this in itself is highly significant since, in ancient Arabia, the ibex was associated with the pre-Islâmic pagan gods. The hunting verse of Ḥaḍramawt, so conventional and stylised as to argue a long ancestry, and to a lesser extent the proverbs of the country, give some indication of the place occupied by the Hunt in the popular mind. The hunting verse resembles the classical *qaṣīdah* in some respects, the latter also embodying references in its prelude to wild animals and rain. The cases cited from the hereditary hunting judges of Madūdah have a special importance as illustrative of a sophisticated and possibly extensive law.

Hunting grounds seem to be jealously regarded, and from one of the inscriptions there may be evidence that this was so in the pre-Islâmic period. Some of the ancient inscriptions come from places at least very near to the districts where the "Ritual Hunt" is still performed today.

Much of the evidence examined in this study is based on a careful consideration of philological data which seems to have a special relevance in such contexts as this.

While this study was at proof stage, Professor Beeston kindly undertook to read it again—most of his suggestions are incorporated in the text, but the paragraph (p. 31) dealing with s̲ha'b/s̲hi'b could not be altered. His argument for s̲ha'b, tribe, not s̲hi'b, pass, convincingly demolishes my own proposal arising from my misunderstanding of the preposition *b m*.

REFERENCES

[1] *Le Muséon* (Louvain, 1948), LXI, 183–96. Cf. also A. W. Macdonald, "Quelques remarques sur les chasses rituelles de l'Inde du nord-est et du centre", *Journal Asiatique* (Paris, 1955), CCXLIII, 101–15, though there is little that has any direct bearing on the Arabian hunt. Professor von Wissmann has drawn my attention to Karl Jettmar, "Megalithsystem und Jagdritual bei den Dardvölken", *Tribus*, Veröffentbeilagen des Lindenmuseums, No. 9 (Stuttgart, 1960), 121–34, for comparison.

[2] W. H. Ingrams, "A Dance of the ibex hunters in the Hadramaut", *Man* (London, 1937), XXXVII, 12–13, and Doreen Ingrams, *A Survey of the social and economic conditions in the Aden Protectorate* (Asmara, 1949), 60.

[3] *Tārīkh al-Yaman* (Cairo, 1346 A.H.), 180–81, and (Cairo, 1947), 293.

[4] *Tārīkh al-Mustabṣir*, edit. O. Löfgren as *Descriptio Arabiae Meridionalis* (Leiden, 1951–54), 199. According to Lane, *Lexicon*, the *iyyal/uyyal* is a *wa^{c}l* or ibex. Professor al-Ghūl has referred me to Ibn al-Athīr, *Nihāyah* (Cairo, 1311 A.H.), I, 28: "He gave him an *arwā* while he was *muḥrim*". The plural, says Ibn al-Athīr, is *urwīyah* and *arāwīy*, this being *ayāyil*, or, it is said, *ghanam al-jabal*, mountain sheep/goats, the latter not a very precise term. David L. Harrison, *The mammals of Arabia* (London, 1964–1972). I, frontispiece and II, 295 has a picture and description of the caracal lynx with which Professor Beeston (above, p. 71) proposes to identify the *fahd*. Al-Saiyid ^{c}Alī b. Aḥmad b. Muḥammad b. al-shaikh Shihāb al-Dīn al-^{c}Alawī (edit.) *Al-Dīwān al-musammā bi-'l-Waqā'i^{c} fī-mā jarā bain Āl Tamīm wa-Yāfi', li-'l-shaikh al-mu'allim ^{c}Abd al-Ḥaqq al-Ḥaḍramī* (n.d. or place of publication), photocopy in my possession of this rare lithograph, 75, has the verse,

> *Wa-fī Yirmān faḍḍ rās al-fahd bi-'l-fās*
> And on Yirmān he split the head of the *fahd* with the axe.

Yirmān is a mountain near Dammūn marked on the von Wissmann map. From this one infers the *fahd* was hunted here last century. The *nimr* skin I saw (above, p. 71) is probably Harrison's *Felis nimr* (op. cit., II, 304).

[5] "Materials for South Arabian History" (1), *B.S.O.A.S.* (London, 1950), XIII/2, 294. I now possess a MS. of the history in question. According to the British Museum MS. of the *Rawḥ al-rūḥ*, folio 10b, a certain Ḥamzah b. ^{c}Abdullāh al-Nāshirī composed for ^{c}Āmir b. ^{c}Abd al-Wahhāb, *Intihāz al-furaṣ fi 'l-ṣaid wa-'l-qanaṣ*. He was a Zabīdī and died in 926 A.H. (A.D. 1520). Cf. Ibn al-^{c}Aidarūs, *al-Nūr al-sāfir*, (Baghdād, 1934), 131. According to the British Museum MS. of *al-Sanā' al-bāhir*, folio 180a, ^{c}Āmir went to hunt *al-ghazlān wa-'l-rīm*, gazelle and white antelope.

[6] See our "New map of Southern Arabia", *Geographical Journal* (London, 1958), CXXIV, 163–71.

[7] I have made no exhaustive enquiries in Arabic works on hunting, but Professor A. K. S. Lambton was so kind as to make a cursory examination for me of the Teheran MS. of *Kitāb al-ṣaid wa-'l-qanṣ* (Brockelmann, *GAL*, Supp., I, 433), the author being a contemporary of al-Ṣūlī. Her brief examination did not elicit any references to the South Arabian Hunt, but her summary of contents is to be recorded.

"The *Kitāb al-ṣaid*, a well-written MS., contains many quotations in verse and otherwise from various sources, and a little verse by the author himself. The main sections are, what game is permitted and what forbidden; a good deal on hunting dogs; the practice of the *Majūsiān* with regard to what game is permitted and forbidden; hunting in the Ḥaramain, the views of the *ahl al-^{c}ilm* on what game is permitted and what forbidden; Christian practices with regard to the same; birds of prey; their food and illnesses, stratagems to catch game, hawks; eagles; wild beasts; wild asses; lions; hunting panthers; propitious times for hunting; game birds. There is a chapter in it, mainly verse, concerning kings and chiefs on hunting."

This is substantially the same type of material as is to be found in Erwin Gräf, *Jagdbeute und Schlachttier im islamischen Recht* (Bonn–Mainz, 1959), which contains a corpus of texts reflecting the attitude towards hunting, formulated in the early stages of the growth of Islāmic law, an attitude which has become orthodoxy. From an admittedly cursory survey of this volume I found nothing with direct bearing on this study, but I had already also examined a representative number of these sources in Arabic.

[8] Al-Bukhārī, *Ṣaḥīḥ* (Cairo, 1345 A.H.), VII, 110 *seq.* Al-Hamdānī, *Iklīl* I, edit. Muḥ. b. ᶜAlī al-Akwaᶜ (Cairo, 1963), 186, or edit. O. Löfgren (Uppsala-Leiden, 1954–65), 72, alludes to the tribe of Abū Thaᶜlabah al-Khushanī, the Companion of the Prophet from whom came the futya 'l-ṣaid. Al-Akwaᶜ thinks this is simply a reference to a *ḥadith* in the *Ṣaḥīḥ*; c. al-Mubarrad, *al-Kāmil*, edit. Aḥmad Muḥ. Shākir (Cairo, 1937–56), III, 893.

[9] Cf. Abū ᶜUbaidah, *Kitāb al-amwāl* (Cairo, 1353 A.H.), 190 *seq.*: *Inna wādiya-hum ḥarām muḥarram li-'llāh kulla-hu, ᶜiḍāha-hu, wa-ṣaida-hu, wa-ẓulm fī-hi, wa-sarq fī-hi aw isā'ah, wa-Thaqīf aḥaqqu 'l-nās bi-Wajj.*

[10] Perhaps the memory of this *ḥaram* still survives in the place near al-Ṭā'if called by M. Tamisier, *Voyage en Arabie* (Paris, 1840–41), I, 330–38, Maṭman al-ghāzale (Maṭman al-Ghazālah). This was still a place of pilgrimage in Tamisier's day. To Dr. Sharīf Rāshid and his friend Ḥamzah Ḥusain al-Fiᶜir (of the Fuᶜūr Ashrāf of Wādī Liyyah at al-Ṭā'if) I am indebted for the information that the correct name is Mawṭi' al-Ghazālah located at Sh hār of al-Ṭā'if. "It is a rock upon which there are footprints as if they were gazelle (*ẓaby*) footprints." He adds that there are popular legends about these footprints, such as the belief that they are those of the female gazelle which spoke to the Prophet while standing there, and complained of her Jewish captor who had hunted her and tied her up. Many stories are told of the Prophet's sympathy for the gazelle. In South Arabia in 1958 I was told the following tale. The Prophet's sandal broke, and he went to many animals to ask for a piece of skin to tie it up. He eventually came to the gazelle which gave him a strip of skin—its mark remains in the dark coloured piece down the animal's left-hand side. In return the Prophet conferred two gifts upon the gazelle—one that it will run faster than its enemies (this is before hunting from motor vehicles), and the other that it will never need to drink.

[11] Cf. below, p. 63; Ibn Ḥabīb, *K. al-Munammaq* (Ḥaidarābād, 1964), 422 *seq.*

[12] A. Guillaume, *The Life of Muhammad* (Oxford, 1955), 131, and Wüstenfeld's text, 184.

[13] Cf. above, p. 32.

[14] A. Guillaume, op. cit., 191.

[15] *The Kitāb al-Maghāzī of al-Wāqidī*, edit. Marsden Jones (London, 1966), 960. Muḥ. b. Ḥabīb, *K. al-Muḥabbar* (Ḥaidarābād, 1942), 319, states that it was customary for the pagan Arabs before returning to their houses to pass by the *ṭawāghīt*—which could mean temples or idols.

[16] Tirmidhī, *Ṣaḥīḥ* (Cairo, 1931–34), IV, 288, footnote quoting Abū Dā'ūd; F. Wüstenfeld, edit. al-Azraqī, *Die Chroniken* . . . (Leipzig, 1858), I, 156.

[17] Cf. below, p. 87.

[18] *Histoire des Seldjoucides de l'Iraq*, Recueil de textes relatifs à l'histoire des Seldjoucides, edit. M. T. Houtsma, II, (Leiden, 1889), 69 *seq.*

[19] Ibn Jubair, *Riḥlah*, 2nd edit., W. Wright and M. J. de Goeje, G.M.S. (Leiden–London, 1907), 210. Professor al-Ghūl showed me the illustrated article of Nājī Maḥfūẓ, "Manārāt al-Qurūn", *Qāfilat al-zait* (Dhahran, 1970), XVIII, IX, 43–5, citing additional references. ᶜAbd al-Ḥaqq al-Baghdādī states that between each two baked bricks was a horn or a hoof. Ibn al-Jawzī estimated

there were 4,000 heads. Ibn Abī Ḥajalah, *Sukkardān al-Sulṭān*, written in 757 A.H. (A.D. 1356), says it still existed in his day and was known as Manārat al-Qurūn. Al-Yāfiᶜī mentions it, and Ibn Saᶜīd al-Maghribī (ob. 685 A.H. (A.D. 1286)) shows it on his map as Manārat Umm al-Qurā. Today, says Nājī Maḥfūẓ, there is a place called Umm al-Kurūn (*sic*), about 14 kilometres from al-Raḥbah, but most people do not know why it is so called.

20 *Al-Zakhārif al-miᶜmārīyah wa-taṭawwuru-hā fī minṭaqat Wādī Ḥalfā*, Sudan Unit, Occasional Papers, No. 1 (Khartoum, 1965), 20, and plates 13 and 40. Horns are commonly used on buildings elsewhere in the Sudan.

21 Ḥassān b. Thābit, *Dīwān*, edit. Hirschfeld (Leiden–London, 1910), introd., 51. This "ghazāl al-Kaᶜbah" was found when the well Zamzam was dug, along with some old swords. Ibn Hishām (Guillaume, op. cit., 47) states that two gazelles and the corner stone of the Kaᶜbah were buried by Jurhum in Zamzam well when they were forced out of Mecca. I wonder if this tale disguises the discovery of an offering or sacrifice made at the foundation of yet more ancient buildings than the Meccan Temple? If so, this is to be compared with the ibex carved at Ḥaid b. ᶜAqīl, cf. p. 3.

22 Maḥmūd b. al-Ḥasan Kushājim, *al-Maṣāyid wa-'l-maṭārid*, edit. Muḥ. Asᶜad Talas (Baghdād, 1954), 202, and Lane, *Lexicon*.

23 A. Guillaume, op. cit., 607; Al-Wāqidī, op. cit., 1025 *seq*. Ukaidir used to train horses for hunting by cutting down their feed.

24 Al-Wāqidī, op. cit., 1027; Damīrī, *Ḥayāt al-ḥayawān* (Būlāq, 1868), I, 172, trans. A. S. G. Jayakar (London, 1904), I, 327.

25 G. Ryckmans, *Noms propres sud-sémitiques* (Louvain, 1934–35), I, 4. The same author, in *Journal of Semitic Studies* (Manchester, 1958), III, III, 227, refers to "Dhū Samay Lord of Baqar-um", taking Baqar-um as the name of a sanctuary; but could it not be "Lord of (wild) cows", i.e. ibex, gazelle, etc.? The title might of course also include domestic cattle.

26 Al-Hamdānī, *Iklīl X*, edit. Muḥibb al-Dīn al-Khaṭīb (Cairo, 1367 A.H.), 96.

27 Op. cit., 140–41. He mentions a place al-Ṣaid (p. 20). Cf. below, p. 75.

28 Op. cit., 158. The citation might be read in the passive, or the subject might be implicit in the verb. The *Gloss. daṭ.*, explains *dasara* as, *heurter*, *frapper avec force*, *donner un coup*, *jeter* (with *bi*). Al-Hamdānī says *dasara* means, *al-dafᶜ wa-'l-ṭaᶜn*, etc. Cf. al-Wāqidī, op. cit., 634, 659, where *ṭaᶜām* and *wadak* are used in the senses of corn and meat.

29 Op. cit., 196. A variant reads, *al-qunnāṣ mim-man nasha'a bi-'l-Yaman*, "hunters of Yemenite rearing". Lane explains *siyāḥah* as—going about the earth in the way of devotees, adding that this is forbidden by the *Ḥadīth*. I am inclined to consider it a plural of *sā'iḥ*, itinerant, of the same class as *baqqārah*, etc.

30 Ibn al-Mujāwir, op. cit., I, 149.

31 There is no need to alter the text, as Löfgren suggests, if *maitah* is read instead of *maiyitah*.

32 A practice still current in Ḥaḍramawt. Women tear the *juyūb* along the seams so that they can be mended without really spoiling the frock!

33 Apart from the collection of *Ḥadīth*, the following interesting sources may be cited: *Kitāb al-Muntakhab* of al-Hādī ila 'l-Ḥaqq, edit. A. K. Kazi, Ph.D., dissertation S.O.A.S., folio 62. This very early Zaidī work mentions the *fahd*. Kushājim, *al-Maṣāyid wa-'l-maṭārid*, 28 *seq*.; this author died in 358 A.H. (A.D. 968–9), but one may search in vain for any trace of the ritual hunt in his work. Al-Shāfiᶜī *al-Umm* (Cairo, 1321 A.H.), II, 155–56, *Fī taḥrīm al-ṣaid*, VII, 221–24, *mā jā'a fi 'l-ṣaid*. Hunting ceases when one is in a state of *iḥrām* on pilgrimage to the Kaᶜbah, but may be taken up again according to al-Marzūqī, *K. al-Azminah wa-'l-amkinah* (Ḥaidarābād, 1332 A.H.), II, 167,

after the Aiyām al-Tashrīq, i.e. Dhu 'l-Ḥijjah 11th–12th, though this is put by Koran commentators as at the end of Muḥarram, cf. *Kor.*, V, 2–3 and 95. ʿAlī b. ʿAbdullāh al-Samhūdī, *Wafā' al-wafā'* (Cairo, 1326 A.H. (A.D. 1908)), 76–7, gives many citations to show that the hunter (*ṣā'id*) in the Medinan *ḥaram* is despoiled (*yuslab*), and so is the cutter of fodder (*kala'*), "just as the slain of the infidels is despoiled so that his horse and weapons are taken, but, it is said, the clothes only". This goes to the taker of the spoils, or to the "needy (*fuqarā'*) of al-Madīnah, just as the compensation for the hunting of Mecca belongs to its 'needy', but it is (also) said that it is deposited in the treasury (*bait al-māl*)". The verse quoted by ʿAbd al-Raḥīm . . . al-ʿAbbāsī, *Maʿāhid al-tanṣīṣ* (Cairo, 1367 A.H.), I, 372 might be cited,

ra'aitu ẓaby-an yaṭūfu fī ḥarami-ka

Damīrī, *Ḥayāt al-ḥayawān*, trans. A. S. G. Jayakar, II, 270, cites Azraqī as reporting that merchants from Syria during the time of Quṣaiy in the pre-Islāmic period were severely punished for slaying a gazelle in Mecca by a sudden calamity which overtook them.

34 *K. al-Muḥabbar*, 314.

35 Pronounced in the Yemen as Ghamdān. The Director of Antiquities in the Yemen Republic, Qāḍī Ismāʿīl al-Akwaʿ, showed me the site which he believed to be that of the old castle, immediately north of al-Masjid al-Kabīr. He maintains that the mosque is constructed of the stones of the ancient castle which is highly probable. The mosque also has two oblong bas-reliefs on the exterior of its north wall, each of a bird in side-view, with a rosette above the tail. These are clearly of foreign inspiration, as a visit to the Byzantine Museum in Athens showed me. There one sees the same motive, but the bird in closely similar carvings is generally the peacock or dove. One would surmise that these carvings came from the old Christian church in Ṣanʿā', as proposed by Hugh Scott, *In the High Yemen* (London, 1942), 128, with illustrations.

36 *K. al-Aṣnām*, edit. Aḥmad Zakī (Cairo, 1914), 58; *Les Idoles de Hicham ibn al-Kalbi*, edit. and trans. Wahib Wahib Atallah (Paris, 1969), 8c, 52c. Balkhaʿ might just possibly be a disguised Ḥaḍramī name commencing with Bā.

37 "Ḥimyar and Kuhlān are called the two *shaʿbs* (confederations) of Saba'," according to al-Hamdānī, *Iklīl* I, edit. al-Akwaʿ, 22. The etymology of this name, and even the correct spelling are dubious. In 1964 a Yemeni told me that Ramlat Sabʿatain (with *ʿain* not *hamzah*) was correct, but he then added that they say Ramlat Sabtain, meaning the Sand of Two Weeks—they believe a Jinnī to be in *sabʿah* seven, so some tribes do not say it, but *sittah wa-thamāniyah wa-'l-ʿadad alladhī baina-hum/wa-mā bain al-sittah wa-'l-thamāniyah*; others say *sittah samḥah*, and others *nuṣf arbaʿatʿash*. Some say Sabʿah is the actual name of a Jinnī, and the Ramlah is so-called because people fear this desert with its difficulties and dangers.

38 *Muʿjam al-buldān*, art. Balkhaʿ.

39 *Ṣifat Jazīrat al-ʿArab*, edit. D. H. Müller as *Al-Hamdânî's Geographie der arabischen Halbinsel* (Leiden, 1884–91), 87.

40 Whatever is made of the problem of the word *labbaika*, for which cf. C. de Landberg, *Glossaire daṯînois* (Leiden, 1920–42), 2612, I incline to the view that it is a request to a god as a *ghawth*, perhaps meaning, "May you give help", making *labbaika* equivalent to *labbaita*, as in the dialect of parts of the Yemen where there is a *t/k* correspondence. I have recorded colloquial verses today announcing the presence or arrival of a pilgrim and requesting a favour.

41 *Ṣīd* can of course be the plural of *aṣyad* as is attested by verses in the *Naqā'iḍ* and *Mufaḍḍalīyāt*, etc.; it can also apply, as an adjective, to hunting dogs and hawks. A verse in *Iklīl* I, edit. al-Akwaʿ, op. cit., 221, in praise of ʿAmr b. Zaid of Khawlān, a Ḥimyar group, in the pre-Islāmic era, might seem best understood in this sense of a plural of *aṣyad*.

In line 3 "a time of ease" corresponds very much to the terms used in the colloquial verse quoted *infra* as *rakhā*, see p. 36, the ease brought by good rains.

42 The lines scan, as I understand them:

— — ᴗ — / — — ᴗ — / —
— — ᴗ — / ᴗ — ᴗ — /
ᴗ — ᴗ — / — ᴗ ᴗ — / ᴗ —
ᴗ — ᴗ — / ᴗ — ᴗ — /
— — ᴗ — / — — ᴗ — / — —

If an extra half-beat is added to each important line (1, 3, 5) it might conform to the stamping of feet as the group proceeds declaiming the verse.

In line 5 one can read *ṣaid/ṣīd*, but Ibn Qutaibah, *Introduction au livre de la poésie et des poètes*, edit. and trans. Gaudefroy Demombynes (Paris, 1947), 30, reckons such as the rhyme *ᶜabīd* and *ṣaid* a fault. From experience of listening to spoken Arabic in many places I have found that to distinguish between the pronunciation of the *ai* and *ī* is difficult. I doubt if the poets of antiquity always made this distinction either, and hence could rhyme the two. Ya'qūbī, *Tārīkh* (Beirut, 1960), I, 256, attributes *talbiyahs* with a monotheistic ring, "*Lā sharika laka*, You have no partner", to Quraish, Kindah and Ḥaḍramawt in the pre-Islāmic age. Of the Islāmic *talbiyahs* quoted in Ibn al-Daibaᶜ, *Taysīr al-wuṣūl* (Cairo, 1346 A.H.), I, 277, one is clearly in *rajaz* metre, and the second, attributed to ᶜAbdullāh b. 'Umar, with two minor adjustments—an extra *labbaika* and alteration in the word order of the last line to read *wa-'l-ᶜamlu wa-'l-raghbā ilaik* is also metrical. In this latter one line runs "*Al-khair fī yadi-ka labbaik*, Well-being is in your hand . . . "*Khair* which, in southern Arabia, can have such meanings as "harvest", is also parallel to *rakhā*'.

43 *Basīṭ* metre. *Maqīl*, the time between 12 noon and 3 p.m., siesta time; *suḥaibī*, syn., *musaibilī*; *ḍiyādah*, the stalk of the *ṭahaf*-millet: *ḥabal*, to make *ḥabīl*, i.e. fodder twisted into a sort of grass rope, given animals at the top of the *maqūd*, the well-ramp; *diqām*, cf. *Gloss. daṭ.*, 826, *daqm*, crête de montagne, pl. *adqām*.

44 *Suḥaibī* will be *Setaria italica*, and *ṭahaf* is *Eragrostis abyssinica*.

45 "Some irrigation systems in Ḥaḍramawt," *B.S.O.A.S.* (London, 1964), XXVII, I, 75.

46 Cf. *Gloss. daṭ.*, 2095, *shārah/ishārah*, and a verse very similar to that quoted here. *Basīṭ* metre. In 1954 I saw the shrine of this saint in Wādī Yashbum. Cf. G. Wyman Bury, *The land of Uz* (London, 1911), and probably also the Admiralty *Handbook of Arabia* (London, 1916–17), I, 518. Bury states that he lived in Yashbum about the end of the 16th century. There is a cairn in his honour on the Maḥjir-Maᶜn frontier. The light on the *manārah* (minaret?) is a *barakah* for the saint.

47 *Al-Kāmil*, edit. Aḥ. Muḥ. Shākir (Cairo, 1937), 951; W. Wright edition, 562–3.

48 Al-Ṭabarī, *Tārīkh al-rusul wa-'l-mulūk*, edit. as *Annales* . . . by M. J. de Goeje et alii (Leiden, 1881–85), III, 399.

49 Cf. *infra*, The *Tarjīᶜ al-aṭyār*, 343, has an interesting verse on hawks:

لو لا الشهامة في البازِ ما اصطاد عِيال الأوعال   من بين كم من نطّاح

50 Cf. *Prose and poetry from Ḥaḍramawt* (London, 1951), introd., 33, for this type of verse. *Bār*, probably from the class. root *bari'a* with the basic sense of "to be quit, free, of"; cf. *Gloss. daṭ.*, *birī*, etc. It was explained to me as, *ismuh saqaṭ ᶜind al-nās*. *Iᶜtibār* was paraphrased as *ᶜibrah*, *burhān*, but these do not seem very appropriate senses. In Madūdah the term *ᶜuzūbah* was also used as a synonym of *qanāṣah*, meaning, "the going forth to hunt".

51 Cf. English, "Laugh and the world laughs with you; weep and you weep alone".

[52] Cf. Ibn al-Athīr, *Nihāyah*, I, 253, إذا اجتمعت حرمتان طرحت الصغرى للكبرى

This is explained as meaning that if there is a matter in which there is profit to most people and harm to a few, the profit of the majority is put first.

[53] Saif b. Ḥusain al-Quᶜaiṭī, *Al-Amthāl wal-'l-aqwāl al-Ḥaḍramīyah*, MS. in Osmania College Ḥaidarābād, provs. Nos. 243, 237, 171, 349–50, 356. *Jull* is rendered by him as *al-ṣaid*, but the word in this sense seems unknown elsewhere apart from this citation.

[54] The vocalisation given this proverb is classical, as only *zurbiṭānah* is vowelled by al-Quᶜaiṭī. He defines it as a sort of *ṣawārīkh* which boys commonly make, but this is a strange word to apply. From al-Quᶜaiṭī's definition it ought to be a sort of squib, but in older times it was a blow-pipe or arquebus. For the *zebratana* in Ḥaḍramawt, see my *Portuguese off the South Arabian coast* (Oxford, 1963), 198.

[55] *Al-jamālah*, says al-Quᶜaiṭī, means *al-najāḥ wa-'l-fawz.*

[56] *Sās*, from *asās*, root, foundation, etc. Cf. "Two tribal law cases" (1), *J.R.A.S.* (London, 1951), 34, where it means the ordering of procedure, etc.

[57] Cf. below, pp. 38, 60, 63.

[58] Cf. p. 60.

[59] Cf. *Prose and poetry* . . . , pref., 59.

[60] Leiden, MS. Or. 20073, 126, in *rajaz* metre. *Mibᶜād*, perhaps for *mā baᶜd.* The riposte to this by ᶜAbd al-Ḥaqq, *al-Waqā'iᶜ*, op. cit., 8, reiterating the line of Rubaiyaᶜ, runs, *Kullin ka'annah wāw fī mirbāt-ah*, which I think must mean, "Each one as if he were (the letter) *wāw* (curled up) in his pass". If this is so then Rubaiyaᶜ's verse ought also to be understood in this way. A *mirbāt*, plural *marābī*, means a narrow pass (*maḍīq*) between the mountains where the hunters sit. Cf. Imra'u 'l-Qais, *Dīwān*, edit. M. de Slane (Paris, 1837), 43,

وقد أغتدى ومعي قانصان وكلٌّ بِمَرْبَأته مُقْتَفِرْ

Lane gives a variant, مَرْبَاة . The *qāniṣān*, or "two hunters", here, are hunting dogs.

[61] *Iklīl*, X, 57.

[62] *Faṣl al-maqāl*, edit. ᶜAbd al-Majīd ᶜĀbidīn and Iḥsān ᶜAbbās (Khartoum, 1958), 39.

[63] Cf. for *ḍaim*, e.g. Naṣr b. Muzāḥim al-Minqarī, *Waqᶜat Ṣiffīn*, 2nd edit. (Cairo, 1382), 386, where Muᶜāwiyah opposes it to *ḥaqq*; Balādhurī, *Ansāb al-ashrāf*, edit. Muḥ. Ḥamīdullāh (Cairo, 1959), 142.

[64] *Ḥaḍramawt* (Damascus, 1949), 56.

[65] *Prose and poetry*, . . . , 165, v. 63, and 63, v. 23.

[66] A long stone, flat on one side, upon which various edibles are pounded.

[67] *Ḥayawān* (Cairo, 1356 A.H./A.D. 1938), VI, 369. For the *wuᶜūl*, ibid, II, 310. Cf. *Waqᶜat Ṣiffīn*, op. cit., 385, *wa-arḍu-hum arḍ-un kathīr-un wibāru-hā.*

[68] Op. cit., 20.

[69] *Maṣād* in Lane, *Lexicon*, also means the upper or highest part of a mountain, where of course the ibex is to be found.

[70] *Qaws muṭᶜimah*, he continues, is applied also to a bow, from *ṭuᶜm*, bait, etc.

[71] *Prose and poetry* . . . , text, 63, v. 16.

[72] Op. cit., 456.

[73] Cf. R. Klinke-Rosenberger, *Das Götzenbuch Kitâb al-Aṣnâm des Ibn al-Kalbî* (Leipzig, 1941), 21, 26, 31, 36, where *al-dawār* is described as circumambulation of *anṣāb* stones. Those unable to build a temple (*bait*) or make an idol (*ṣanam*) set up a stone (*ḥajar*) in front of the Ḥaram and any other place they approved, and made a circumambulation of it as they did of the temple, and they called them *anṣāb*. This seems to be a general statement not applying to the Ḥaram of Mecca in particular. In Dat͟hīnah there is a village, am-Madārah, where there is a saint's shrine.

Another definition says the *dawār* is an idol (*ṣanam*) around which the Arabs used to set a place in which they circumambulated, the name of both the idol and place being *al-dawār*. Cf. Al-Kumait, *S͟harḥ al-Hās͟himīyāt*, edit. Muḥ. Maḥmūd al-Rāfiᶜī, reprint of 1329 edit. (Cairo, n.d.), 60: "The *dawār* and standing stones (*nuṣub*) are repudiated among us, after the time when we were intent on worshipping (ᶜ*ākif*) them with sacrificial beasts (ᶜ*itr*), these useless places of immolation (*manāsik*)." The tops of the *nuṣub* were blooded with the blood of the animals sacrificed like, perhaps, the top of the *bakarah* has oil poured over it in the Wāḥidī Sulṭanate. Cf. my "The 'White Dune' at Abyan; an ancient place of pilgrimage in southern Arabia", *Journal of Semitic Studies* (Manchester, 1971), XVI, 1, 80, illustrated.

[74] A. Jamme, "L'Inscription Ḥadramoutique Ingrams I et la chasse rituelle sud-arabe", *Le Muséon* (Louvain, 1956), LXIX, 99–108. He suggests (p. 103) that RES 4176–/6–7 "Samᶜay n'est pas autorisée à empiéter sur la chasse de Ta'lab", indique que le dieu Ta'lab possédait une chasse sur laquelle une tribu ne peut impiéter.

Professor Maḥmūd al-G͟hūl, however, offers an interpretation of this inscription to which I should prefer to subscribe. *Ṣaid* he understands as "game", and renders the text as, "It is not, lawful for (the tribe) SMᶜY to ambush the game of Ta'lab". ḤBN is to be compared with the Arabic *k͟habana*, hid, concealed, and the Ḥaḍramī *ik͟htabā* and *kabban*, to lay an ambush.

SMᶜY was the tribe responsible for the administration of Ta'lab's pilgrimage. Cf. the parallel restriction on pilgrims already under vow, not only to refrain from killing game, especially in al-Ḥaram, but even to be a party in any way to ambushing it or inciting anyone to hunt it, as in al-Buk͟hārī, *Ṣaḥīḥ* (Leiden, 1862), I, 456–57.

[75] In Tarīm, Raḥaiyam said *t͟hib* simply means *qum*, as in standard Arabic.

[76] *Loc. laud.*, cf., p. 29

[77] See C. de Landberg, *Daṭīnah* (Leiden, 1909), I, 1467 *seq.*, especially p. 1469 with an allusion to *wi*ᶜ*l*, used probably in the sense of warrior, hero, in pre-Islāmic inscriptions. Cf. the excellent article in *Tāj al-*ᶜ*arūs*, VIII, 157–58.

[78] Leiden MS. Ar.2932, p. 1. It commences: بنى مغراه من لا قنع مبيوع دينه

There is a copy of another MS. also in Leiden, transcribed by an Indonesian (alas very inaccurately) for C. Snouck Hurgronje. I am greatly indebted to the late Dr. C. Voorhoeve for his kindness in acquainting me with the existence of this and similar MSS., and for placing them at my disposal.

[79] For the Banī Mig͟hrāh metre, and the nature of this type of poetry see *Prose and poetry*, introd., 25, and below, p. 39 *seq.*

[80] ᶜAbdullāh b. Ḥusain b. Ṭāhir b. Muḥ. Bā ᶜAlawī (ob. 1272 A.H. (A.D. 1855)), *Majmū*ᶜ *yas͟htamil* ᶜ*alā t͟halāt͟hah wa-*ᶜ*is͟hrīn risālah* (Cairo, 1340 A.H.). Cf. Brockelmann, *GAL*, Suppl., II, 820. While ᶜ*āqil* in classical Arabic means intelligent, it also means a "headman" in South Arabian colloquial Arabic.

[81] *Arbāb al-qaniṣ*, an expression used in colloquial Arabic also, means "those in charge of the Hunt". The slaves intended are the slave troops of the Sulṭāns.

[82] These verses of course are primarily intended as an attack on tribal law (*ṭāg͟hūt*) as well as the Hunt.

[83] ᶜAbd al-Raḥmān b. Muḥ. b. Ḥusain b. ᶜUmar al-Mashhūr Bā ᶜAlawī, *Bughyat al-Mustarshidīn* (2nd ed., Cairo, 1936), 255 (p. 248 of the earlier edition). A passage to much the same effects occurs in ᶜAbdullāh b. ᶜUmar b. ᶜAbdullāh Bā Jummāḥ (? vocalisation) al-ᶜAmūdī, *ᶜUmdat al-ṭālibīn fī maᶜrifat baᶜḍ aḥkām al-dīn* (Cairo, 1332 A.H.), 105.

[84] The following is probably one of the practices to which the author refers, and is taken from my Tarīm field books. If you should fall sick you send your cap (*kūfīyah*) to Bin Sumaiṭ, i.e. to a member of this well-known family of Saiyids. Bin Sumaiṭ recites first, then he measures it with his hand (*yishbur*), i.e. he folds the *kūfīyah* which has the shape (Fig. No. VIII) over once or twice, and finds perhaps that it is three fingers (*aṣābiᶜ*) wide. Then he recites and measures again, and finds perhaps that it is only two fingers wide. In such circumstances he knows that it is the evil eye (*al-ᶜain*); but if each time he measures it he finds that it is the breadth of three fingers he knows there is really nothing wrong. Sometimes he recites (*yiqrā*) and then spits on the *kūfīyah* and sends it back, sometimes he writes an amulet (*ḥirz*) without any *nuqaṭ* (diacritical points) on the letters and sends it back. He may "measure" a woman's necklace (*marīyah ḥaqq marāh*)—her upper (*ṭāliᶜī*) or lower (*ḥābiṭī*) necklace, or if it is a small child, his *marīyah*—for little boys wear necklaces for superstitious reasons, loaded sometimes with amulets, or his *thawb* (smock). Poor people of course bring him their own *kūfīyahs* and the like. If it is an animal which is not eating they take its tether rope to Bin Sumaiṭ and he asks about "envy" (*ḥaṣad*, the evil eye) and gives directions accordingly. People often say, on discovering that something of theirs has been afflicted with the evil eye, *Yā ᶜain al-saw firrī fī 'l-jaw*, "O Eye of Evil, fly away into the sky!" From this practice arises the saying with which I confess to having teased my friend ᶜAlī b. Sumaiṭ of Tarīm, *Bin Sumaiṭ mā yinfaᶜ nafsuh*, "Bin Sumaiṭ can't do himself any good!" Physician heal thyself! Another old Tarīm friend, an educated young Saiyid maintained that by reciting—the Koran, I take it for granted—he could effect cures in simple things at least, and this seemed generally believed. He modestly disclaimed any particular merit, but considered this was merely a peculiar property with which he was born. It was suggested he should recite (*yirqī*) over my servant's scorpion bite. *Al-Jawhar al-shaffāf*, MS. in photocopy in S.O.A.S. Library, story 285, has a reference to spitting on a sheep to cure it of an ailment. Story 404 concerns a saint who "recited over a horse and massaged (rubbed) it with his blessed hand (*qarā ᶜalā ḥuṣān wa-masaḥ ᶜalaihi bi-yadi-hi 'l-mubārakah*)". If justification is required for this practice it can be found in the Prophet's action in spitting into a wound in a man's face which remained free of pus after that; he also massaged (*masaḥ*) his face, blessed him, and gave him a piece of his stick (Al-Wāqidī, op. cit., 568, cf. 190).

[85] His *Fatāwī* are known (in MS.) in various recensions, and still used by scholars. A set of photographs of one recension of this work is in the Library of the S.O.A.S.

[86] This actually happens. About New Year 1940–41 I visited a guard post at Dirjāj near Abyan. At the top of the stair I saw a splash of dried blood above the corner where it turned onto the roof—there was also a little garde-robe at this corner. On questioning the *nā'ib* of the post, Ḥusain Ḥaidarah al-Quṭaibī, he informed me that all the men had been ill with fever (for it is a malarious spot). They thought there must be some evil about the place so, to drive away the *shayāṭīn*, they slaughtered this goat, saying, *Bismillāh al-Raḥīm - hādhā ᶜalaik fidā min kulli sharr*, "In the name of God the Compassionate this is a ransom for you from any ill". Ibn al-Mujāwir, op. cit., I, 150, uses *fidyah* as a term for a sacrifice in consecrating a road.

[87] A pleasant South Arabian custom, indicative of the standing of scholarship in local society!

[88] In the Western Aden Protectorate such a case might be the hocking and slaying of the *ʿaqīrah*. I heard that at Maḥfid they provided a number of *ʿaqīrahs* on the Governor's visit there (prior to 1954).

[89] *Prose and poetry*, introd., p. 29.

[90] Leiden MS. 2932, p. 183, mentions and quotes a poem of Bū Nāṣir al-Fāris, perhaps this man. He calls himself in the course of the poem Bin Nāṣir. He is said never to have let his horse enter his fort by its gate (*siddah*), but always to have made it jump the surrounding wall (*dawr*).

[91] *Naṣīf Allāh*, syn. *naṣfah*, paraphrased as *intiṣār al-maẓlūm min al-ẓālim*. *Naṣfah* means punishment (for example, from God) of someone who has wronged you. The commentary on ʿAbd al-Raḥmān b. Yaḥyā al-Ānisī, *Tarjīʿ al-aṭyār bi-murqiṣ al-ashʿār*, edit. ʿAbd al-Raḥmān al-Iryānī and ʿAbdullāh . . . al-Aghbarī al-Fā'ishī (Cairo, 1369 A.H.), 61, explains *ḥukm al-naṣaf* as *al-inṣāf*, and the poet (431) says, *wa-'l-naṣaf majmaʿ al-khair kāfah* (*kāffat*).

[92] *Farfārah* or *farfīrah*, also known, because of its length, as *ṭawīlah*, is the Saiyid coat; it is also worn by the Mashāyikh. The other Ḥaḍramīs wear a sort of jacket. A Saiyid told me an amusing tale of a certain learned scholar who came from Saiwūn to Tarīm riding his donkey. All unbeknown to him, his *ṭawīlah*, instead of being tucked under him on the saddle, lay over the donkey's rear quarters and got bespattered with dung. His embarrassed friends on his arrival in Tarīm were unable to draw attention to his condition.

[93] *Taḥaiyāl*, syn. *mughādarah*, trickery. *ʿAtrūr*, pl. *ʿatārīr*, syn. *shiḥrah* (for the latter cf. *Gloss. daṯ*, 2025, the road below Madūdah), a short road in the mountains, or a small trickle after rain. It is also said to mean *maʿārik*.

[94] The metre is wrong here, and perhaps one should read simply, *qanāṣah*, or perhaps if the *nā* is short, *ʿilluh*.

[95] *Yaʿilluh* was paraphrased as *ʿasā yakūn fī wasaṭ bīr*. It looks like the classical *laʿallā*.

[96] The vocalisation of *yitabʿūn* is mine, and I have given it this vowel scheme the sake of the metre, basing it on a recollection of what I have frequently heard. *Tamwīr*, pl. *tamāwīr* was said to mean *khayāl*, or *tafkīr baṭṭālī*, imagining or evil thought.

[97] Although I have given my rendering in rhyming couplets the verses are in fact *mashṭūr*, but the poverty of rhyme in English makes rhyming translation without distortion of the sense extremely difficult.

[98] It seems appropriate to reproduce the Arabic in which the introduction to this tale was narrated to me for dictation:

لما استولت الدولة الكَثيرية على تريم قام جماعة من رجال العلم والدين فاوعدوا إلى الدولة بأن تبطّل القنيص المعهود من قديم وما احتوى عليه من حفلات لِما يرونه فيها من المضارّ دينية واقتصادية واجتماعية . وفعلاً أعلنت الدولة الكثيرية بتبطيله وضجّ العامّة ضجيجاً عظيماً من هذا المنع وقام شعراؤهم بالتنديد والانكاف . وممّا قاله بعض الشعراء مشيراً فيها إلى العلماء والفضلاء إلى ان قال :

[99] These tussles in which men were sometimes killed, figure in my collection of Quarter documents of the last two centuries.

[100] Cf. above, p. 13.

[101] *Aden Chronicle*, March 1, 1962, XI, No. 476, 5.

102 A. J. Drewes, "Some Ḥaḍramī inscriptions", *Bibliotheca orientalis* (Leiden, 1954), XI 3–4, 93–94.

103 Ibn al-Athīr, *Kāmil* (Cairo, 1290 A.H.), XII, 84.

104 Cf. G. Makdisi, "Topography of Eleventh Century Baghdad", *Arabica* (Leiden, 1959), VI, II–III, 17, 25, 28, 30. G. Le Strange, *Baghdad* (Oxford, 1924), east side.

105 Makdisi, op. cit., 17, 28, 30. Le Strange, west side.

106 "*Sabu*ᶜ," i.e. a lion, leopard, lynx or other ferocious beast.

107 *Kāmil*, op. cit., 136.

108 A. Guillaume, *Life of Muhammad*, 15.

109 Similar graffiti figure in H. St. J. B. Philby, *Sheba's daughters* (London, 1939), 28–29, 42–43, 56. Those at Qarn al-Binā', near Bīr ᶜAsākir are especially similar to those I have seen in Ḥaḍramawt. Bertram Thomas, *Alarms and excursions in Arabia* (London, 1931), 199, reproduces graffiti just to the west of the Musandam peninsula with what may be ibex symbols of the same type as those in Wādī Thibī. Cf. E. Anati, *Rock-art in Central Arabia*, I, "The oval-headed people of Arabia", II, I, "Fat-tailed sheep in Arabia", II, I, "The realistic-dynamic style of rock-art in the Jebel Qara". *Bibliothèque du Muséon*, L.I, Géographie et archéologie, III (Louvain, 1968).

In the corpus of approximately 2,000 Thamūdic inscriptions from north-west Arabia (A. van den Branden, *Les inscriptions Thamoudéennes* (Louvain–Heverlé, 1950)), the ibex (*wi*ᶜ*l*) is four times mentioned, the gazelle not at all, and the lion once. Other animals, such as camels, figure in these inscriptions, and also *bqr* with an accompanying *wasm* or brand-mark, but it does not seem reasonable to me to translate *bqr* as camels rather than cattle.

In three cases the formula is, "The ibex belongs to . . . " In one case we find, *Ṣyd* (*w*ᶜ)l. I feel this should be translated rather as, "An ibex-hunt", instead of, "*Un chamois est pris*". Likewise I should prefer to take *Qnṣ 'asad* as "A lion-hunt". I suggest these were made to record important bags by hunting parties, though it is an open question as to whether there was any ritual association with these rock inscriptions.

See also A. van den Branden, *Histoire de Thamoud*, Publications de l'Université Libanaise, Section des Etudes Historiques, VI (Beyrouth, 1960), 50–54, La chasse, with mention of the proper name *Ṣyd'l*, "*chasseur de 'Il*", and rock drawings suggesting a beater scaring game, etc.

110 Landberg, *Daṯīnah*, 1468, says that in Ḥaḍramawt, *ṣaidah* is the feminine of *wi*ᶜ*l*. See Ibn Sīdah, *Mukhaṣṣaṣ*, VIII, 29–31.

111 Acephalous MS. in my possession, folios 3–4.

112 I suggested in *Prose and poetry*, introd., 34, that bowmen, before the introduction of the gun, had the same stance as the guns have nowadays. Shanbal the Ḥaḍramī historian frequently uses the word *rāmī* for archer, and the archers seem to have formed a sort of special corps as they are often specifically mentioned in the lists of men slain in an affray. They seem to be distinguished from the gun-men when, about the time of the Portuguese, guns first came to Ḥaḍramawt. My surmise was to some extent confirmed on my last visit to Ḥuṣn al-ᶜUrr, where among the carvings, was a man in a sort of kilt shooting at an ibex with bow and arrow. Others fighting the lion which is now, like the ostrich, extinct, can be seen on the capital (D. van der Meulen and H. von Wissmann, *Hadramaut* (Leiden, 1932), 178), with spears and shields (Plate No. IX). Shields are now unknown but round targes perhaps identical with these are still to be seen in the ᶜUmān regions. W. Thesiger, *Arabian Sands* (London, 1959), 2, says the Qarā tribesmen of Ẓufār have the round shield, and, p. 67, it is made of wickerwork covered with hide (an illustration of this shield being given). G. de Gaury, *Rulers of Mecca* (London, 1951), 139, also shows a round shield, bow and arrow, and javelin in the hands of a Yemenite Janissary, and the mediaeval geographers allude to the round shield.

Mr. Stephen Day, some years ago, purchased a shield from Upper Yāfiᶜ (Plate No. XIX) which is described by the words *turs, daraqah* (pl. *diraq*), and *jawb* (pl. *ajwāb*). This shield must be Indian. At Mūdiyah I saw a MS. work with the Qāḍī entitled *al-Masā'il al-Malībārīyah*, the title is dubious and the work is not known to Brockelmann, but it may belong to the mid-10th/16th century, and it propounds the question as to whether hunting with the gun is lawful:

م. بنادق الأروام والافرنج التي فيها الباروت والنار هل يحل الاصطياد بها ، وهل هي المراد بما في فتاوى النووي ؟

ج. لا خلاف في حرمة الرمي إلى الصيد بالبندق الذي فيه الباروت ، وانما الخلاف في البندق الذي من الطين . فصاحب الذخائر يقول لا يحل لأن فيه تعريض الحيوان للهلاك ، والنووي يقول يحل .

I have since discovered this question in Ibn Ḥajar al-Haitamī, *Al-Fatāwā al-kubrā al-fiqhīyah* (Cairo, 1938), IV, 250. The question is further discussed in al-Ḥusain b. Muḥ. b. Ḥusain al-Ibrīqī al-Ḥabbānī al-Ḥaḍramī, *al-Adāb al-muḥaqqaqah*, a MS. in photo-copy in my possession from a Tarīm original, quoting Ibn Ḥajar's *Tuḥfah*, K. al-Ṣaid (photo-copy sheet 7), and Al-Shawkānī, *Nail al-awṭār* (Cairo, 1357 A.H.), VIII, 137, *Bāb al-nahy ᶜan al-ramy bi-'l-bunduq*. See also D. Ayalon, *Gunpowder and firearms in the Mamluk kingdom* (London, 1956), 59.

[113] In Tarīm the beater at the top of the mountain is called *al-nashshāsh*.

[114] Leiden MS. Ar.20073.

[115] *Mutadārik* metre. *Malaq* means *maḥall wa-waqt*, and one says, "*Mā yā-nā malaq*", meaning, "*mā wāfaq-nī*, it did not suit me".

[116] The occasion is the Kathīrī–Quᶜaiṭī wars of last century when the Kathīrīs were supported with money from Ḥaidarābād.

[117] Cf. "*The Quarters of Tarīm and their tanṣūrahs*", *Le Muséon* (Louvain, 1950), LXIII, III–IV, 277 *seq.*

[118] *Al-jamīlah* was explained to me as *fawz bi-taḥṣīl al-ṣaid*. Cf. footnote No. 55, above. Leiden MS. Ar.2932, folio 210 *seq.* has a poem of a certain ᶜAwaḍ Ṣāliḥ b. Biqīᶜ of al-Mishṭah which contains the line (folio 211, 7):

حصلت جميله ضافيه نعتادها ترجع بزف

[119] *Gloss. daṯ., sharᶜ-ah qaṣīr, il fait fi de son honneur. Khaibah* is explained as "ugly", but it seems to me to have the sense of "failure" here. The dual seems used in the same way as one says "*marḥabatain*".

[120] Op. cit., 56. Cf. E. V. Stace, *English–Arabic vocabulary* (London, 1893), 144; ring in a horn, *rajabah*.

[121] *Prose and poetry*, introd., 33. Cf. Leiden MS. Ar.20074, for verses.

[122] T. R. H. Owen, "The Red Sea ibex", *Sudan notes and records* (Khartoum, 1937), XX, 159–65, though not very informative, states that the Beja think the ibex has only at most 32 rings on its horns. He says the Beja state that the ibex, jumping from a height, will deliberately land on its horns—this is more or less what al-Nuwairī, *Nihāyat al-arab* (Cairo, 1923–54), IX, 329, says in the 7th–8th century A.H.; Cf. Jāḥiẓ, *Ḥayawān*, VII, 248. I do not know if it is true or merely legendary that the ibex lands on its horns as described, but Owen seems to think there may be reason to believe that it does. Al-Nuwairī also described its filial piety towards its parents, and says that the ibex chooses to be taken in the net with its young if they are trapped.

123 The *naqar* is said to be the piece from the joint downwards in any limb of the body.

124 Landberg, *Daṯînah*, 1469, says *qashᶜah* means horns in Dathinah and Ḥaḍramawt.

125 In the Yemen the ibex-horn is considered lucky. The 15th–16th-century writer Baḥraq, of al-Shiḥr and Aden, recommends that a pregnant woman suspend an ibex horn on her person in order to ease delivery. Cf. "Folk Remedies from Ḥaḍramawt", *B.S.O.A.S.* (London, 1956), XVIII, I, 8. Landberg, *Daṯînah*, loc. laud., has made some notes on the setting of the ibex-horn on the corners of houses. Nabhānī (G. Rentz, "Pearling in the Persian Gulf", *University of California Semitic and Oriental Studies* (Berkeley, 1951), XI, 22), says that in the Persian Gulf the nose-stopper (*fiṭām*) of divers is made of *qurūn al-wiᶜl aw min al-dhabil, ay ᶜaẓm al-sulaḥfāh*, "ibex-horn or turtle-shell".

126 See illustration No. VII, a tomb of a Buraikī shaikh. *Al-Shaikh Buraik min ahl Shabwah* is mentioned in the Saiwūn copy of the *Manāqib Bā ᶜAbbād*. Maqrīzī's Buraikī informant from Shabwah is to be found in al-Sakhāwī, *al-Ḍaw' al-lāmiᶜ* (Cairo, 1353–55 A.H.), V, 52. A curious custom, mainly I suppose, of the coastal areas, is to place the formidable-looking sword of the sword-fish inside a *qubbah* of a saint. I have also seen this in East Africa. My enquiries on many occasions as to why the sword should be kept there met with no response worth recording until, in 1964, when at one of the Saiyid *qubbahs* in al-Shiḥr I chanced on a woman who seemed to be embracing the sword, and it is probably therefore linked to ideas of fertility, but Ḥaḍramīs of the educated classes, are, not unnaturally, anxious to conceal such superstitions prevalent at shrines, so I have no more precise information even now.

127 "The Moon-God on Coins of the Ḥaḍramaut," *B.S.O.A.S.* (London, 1952), XIV, III, 623–26.

128 Cf. Lane, *Lexicon*, *ᶜajm*, *shariq*, and *quṣrā*. This white fat has a pleasant sweet tender taste.

129 The Qiblī is all lying west of, say, Shibām. ᶜAlwā is the upper part of the Wādī Ḥaḍramawt.

130 *The Ritual Hunt*, 195. To understand *bdltn* in the sense of the Arabic *badanah* a sacrificial animal, seems to me attractive, and the permutation *l/n* is common in the South (Cf. *Gloss. daṯ.* art. *lām*). In the *Koran* (XXII, 36) we find it in the verse, *Wa-'l-budna jaᶜalnā-hā lakum min shaᶜā'ir Allāh*, etc. Another example of the usage I have taken from A. K. Kazi, *Al-Muntakhab min al-fiqh* of al-Hādī ila 'l-Ḥaqq (University of London, Ph.D. thesis), folio 59:

وأمّا القارن فإذا أراد الإهلال بالحجّ والعمرة معاً فلا يجوز ذلك عندنا إلا أن يسوق
بدنة يسوقها من موضعه الّذي أحرم فيه.

Al-Wāqidī, op. cit., reports several curious customs or regulations on the *badanah* which closely resemble, in one or two respects, what is done in South Arabia today with animals destined to be sacrificed at a saint's shrine. Cf. pp. 578, 614, 733, and 573, where there is an allusion to the marks made on animals for sacrifice (verb *ashᶜar*), and that the Prophet "garlanded" the *budn* with sandals (*niᶜāl*). The oath *ᶜalā dimā' al-budn* is reported by such as Sībawaihi, *al-Kitāb* (Būlāq, 1316–17 A.H.), 336. I was told in the Wādī Maifaᶜah in 1964 that, in the olden days, if a man had a son who fell ill he would make a cut in the ear of an animal between the lobe of its ear and its body, and say, *Yā Bin Hūd idhā kān yislam waladī hādha 'l-tais lak nidhr*, "O Bin Hūd, if this boy of mine gets better this male goat is yours as a votive offering". It was added that this is not done very much today. Bin Hūd is the pre-Islāmic prophet I visited in the Wādī Hadā in 1947.

I have jotted down in my notes that *badan* is the part of the meat given the Manṣab, possibly a note taken during my brief 1957 visit to Tarīm, but I hesitate to place any reliance on it.

Ibn Sīdah, *Mukhaṣṣaṣ*, VIII, 30, says, *al-badan* means *al-wa*ᶜ*il al-musinn*, an old ibex, its young (*walad al-wa*ᶜ*il*) being known as *furhud*. Lane quotes *wa*ᶜ*il badan*, an old ibex. Landberg treats of the *wa*ᶜ*il* at length in *Daṭînah*, 1467–71. It seems also to mean *Ashrāf al-nās*, the nobles of the people. Professor Jibrail Jabbur of Beirut, in conversation, told me that at Qaryatain, in eastern Syria, in his youth, he used to hunt gazelle which, as they crossed the mountain, were led into traps by stone walls, and killed. The gazelle migrated by this route to and fro. There were few or no *wu*ᶜ*ūl* up there, but there is a place called ᶜAin al-Wuᶜūl near Tadmor. In that district *wu*ᶜ*ūl* are called *badan*, singular *badanah*.

Very strange is the name *wi*ᶜ*l* given to Shawwāl and Shaᶜbān, so that one says, Wiᶜl Shaᶜbān and Wiᶜl Shawwāl (*Tāj al-*ᶜ*arūs*). Lane says the tribe of ᶜĀd called the tenth month, corresponding to Shawwāl, Waᶜl. Al-Marzūqī, *K. al-Azminah wa-'l-amkinah*, I, 282, deals with this subject at some length. "Shaᶜbān is called Waᶜil, with an *i* after the ᶜ*ain*, plural Awᶜāl. Al-Farrā' said, 'Some of them say *wi*ᶜ*lān*'. One also says, *wa*ᶜ*l*—which is a place of refuge. One says 'I have no *wa*ᶜ*l*', i.e. refuge, 'from him', and 'I found no *wa*ᶜ*l*', i.e. means of access, 'to him'. It seems as if the month was so called because during it, raiding was frequent, and every tribe (*qawm*) used to take refuge in places in which they would be fortified."

There is one Tradition which explains *Koran*, LXIX, 17, describing the Day of Judgement, "On that day eight shall bear up the throne of thy Lord", as eight *aw*ᶜ*āl*—in the plain sense, "ibexes", but in this context it is said to mean "angels". I do not suggest that this is what the author of the Koran meant, but that such an interpretation of the "eight" could be given, and later one presumes, rejected by orthodoxy, is remarkable.

131 *Khuṣār* is anything eaten to flavour bread, e.g. meat, fish, or vegetables.

132 *Iklīl* I, edit. al-Akwaᶜ, 22. *Sha*ᶜ*b* would be more like a confederation of tribes. Kinānah is a *qabīlah*, Quraish an ᶜ*imārah*, Quṣaiy a *bait*, Hāshim a *fakhidh*, and al-ᶜAbbās a *faṣīlah*, according to Abu 'l-Walīd al-Waqshī and Ibn al-Sīd al-Baṭalyūsī, *al-Qurṭ* ᶜ*ala 'l-Kāmil*, edit. Ẓuhūr Aḥmad Azhar, University of Panjab thesis, 345.

133 For his biography cf. *Prose and poetry*, introd., 62.

134 See *Prose and poetry*, introd., 26.

135 ᶜAbd al-Ḥaqq alludes to the Qiṭmīr breed (*Prose and poetry*, text, 73).

136 *Ansāb al-ashrāf*, edit. M. Ḥamīdullāh, op. cit., 15 and 23.

137 *Iklīl* II, edit. al-Akwaᶜ, 14.

138 Cf. *supra*.

139 *Arabica V* (Leiden, 1898), 214.

140 *Arabica V*, 203–4. Kadūr is the *ḥabaṭ* protected by four saints of Lihyah. I am indebted to Captain Julian Johnston for making some further enquiries on my behalf about Kadūr. He writes, "It is strange that although the Bedouin of the area, including the Qumaishīs and the Ahl Aḥmar, agree that ibex-hunting does take place there, I can find no one who can say with any authority that it is a *ḥabaṭ*. Sulṭān Nāṣir is positive that Kadūr is not a *ḥabaṭ*, and so are all the tribal *muqaddams*. There is however a *ḥabaṭ* at al-Sharīrah which is an area of ground below Kadūr, which boasts no buildings except a *walī*." Of Kadūr and its ibex he writes, "They do net them there, but only infrequently, usually under the aegis of the Mashāyikh of Hadā".

141 It is marked on von Wissmann's map, south of Lamāṭir, really a spur of Jabal Kadūr, where it is written Muḥarraq.

142 Qirfah is on the map, south of Ḥawṭat al-Faqīh ᶜAlī, and Kibrān north of it. Al-Saqāh and Madbī are not elsewhere reported.

[143] *Arabica* V, 193.

[144] "The Ritual Hunt," 188.

[145] This word is new to me, and I am not sure of its more precise sense.

[146] ᶜAbd al-Ḥaqq, *al-Waqā'iᶜ*, op. cit., 81, immediately after recounting the head of game which were killed on a certain hunt, goes on to say (metre *rajaz*):

يا اللهْ برَحْمهْ سابغهْ كلٍّ بها يقْضي وطرْ
وتشرب الودْيان للشّيبان جزْلات العجرْ
وتشْرب النّخْله لحتّى يزْجى النّخْل الثّمرْ
ويرْخص الْحبّ الّذي قدْ كان مدّيْن اسْتعرْ

Not having read the verses with Ḥaḍramīs, I must content myself with giving the general import only: "O God give us ample rain whereby everyone's aims will be achieved, and on account of the old men (ibex?) with large rings (on their horns) the *wādīs* will drink, the palms will drink and give abundantly of fruit, and corn which was sold at two *mudds* (to the *riyāl?*) will become cheap."

[147] Al-Wāqidī, op. cit., 561.

[148] *Al-Imāmah wa-khaṭaru-hā ᶜalā waḥdat al-Yaman* (Beirut, n.d. but not earlier than 1958), 8. Zubairī's strictures on the *imāmate* are not of course to be accepted at their face value. Cf. al-Wāqidī, op. cit., 1008–9, and *K. al-Amālī ᶜan Abī ᶜAbdillāh Muḥ. b. al-ᶜAbbās al-Yazīdī* (Ḥaidarābād, 1367 A.H./A.D. 1948), 47.

[149] Aden, 14th January, 1958, No. 166, 6.

[150] A troop, band, cf. Ḥaḍramī *khibrah.*

[151] The *ḥawīk* are really the artisan class as a whole. In al-Rawḍah and al-Ḥawṭah, the headman, known as Amīr al-Ḥawīk, is also the herald (*muṭarrib*) who announces any public events or incidents, and anything lost or stolen.

[152] *Prose and poetry*, introd., 22. The sharḥ is described.

[153] These two names should mean "The People of the Lower/Upper" part (?).

[154] Cf. my "Société et gouvernement en Arabie du Sud", *Arabica* (Paris, 1967), XIV, III, 284–97, for their place in the social structure of the country.

[155] "The Quarters of Tarīm . . . ", op. cit., 282.

[156] *Gloss. daṯ.*, 2824.

[157] ᶜAbd al-Ḥaqq, *al-Waqā'iᶜ*, op. cit., 99, has a typical verse (in Banī Mighrāh metre),

إلى وادي سقاه الْحيا منْ مزْن سحّابْ
قنفْ من قال شى لهْ مثل كذّاب كذّابْ

* * *

يكون الله في سعْفهم وآبْليس قدْ غابْ

This poem was not read with Ḥaḍramīs. The general drift of the lines whoever is: When you go to a *wādī* (to hunt), may it have rain, then abstain (taking *q n f* as in Dozy, *Supplément*) from anyone who says words like "liar, liar". The last verse quoted expresses a constantly recurring theme in ᶜAbd al-Ḥaqq's poems—that Allāh is with the hunters and Iblīs has departed or fled.

158 This is probably to be derived from *badā* (not *bada*[c]*a*), *Gloss. daṯ.*, 141, *commencer la guerre.*

159 *Gloss. daṯ.*, 1087.

160 Cf. *Prose and poetry*, introd., 36, *ḥaffah.*

161 The Manṣab mentioned to me the word *khanabah* which he paraphrased as a *jalabah* or a *shāh*, but I think he meant an ibex or possibly a gazelle.

162 Cf. Lane, *Lexicon*, 1175, for full description, though I do not know if this is the same as what is used in Ḥaḍramawt. A plant we collected on the San[c]ā'-Ḥudaidah road recently had light grey-green leaves and cottony spikes of flowers though it had no resemblance to the cotton-plant. This was described as *rā*[c] (with [c]*ain*) and as useful for stuffing pillows, etc.

163 *Prose and poetry*, introd., 25.

164 Mighrāh = Mughrāh might perhaps then mean a bitch set to hunting.

165 Arabic text in *Prose and poetry*, 71; *al-Waqā'i*[c], op. cit., 121.

166 The hallooing is an indication that the flood is coming down the valley, an occasion for rejoicing.

167 The indigo-dyed cloth has a smoothness and sheen when just freshly beaten.

168 *Prose and poetry*, introd., 25. *Al-Waqā'i*[c]. op. cit., 76, has a verse similar to verse 19, *Wa-ba*[c]*d al-sā, yā mu*[c]*tanī qum shill qirṭās*, "Now, o troubled one, up and take a paper". So even this sending a message to the hunters may be a poetic convention.

169 *Iklīl II*, edit. al-Akwa[c], 19, 38. Mawlā Madūdah is mentioned, some 500 years ago, by Sa[c]d al-Suwainī (*Prose and poetry*, text, 163). I do not know whether the Manṣab or the village in general is intended, and the verse may not be genuinely of Sa[c]d.

170 See below, p. 55.

171 *Ḥayawān*, VI, 466.

172 I have taken *raqaṣ* as hand-clapping as in South Arabia, and *la*[c]*iba* as to dance—as it is there also.

173 It is just possible this was a polite excuse to avoid showing the book, but many MSS. have actually been lost this way.

174 The Wādī Ju[c]aimah lies to the north of Madūdah. A proverb in al-Qu[c]aiṭī's collection, op. cit., 268, runs *Al-sail jā' min Ju*[c]*aimah wa-'l-jamālah li-Sar*, "The flood (really) comes from Ju[c]aimah but (Wādī) Sar/Sarr gets all the credit". *Jamālah* in this context is explained as *al-dhikr, ḥusn al-ṣīt*. W. Ju[c]aimah flows into the main Wādī Ḥaḍramawt as also does the W. Sarr above and to the west of it—as can be seen on von Wissmann's map. [c]Alawī b. Ṭāhir's *al-Shāmil*, of which the first 150 pages of proofs pulled in Singapore 1941, but never published, are now in microfilm at the S.O.A.S., 84, gives the word *khiṭmah*, plural *khiṭam*, which he defines as *al-jibāl wa-ṣaḥārī-hā ka-'l-bādiyah*. I was told it meant a *shi*[c]*b*, pass or mountain-side. Cf. also *Prose and poetry*, introd., 34, vocalised *khaṭmah* and given the sense of "field of fire".

175 The five headmen (*ubwah*) over the five tribes (*qabā'il*).

176 For a definition, in brief, of a Manṣab of Mashāyikh, see "Two Tribal Law Cases" (II), *J.R.A.S.* (London, 1951), 166.

177 Text, *fīhi salā*. Paraphrased as *yuḥibb*.

178 Lit. "the people of the fifths".

179 The Arabic day commences at 6 p.m. I am however in some confusion here, for it seems that the author, further on, quite definitely means by Tuesday evening, for example, not Monday evening—as an Arab would understand it—the evening preceding the day of Monday, but our Tuesday evening.

180 The *ṭaw*[c]*ah*-pole (syn. *quṭb*) is laid flat on the ground.

181 This use of *taḥt* is frequent. The reception room is on the first storey.

[182] See *The Quarters of Tarīm*, 279 *seq*. If these songs are correctly reported I have been unable to discover that they have a consistent metre. Perhaps *kam* should be read for *kammin*.

[183] *Ḍāfī*, paraphrased as, *nafīs*, *muttasi*^{c}, wide. *Gloss. daṭ.*, gives *ḍafā* as having the sense of *couvrir* in Ḥaḍramawt. In explanation it was said to me, *yiḍaffūn al-ṭarīq bi-'l-shabak*. *Ḍāfī* seems to be the stock epithet of the hunting-net. Leiden MS. 20073, p. 57 has, in a poem of Bā Jarād, *al-wushūr al-ḍāfiyah*, and, in the preceding poem of b. Shihāb, to which Bā Jarād's verses are the riposte, appears the *rajaz* verse:

إذا حمل ألطَّوْع والوَشْر المُلَمَّع بالسَّوَاد

"When he bears the pole and the net shining black."

For the mesh of the net (*maiḥ*, plural *miyāḥ*, *amyāḥ*, *muyūḥ*), cf. *Daṭînah*, 1511.

Damār, syn. *qatl*. Al-Aḥqāf is a name applied to Ḥaḍramawt and has been extensively discussed by scholars. My informants said it meant "the mountains", but I am dubious about this.

[184] *Zahīyah*, syns. *faraḥ wa-surūr*. Shaikh Hādī said that the *marba*^{c}*īyah* is a sort of ibex, *marba*^{c}*ī* meaning an animal, or horn perhaps, with four finger-breadths between each ring—the young ibex he said, have only two finger-breadths between each ring of the horns. *Marba*^{c}*ah* was said to be a local variant. Leiden MS. Ar.20074, 22, in a poem by ^{c}Alī al-Bu^{c}sī (a Yāfi^{c}ī), speaking of a *zaff* in al-Dimnah (the nickname of Shibām), says (metre, *basīṭ*):

ضَلَّتْ بني مالك الجاويد تَتفخَرْ   بالمَرْبَعيه وَسَطها داخل الأدوارْ

[185] Note the phrase *ṭabakh al-qahwah*.

[186] *Aḥwāl-hum mut*^{c}*assirah*.

[187] *Razīnah*, syn. *muttasirah*.

[188] He will pray for God to give them game (*ṣaid*).

[189] It will be recalled that the complaint of the ulema (see p. 22) includes the hunters' neglect of the prayer.

[190] ^{c}*Ammārah*, ^{c}*ammāriyah*, cupboard. I think the Mashāyikh ancestors of the Manṣab must be intended. The phrase was explained to me as *maḥall al-kutub*, but unfortunately I never saw it.

[191] This is said to mean, *ilā ḥaḍrat al-Nabī*.

[192] The Koran.

[193] I have recordings of some Banī Mighrāh songs.

[194] See *Prose and poetry*, introd., 18 *seq*. Some examples, collected by the late Mrs M. de Sturler Raemakers, are now in the Museum of Ethnology at Cambridge.

[195] The net-men are of course *masākīn*, not tribesmen.

[196] *Sālī*, rendered as, one who wishes and has a desire (*gharbah*) to enjoy something.

[197] I.e. the Headman of the Hunt as *supra*.

[198] *Farraq*, to divide out (the contribution payable by each man). From this comes the type of tax or impost known as *firqah*, a sort of levy of money; the term is widely used in the Protectorates. A parallel term is to be found in

Miftāḥ al-saᶜādah wa-'l-khair fī manāqib al-Sādah Banī Qushair, a MS. of which I saw in Ḥuraiḍah: دفع اهل عجز دفعة كبيرة

"He made the people of ᶜIjiz pay a large impost."

199 The *khubrah* or date-cluster cover is one of Madūdah's exports to other parts of Ḥaḍramawt. These are made of plaited palm-leaf and it occurred to me that they might perhaps be the objects represented on the Kharibat Āl ᶜAlī jamb, globular in shape (see Fig. No. IX), but I now think this unlikely.

200 *Mīzān* may be added to differentiate the weight from some other weight formerly in use.

201 Munaibārī, or Minaibārī. Ḥ. b. Minaibārī is marked on von Wissmann's map.

202 A tribe of the Āl Kathīr. It may be possible to trace them in Muḥ. b. Hāshim, *Tārīkh al-Dawlat al-Kathīrīyah* (Cairo, 1948).

203 The use of *am* for *al* is curious here, but it is traditional in this part of South Arabia.

204 Ṣiqair is marked on von Wissmann's map. It seems to have lost most of its inhabitants, probably quite recently. Bait b. Ḥuṣn is also marked.

205 Written *qahāw*, an odd plural, probably *qahāwī* is meant.

206 I do not know what tribe this is.

207 All those presented with a *dair* of coffee contribute a *ṭabaq* of dates worth about 5/- (1954) to the Hunt.

208 So expressed in the Arab way, but our Thursday evening is intended.

209 I.e. 9 p.m. until midnight.

210 Announce (*ikhtaṣar*), explained as *yinādūn*.

211 The *dallāl* often, perhaps normally indeed, acts as the herald.

212 This is a conventional form. The Arabic text runs:

اسمعوا يا حاضرين ! ان اهل البلاد اجتمع رايهم عند المنصب على قناصه ، والسمر الكبير عشية الجمعه تحت بيت الشيخ محمد بن ابي بكر با حميد . والحاضر يحكي للغايب !

213 Perhaps to be understood as our Thursday evening.

214 I.e. he hands out pieces of meat without knowing what he is going to give. Meat of course is usually divided out according to strict rules, but see below, pp. 63–4.

215 The sense of *yibaiyin-hā* is *yibaiyin karāmah*, manifests a miracle.

216 The *mibaddā* is the name of the first net set up in a pass, and the *ẓuhār* is the second—which may catch the game if it escapes the net-men at the *mibaddā*.

217 Text, *yidīrūn*, explained as *yidarijūn*.

218 Midnight.

219 Cf. *Prose and poetry*, text, 157 for a poem of his.

220 Sulmān, a *miskīn*, was still alive in 1954.

221 For the *marzaḥah* see *Prose and poetry*, introd., 30.

222 Text *daryāt*, i.e. *darjah* (sing.) as in C. de Landberg, *Ḥaḍramoût* (Leiden, 1901), glossary.

223 Ar. *yidᶜī min* = *nadā ᶜalā*.

224 The author means, after the Midday Prayer.

225 The Arabic text commences,

الأوّله صلّوا عليه . والثّانيه صلّوا عليه . والثّالثه صلّوا عليه . ما تسمعون إلا خير .
يقولون أهالي بلدة مدوده اعتصب رأيهم على قناصه إلى جعيمه . . .

226 I.e. 2 p.m.

227 Syn. *mashaw*, they walked. Amongst other senses *Gloss. daṭ.*, gives *partir*.

228 I.e. 12 noon.

229 *Muḍwā*, an evening journey, cf. Landberg, *Ḥaḍramoût*, glossary.

230 My informants said that this phrase *man lā* ᶜ*alam* ᶜ*alā bunduqīyat-ah* means that if there is no trace of his bullet then he cannot claim to have hit the beast. Cf. *Prose and poetry*, introd., 35, on such issues.

231 For this dance cf. *Prose and poetry*, introd., 29 *seq.*

232 Syn. *al-ḥalqah.*

233 I.e. skirting along the lower part of the mountain, following the *wādī.*

234 The *sāḥah* is an open space behind Madūdah—my informants actually took me there.

235 *Khanab*, rendered *al-ṣaid alladhī fi 'l-jabal.* Cf. above, footnote 161.

236 In Tarīm I heard the word *manwī* used, which I understood in the sense of intending to go on the hunt of an animal though I had no second chance to check this. I do not find the classical dictionaries very helpful here, but in any event it is interesting to find *nīyah*, which also has a special religious connotation in the Islāmic prayer, used here. The *Tāj al-*ᶜ*arūs* says that *anwā ḥājah*, means *qaḍā-hā.*

237 Syn. *yiṭla*ᶜ*ūn.*

238 I.e. between 5 and 6 p.m.

239 I.e. 9 p.m.

240 A *murabba*ᶜ*ah* is a small square or oblong cabin of stone with a mud roof, usually a sort of shelter, on the Jōl. Cf. van der Meulen and von Wissmann, *Hadramaut*, index.

241 I.e. 10 p.m.

242 See footnote 216.

243 A *kalb* is a forked branch suspended on a rope, upon which one hangs a water-skin.

244 See footnote 60. In Aden Federation the word *maḥājī* means *khanādiq*, trenches.

245 *Fī ṣadaf*—if you were to sit behind a chair, e.g. that keeps you from being seen by someone on the other side, then this is a *ṣadaf*. Cf. Lane, *Lexicon*. The stones were described as a *mirsā* or *mirbā*, a sangar or breastwork.

246 ᶜAlawī b. Ṭāhir, *al-Shāmil*, 204, says صلقهن is *zaghārīt al-nisā'*.

247 *Al-Ḥājib* is an excrescence on the top of the Jōl. The look-out man is called *al-*ᶜ*aiyān*, and his task, *al-*ᶜ*iyānah*. A look-out man at sea is called *shawwāf* (G. Ferrand, *Instructions nautiques* (Paris, 1921–28), I, 86 a).

248 As the ibex has a sort of beard the Arab thinks of him as a venerable old man. Cf. the Kharibat Āl ᶜAlī jamb (Fig. No. IX) where the beard clearly shows. Cf. *Al-Waqā'i*ᶜ, 86:

ولحيه فيه تصلح لصاحب عرْس عذْبه

Fig. IX

Door jambs from Kharibat Āl ᶜAlī near al-Ḥazm in Jawf Bin Nāṣir.

(a) The male figures wearing waistwrappers (*miᶜwaz*) and carrying curved sticks. From the rafters of the roof above them hang pottery waterjars as in the present-day hostelries (samsarah) in Ṣan'ā'. A pair of male ibexes sit couched beneath them.

(b) Two ibexes sitting couched below what may be a formalised representation of a hunting net, but this is uncertain.

[249] Bin Ḥumr is the name of the ibex. The hunter says, "Raise your neck", taking hold of the ibex by the beard (*liḥyah*), because it is all crouched together in expectation of its death blow.

[250] He means that the Hunt is over and they must now return. One often hears the phrase *al-lail yā ᶜiyāl* addressed, for instance, to a body of soldiers, to get them moving quickly.

[251] The tribes get wildly excited on such occasions, and will recklessly fire off many rounds with no thought of the cost, though usually careful to husband their ammunition.

[252] This might have been read as from the root *ḍallā*, for which see Landberg, *Ḥaḍramoût*, glossary.

[253] The man whose shot first hits the animal always bears its head.

[254] I.e. 2 p.m.

[255] Named in all probability, after the famous family of Mas͟hāyik͟h. See "Hūd" . . . , *Le Muséon* (Louvain, 1954), LXVII, 129 *seq.*

[256] I do not know these passes, nor are they marked even on the most recent maps at my disposal. In consequence the interpretation of the literal translation given here is just a little dubious.

[257] By game, gazelle merely, or even something lesser, is intended.

[258] I.e. 7–8 p.m.

[259] A famous Mas͟hāyik͟h family.

[260] I.e. 11 p.m.

[261] A *duqum* is a sort of peak, cf. footnote 43, but *maqṭaᶜ* might be a cut in the surrounding bank of a field as well as some cut in the actual peak itself. If it is a field *maqṭaᶜ* it might perhaps be translated as spill-way.

[262] This ᶜUmar, it would appear, is the ancestor of Mawlā Ṭuyūrah.

[263] According to ᶜAlī b. ᶜAqīl, *loc. laud.*, the *duk͟hlah* is the entry made when the ibex has less than forty rings on its horns.

[264] I.e. 2 p.m.

[265] The name of a *s͟hiᶜb* or pass.

[266] Lit. "Go with God!" Von Wissmann's maps report a similar name, Maᶜa 'llāh, in the Saibān area. The name is confirmed by the *S͟hāmil* of ᶜAlawī b. Ṭāhir. I imagine that this imperative feminine is conceived of as the rider addressing his beast, but I do not really know. Similarly Tawak͟hk͟harī should mean something like, "Hold back!"

[267] This might be rendered better as, "They again hunt . . . "

[268] *Maṭāriḥ*, plural of *maṭraḥ*, often used in the Western Protectorate for a camping site; such sites sometimes seem to become villages but the name sticks.

[269] This is a mountain. ᶜAlawī b. Ṭāhir, *al-S͟hāmil* (S.O.A.S. photo-copy), 90, gives *ᶜirqah* the sense of "a narrow road in the mountains which animals find difficult".

[270] An entry with *zāmils*, according to my commentator.

[271] I.e. 10 a.m.

[272] For an exact description of the *zaff* cf. *Prose and poetry*, 33.

[273] I.e. 7 a.m.

[274] The sing. of *maᶜāris* was given me as *muᶜarris*, and the word was said to be synonymous with *ᶜarūs*, plural *ᶜarāwis*.

[275] *Huqlah* also appears in *Prose and poetry*, text, 23. Here it means a mock representation of the Hunt with firing of crackers, etc.

[276] *Mutahaqqilīn* was paraphrased to me as *Zanādiqah*. I find this a little difficult.

[277] It is curious to see how this word has come back into Arabic, probably from India, in a somewhat modified form.

[278] I.e. 12 noon.

[279] I.e. 6.30 p.m.

[280] In such cases as the Hunt has taken three head.

[281] His share is given below. This should be compared with the Manṣab's share on p. 31.

[282] The *qaṣmah* in Classical Arabic is, literally, "a fragment, piece".

[283] This is a large vessel which their ancestor gave as a *waqf*.

[284] These are the poets, camel-men (*jammālah*), the Bedu, and the hunters of Juᶜaimah.

[285] The meat is divided, *ᶜalā ᶜadad al-ḥāḍirīn*, according to the number of those present, but a third or a quarter is left out of the division, known as *al-khimmah*. This *khimmah* is taken to Madūdah and divided between the Manāṣib, the Headman, and the Five Members, as above.

[286] In the event of his having struck the first blow.

[287] This type of term is used to denote the members of the Quarter organisation of such towns as Tarīm, where *ᶜiyāl* is actually used.

[288] A curious custom is that the Headman or Abū pays for the shoes of the Bedouin, being reimbursed of course, from the funds of the Hunt.

[289] This term in the form *fidā* (see footnote 86), has already been noted as employed for a sacrifice. Here it was said to be a *rās ghanam*. Cf. *Gloss. daṭ*.

[290] I.e. a *miskīn*, translated elsewhere as "petty tradesman". He would not be a *rāmī* of course, as these are tribesmen only, even if they be settled tribesmen.

[291] If a gun should "attaint" himself he may fall on the mountain, or his bullet simply does not hit the mark, but the point is that his "taint" does not affect the Hunt as a whole.

[292] I.e. the guns, tribesmen.

[293] Amplified by my informant who says even a single drop (*qaṭrah*), is enough to qualify the gun for the honour of having first hit the animal.

[294] The gun claims that he has hit the animal in such and such a portion of its body, but if, after examination, no bullet be found in that place, his claim to have hit the animal is rejected. He may even take the precaution of carrying with him a stone with the animal's blood on it, to prove his case.

Al-Damīrī, op. cit., text, II, 88, reports the case where two wounds are inflicted upon a hunted animal. I have not scrutinised the Arabic texts for the laws of hunting, but the dissimilarity between mediaeval hunting law and Ḥaḍramī custom in this individual instance makes it worth while to reproduce al-Damīrī's text.

"It may be that two wounds (inflicted) by two (separate) men would follow one upon the other. The first of these must be either mortal or maiming (*mudhfif aw muzmin*), or neither mortal nor maiming. If it be neither mortal nor maiming, not being effective in stopping it, then, if the (second) wound be mortal or maiming, the game belongs to the second man, but the first is not liable for anything on account of the wound he (inflicted). But if the wound (inflicted) by the first man be mortal, then the game belongs to the first man, and the second man must pay the fine for the wound (*arsh*) of any fault (*naqaṣa*) (caused) to its skin or flesh. If the first man's wound be maiming he possesses the game thereby, and the second (wound) is scrutinised, and if it be despatched by cutting the windpipe and the gullet it is lawful (*ḥalāl*), and the second man must pay the difference between its value slaughtered and maimed."

[295] See footnote 157.

[296] The offender is given a number of gentle blows on the shoulder with the *ṭawᶜ* to show that he admits his error.

297 On its horns.

298 ^{c}Abd al-Ḥabīb is an interesting name. *Ḥabīb* is the honorific title of Saiyids, and, it is said, at one time of the Mashāyikh, though this latter assertion is by no means proven. The word *Ḥabīb* could, I suppose, be understood as God. In spoken Arabic one abbreviates *Ḥabībī* to *Ḥibī* sometimes.

299 Bā Akhḍar, a family of Mashāyikh to which one of my informants belongs.

300 This man was of course a *ḍa^{c}īf*. His name, Musaibilī, means bulrush-millet.

301 This was the sense given me for *qirih*. South of Wādī Daw^{c}an von Wissmann has recorded two such features.

302 *Ṣud^{c}*, a split or fissure, is a common topographical term.

303 The Shibām *dallāls* are a well organised group of *masākīn*, belonging to a limited number of family groups. As trading rather than craftsmanship is the great activity of the town it is natural that they should organise the Hunt, but even in Tarīm many of the Quarter notables are *dallāls*.

304 I cannot be sure whether *ṣaidah* is a feminine noun or merely the *ism al-waḥdah* of *ṣaid*. This in itself is obviously an interesting point.

305 The reason given me for the use of the incense was in order to whiten face.

306 Ar. *^{c}iwaḍ-an ^{c}an*, syn. *badal ^{c}an*.

307 I.e. Maria Theresa dollars.

308 He is buried in the cemetery known as Jarb Haiṣam, west of Shibām, and was described to me as *aqdam man kān fi 'l-bilād*. *Tārikh Shanbal* (edition in preparation), gives the date of his death as 687 A.H. (A.D. 1288–9). He actually died in al-Ḥawl (al-Ghurfah) but was taken to Shibām, the town of his ancestors. Not infrequently the hagiologies allude to burial of saints in cemeteries at some distance from their death-beds.

309 Wādī Bin ^{c}Alī contains quite a number of villages. The use of the word *Ḥāfah* here is curious; my rendering as Quarter or Ward may not, in point of fact, quite coincide with the Ḥaḍramī conception of the term.

310 I.e. the whole Wādī Bin ^{c}Alī district.

311 Ṣamīl is another significant *miskīn* name, for the club is the characteristic weapon of this class.

312 A tribe of *masākīn*.

313 Note the title applied to the Saiyid.

314 Āl Ḥāmid are also found in Tarīm and Saiwūn, and I have even met a Mahrah-speaking Ḥāmidī Saiyid from Saiḥūt.

315 The procedure is worthy of remark. A Saiyid sends a Hunt case, and were he an orthodox Saiyid he would probably disapprove of the Hunt, to a Headman and to the Shaikh of a village where the Mashāyikh are still paramount. The Āl Ḥāmid of Tarīm are a fairly strict family in a religious sense, if my informants are correct.

316 This phrase is difficult to understand precisely. For the possible sense of *wijh* see *Gloss. daṭ.*, *Ṣalāḥ* would mean perhaps, the interests, welfare, temporal and spiritual, of the tribe.

317 Instead of the usual term *ṭahhar*, the word *ṣufiyat* is employed.

318 *The Ritual Hunt*, 191 *seq.*

319 Mediaeval work on tribal law.

320 Lane, *Lexicon*, 1902; Muḥ. b. Ḥabīb, *Kitāb al-Muḥabbar* (Ḥaidarābād, 1942), 166, Ibn Hishām, *Sīrah*, edit. F. Wüstenfeld (Göttingen, 1858–60), 84–5; *Tāj al-^{c}arūs*, I, 360, and VI, 75.

321 Another version calls it a *qadaḥ*.

322 E. Gräf, *Das Rechtswesen der heutigen Beduinen* (Walldorf-Hessen, n.d.), glossary. I have found this term in a number of other places, including some of my Ḥaḍramī MSS. Raḥaiyam quoted as current in Tarīm, ^{c}*ala 'l-ṭīb wa-'l-naqā*, in friendship and sincerity, and a *ḥilf ṭīb* is a pact of *ṣidq*, sincerity, *shar*^{c}, law (?), *ṣadāqah*, friendship, without *khiyānah*, deceit, treachery.

323 Al-Samhūdī, op. cit., 12.

324 Abu 'l-Faraj al-Iṣfahānī, *al-Aghānī* (Cairo, 1285 A.H.), XIX, 75; *laṭīmah*-perfume. Cf. al-Wāqidī, op. cit., 39, for Yemen perfume (^{c}*iṭr*) sold in Mecca.

325 Aḥmad b. ^{c}Abdullāh al-Ṭabarī, *al-Qirā li-qāṣid Umm al-Qurā* (Cairo, 1948), 479 *seq.* has a section on this theme.

326 This may be read *al-^{c}ūd al-ṭīb* or *al-ṭaiyib*.

327 Cf. Ahmad Fakhry, *An Archaeological Journey to Yemen* (Cairo, 1951–52), III, plate xxxiv.

328 B. Thomas, *Arabia Felix* (London, 1938), 260. Cf. W. Thesiger, *Arabian sands* (London, 1959), 151.

329 Op. cit., 196.

330 *Arabian sands*, 71 and 135. Cf. my "Hūd and other pre-Islāmic prophets", 168.

331 *Prose and poetry*, 116. Cf. *al-Fawā'id al-sanīyah*, MS. folio 63b, *maḍbī*.

332 So vocalised from N. Rhodokanakis, *Der vülgarabische Dialekt im Dofâr* (*Ẓfâr*), Südarabische Expedition (Wien, 1908–11), II, *Glossar*, 65, *Stück Fleisch*. Cf. *Gloss. daṭ.*, *waqaṣ*, *rester tantôt ici*, *tantôt là*. J. Robson, trans. *Mishkāt al-maṣābīḥ* (Lahore, 1963–65), I. 383, "A *waqṣ* of cattle was brought to Mu^{c}ādh b. Jabal". Here *waqṣ* is a term applied to odd numbers of cattle between one limit of assessment and the next. Cf. A. Ben Shemesh, *Taxation in Islam*, II ((Leiden, 1965), 46; *Tarjī^{c} al-aṭyār*, 300; I am uncertain of the vocalisation of *habārish*.

333 Yūsuf b. ^{c}Abdullāh b. Muḥ. b. ^{c}Abd al-Barr al-Namirī al-Qurṭubī, *Bahjat al-majālis wa-uns al-mujālis*, edit. Muḥ. Mursī al-Khūlī and ^{c}Abd al-Qādir al-Quṭṭ (Cairo, 1969), 286.

334 Cf. H. de Monfried, *Secrets of the Red Sea* (London, 1934), 304, "*mogma*", Somali meat, cut in squares, fried in butter and kept for months.

335 "The red granite stela of Ma^{c}īn," in *Journal of Near Eastern Studies* (Chicago, 1953), XII, 194–96. This may be compared with the Aden Department of Antiquities, *Bulletin* 3 (Aden, July 1964).

336 Perhaps even this colour is not fortuitous, for the ibex in Madūdah, possibly elsewhere too, is known as Bin Ḥumr. Cf. footnote 249. In 1966 I saw at Ḥaifah of Arḥab a flat rose-red altar used as a paving stone in the mosque.

337 Mohammed Tawfik, *Les Monuments de Ma^{c}īn* (Yemen) (Le Caire, 1951), 21, Fig. No. 27 (Fig. No. I of this study).

338 For the geography of the area consult H. von Wissmann and M. Höfner, *Beiträge zur historischen Geographie des vorislamischen Südarabien*, Akademie der Wissenschaften und der Literatur in Mainz (Wiesbaden, 1952), IV.

339 Op. cit. I, 144, Figs. 99–100, III, plates lxii–lxiii.

340 Cf. "Star-Calendars and an Almanac from South-West Arabia", *Anthropos* (Posieux (Fribourg), 1954), XLIX, 433–59.

341 "*The Quarters of Tarīm*," 282. He died in 641 A.H. (A.D. 1243–44).

342 Such ornaments are found on the poles (*bairaq*) kept at the tombs of saints, often with a crescent moon. The most convenient reference to this type of ornament is E. Brauer, *Ethnologie der jemenitischen Juden* (Heidelberg, 1934), *Tafel* viii, where copper knobs, *rimmonim*, of *Torah*-Scrolls are shown. I saw similar knobs of silver in one of the Ḥabbān synagogues.

343 Ahmed Fakhry, op. cit., I, Figs. 99–100.

344 *Prose and poetry*, introd., 29 *seq.*

[345] Weaving the hair in dancing is not confined to Arabia. For example the Sudanese hagiology, Muḥ. b. Ḍaifullāh, *Ṭabaqāt Wadd Ḍaifullāh*, edit. Dāwūd Mindīl (Cairo, 1930), 48, speaks of a shaikh who says to the mother of a young girl, *Ṣaffiqī lahā, tarquṣ wa-takibb fawq dhālik al-faqīr*, "Clap for her so that she may dance and throw loose her hair over that (young) *faqīr's* head". It is also, for example, found among Saharan women. Cf. C. Martin, "Nomad women of the Sahara", *Geographical Magazine* (London, 1956), XXVIII, IX, 457. On the coast of Ḥaḍramawt the action is called *tanwīsh*, and in the interior *na^{c}ish*. A. van den Branden, *Histoire de Ṭhamoud*, op. cit., 80–84, shows rock drawings of nude female figures with hair unloosed as they dance—which may indicate that this was a custom going back to those times.

[346] Op. cit., 827, 831, 841.

[347] *Iklīl X*, 13, *Ṣifat Jazīrat al-^{c}Arab*, op. cit., 72.

[348] G. Ryckmans, "Heaven and Earth in the South Arabian inscriptions", *Journal of Semitic Studies* (Manchester, 1958), III/3, 72.

[349] See above, p. 7.

[350] MS., cited above, folio 79a.

[351] A. Jamme, "La religion sud-arabe pré-islamique", *Hist. des religions* (Paris, 1956), IV, 281.

[352] E. Kühnel and L. Bellinger, *The Textile Museum*, *Catalogue of dated tiraz fabrics* (Washington, 1952), plates XLVI–II. These fabrics belong to the 10th century A.D., but ikated tissues were known long before then. Cf. "Materials for a History of Islamic Textiles", *Ars Islamica* (Michigan, 1948), XIII–IV, 76 or reprint (Beirut, 1973), 123.

[353] *Sheba's daughters*, index. Al-Wāqidī, op. cit., alludes, in describing the Prophet's raids, to the hiding of ostrich eggs in the desert to hold supplies of water.

[354] C. Doughty, *Arabia Deserta* (London, 1936), I, 173–74.

[355] *An account of the British settlement of Aden in Arabia* (London), 1877, 109.

[356] Sometimes this name seems to appear as al-Makārim, but this latter form of it has not so far been recorded. It may of course be a question of two different groups.

[357] W. J. Fischel, "Über die Gruppe der Kārimī-Kaufleute", *Studia Arabica*, I (Rome, 1937), 67–82.

[358] In a paper delivered in June 1970 at the Cambridge meeting of the Arabian Seminar ("Some recent views on the public institutions of Saba"), *Proceedings of the Seminar for Arabian Studies held at the Middle East Centre, Cambridge, 22nd and 23rd June, 1970*, 24–26, Jacques Ryckmans says, "A specific activity of the *mukarribs* is expressed by the so-called 'federation formula' (*ywm hwṣt kl gwm ḏ'lm wšymm wḏ ḥblm wḥmrm*), 'when he (i.e. the *mukarrib*) established every community of god or of patron, of treaty or of alliance'. This action alludes to a federation, a synoekesis of tribes in a hierarchy in accordance with the form of the treaty which united them together, and in accordance with the hierarchical station of the divinity whom the tribe worshipped. These elements are parallel to those which are found in the composition of the 'council' of Saba." I incline also to Miss Pirenne's idea that the *mukarrib* might be rendered the "unifier" of the country. Quṣaiy the ancestor of Quraish was a *mujammi^{c}*; *Iklīl X*, 18, states that the equivalent of *mujammi^{c}* in the dialect *lughah* of Ḥimyar is *musallibī*. See also G. Ryckmans, "Inscriptions sud-arabes, dix-septième série", *Le Muséon* (Louvain, 1959), LXXII, 167, the "Community of God" (*gwm ḏ-'lm*).

[359] "The Quarters of Tarīm," 280 *seq.*

[360] Cf. Masjid al-Kabsh at Mecca, *Al-Qirā li-qāṣid Umm al-Qurā*, 496. P. Brönnle, *Commentary on Ibn Hisham's Biography of Muhammad* (Abū Dharr) (Cairo, 1911, and 1970 reprint), 384, *ḍāris*, of a high piece of land, means "that which has jagged stones (*ḥijārah muḥaddadah*)". Cf. al-Wāqidī, op. cit., 887.

361 *Sheba's daughters*, 451.

362 *The al-ᶜUqlah texts*, Documentation sud-arabe, III (Washington, D.C., 1963), 49. The most recent examination of the inscriptions at al-ᶜUqlah is that of Muḥ. b. ᶜAbd al-Qādir Bā Faqīh, *Athār wa-nuqūsh al-ᶜUqlah* (Cairo, 1967). This does not seem to be a publication of much value unless, possibly, it has alternative readings.

363 The verb *kharra*, the sense of which Beeston has taken from Lane's *Lexicon*, exactly fits the circumstances here. "The *Aᶜrāb* (tribal Arabs) come down or descend, from the deserts to the towns or villages (*min al-bawādī ilā 'l-qurā*)." Shabwah can only be approached in this way.

364 In these two cases Jamme's reading for Philby's text is used.

365 Philby's text had *hwrw*.

366 Cf. Lane, *Lexicon*, *taḍāras al-binā'*, "the building was, became uneven, having in it what resembled *aḍrās*, teeth".

367 This was defined to me as "neither stone nor clay".

368 Studied by Brian Doe and the writer, to form a separate publication.

369 Cf. above, p. 9.

370 *Al-Shāmil*, 127.

371 *Koran*, XVII, 104. *Mathbūr* is explained by al-Baiḍāwī, *Anwār al-tanzīl* (Leipzig, 1846–48), I, 552, as *maṣrūf-an ᶜani 'l-khair*, which suits this context well.

372 *Tarjīᶜ al-aṭyār*.

373 Shabwah lies in the territory of the Kurab/Karab, an important section of the Bal-ᶜUbaid confederation. In 1937 the inhabitants of Shabwah were reported to consist of less than 50 males of the Ahl Buraik, Manṣabs, living under the protection of the Kurab. The Bal-ᶜUbaid were, in 1937, independent, but subsequently came under Quᶜaiṭī control. Philby's visit in 1937 led the Imām of the Yemen and the Aden Government to interest themselves in Shabwah. My 1964 notes run as follows: "The Ahl im-Buraik are accounted Mashāyikh but are *ḍuᶜāf* in the sense that they do not bear arms. People repair to the tomb of the ancestor at Shabwah for dealing with illness. They have a special *wasm* (brand) o–o on their camels—these pasture freely in the desert area about Shabwah and whatever raiders come their way do not molest the camels, but leave them alone. There are three other tribes of Mashāyikh in the area, Āl ᶜAbd al-Qādir, Āl ᶜAqīl, and Āl Rabīᶜ. The first has a *wasm S* on the right limb (*al-fakhidh al-ayman*) of their camels, the Āl ᶜAqīl a smaller *wasm* of the same, and the Āl ᶜAbd al-Qadīr a S shape, the end not quite touching. They are 'respected' (*muḥtaramīn*) because, though called *masākīn* (they have no cultivated land), they do not fight (*mā yiḥāribū*). Each year they give an *ᶜirwah* (so many *riyāls*) to various tribes to ask for protection; this is accepted (*maqbūlah*) and the tribes undertake not to molest them. Nowadays (1964) this custom may be disappearing in some places with the introduction of the security of the *Ḥukūmah*." According to *Military report on the British Protectorate of Aden*, etc., General Staff India (Simla, 1915), *arwa* (*sic*) was a term signifying a formal appeal to the Amīr (of Ḍālīᶜ) or granting of a petition by slaying a bullock in his presence as an offering. A Yāfiᶜī source told me that the Bin Buraik were of Yāfiᶜ but left the country and went to Shabwah and other places as a result of a disaster to their lands. These Mashāyikh concealed their name so as not to be molested and called themselves after a slave of theirs in Yāfiᶜ. This was denied by other informants better placed to know, and would seem to be legendary. Al-Sharīf al-Habīlī b. Ḥusain of al-Nuqūb (now in exile in al-Ṭā'if) told me that the Mashāyikh of groups we were discussing, including especially Buraik, known as Mashāyikh fuqarā', though, he added, they are "respected", gave each tribe, e.g. the Karab, ᶜAwāliq, but not the Yām and Manāhīl, an *ᶜirwah* each year of two *riyāls* which was equivalent to a *thawb*. They had *hijrah* with these tribes who would

rise and defend them, or, if anything by way of injury were done them they would receive compensation from the tribes, if, for example, any of their animals were stolen. They were known by the significant term of *Mashāyikh hijrah*. It appears that the class known as *qarār* (*hommes de métier*) also followed this procedure.

The verb is تعروى , to send an ᶜ*irwah*. One also says, "ᶜ*Irwatī filān*, So and so is my ᶜ*irwah*". "*Anta* ᶜ*irwat abūī/jaddī*, You are my father's/grandfather's ᶜ*irwah*." This is because a man inherits from him (*yistārith-ah*). These Mashāyikh might, for example, say to their tribe *Khadh-nī jimālī wāḥid min al-Ashrāf/al-qabā'il*, "One of the Ashrāf/tribes has taken my camels from me". The *qabīlī* would reply to them, *Hādhā lak siyāq* (I do not seem to have asked for the precise sense of *siyāq* in the context) and would give the Mashāyikh his dagger or his camels by way of compensation, while he was recovering the camels from the persons who had stolen them from the Mashāyikh. To those who had taken the camels, tribesmen of course, the *qabīlī* would say, *Anā muta*ᶜ*aiyib fī jimāl* ᶜ*irwatī*, "I have been shamed in respect of the camels of my ᶜ*irwah*".

I have wondered if the phrase in the Prophet's treaty with the Najrān Christians, "*ḥulal al-awāqī*" means *ḥullahs*, i.e. cloaks, worth an *ūqīyah* of silver each (cf. Muḥ. Ḥamīdullāh, *Majmū*ᶜ *al-wathā'iq al-siyāsīyah* (Cairo, 1956), III), just as the ᶜ*irwah* means two *riyāls*. It looks as if the *hajar* of Shabwah and perhaps the two other villages there, Maᶜwān and al-Mathnā, could have, from ancient time, enjoyed the status of a *hijrah*, i.e. a protected enclave.

In the first issues of *al-Nahḍah* (Aden, 1st December, 1949), No. 1 *seq*. the overlordship of Shabwah is disputed. Its inhabitants are stated to be Āl Bū Bakr (? ᶜAwlaqīs) and Kurab, the power lying with the latter who have old treaties with the ᶜAwlaqī sulṭān. In 1939 the ᶜAwlaqīs assisted in expelling al-Qardaᶜī's Yemeni force from Shabwah. Another writer avers that the Aden Government asked the ᶜAwlaqīs to intervene only in accordance with the established practice of *ṭalab najdah*. This did not imply recognition of ᶜAwlaqī overlordship since the real power is in the hands of the headmen (ᶜ*uqqāl*) of Al-Quṭaiyān (Kurab) who belong to neither the Quᶜaiṭī nor the ᶜAwlaqī tribes. It is further alleged that there are documents showing that Shabwah is Baiḥānī, and that, if Shabwah people paid tax to Quᶜaiṭī or ᶜAwlaqī, it is only because it is customary usage for tribes passing through the territories of others to do so.

374 Cf. "Building and builders in Ḥaḍramawt", *Le Muséon* (Louvain, 1949), LXII, 276.

375 R. A. B. Hamilton (Lord Belhaven), *Kingdom of Melchior* (London, 1949), 162, seems to suggest that the people in the Shabwah area, "still dance the dance of the ibex with horned heads", but this may just be a quotation from some remark of W. H. Ingrams.

376 G. Ryckmans, "Inscriptions sud-arabes", *Le Muséon* (Louvain, 1957), LXX, 109 *seq*. To resolve possible syntactical difficulties, I propose that the latter formula be understood to mean *ṣyd* ᶜ*thtr w-*(*ṣyd*) *krwm*. If my theory be correct, I then suggest that an ᶜAthtar hunt was not always a *ṣyd krwm*, and that the term was only added in the circumstances when the special *ṣyd krwm* took place.

377 Professor M. A. al-Ghūl first hazarded the suggestion that the *karawān* might be intended. *Tāj al-*ᶜ*arūs*, X, 314, gives it a plural *karā* which would fit here, and a verse indicating, as he explains it, that it was hunted with the hawk (*bāzīy*); it is also described as having a pleasant call and it seems that the poem cited below refers to this.

378 Al-Thaᶜālibī, *Yatīmat al-dahr* (Cairo, 1947), I, 414.

[379] *Burj* of course means a sign of the Zodiac but I do not understand this phrase, unless it be "the Mansions of perfection".

[380] Here I would suggest that the bustard is called "the maternal aunt" of the *karawān* because it resembles it. Ḥaḍramī fishermen use *khāl* and *khālah*, etc., in this way sometimes in cases where two different species of fish somewhat resemble each other. Rafīq Shākir al-Natshah, *Riḥlah ila 'l-Rub^{c} al-Khālī* (al-Dawḥah, n.d. perhaps 1966?), 32, calls the *karawān* by another version of the same epithet—*ibn ukht al-ḥubārā*, describing it as smaller than a bustard but bigger than a pigeon. This author speaks of returning triumphant (*raja^{c}nā sālimīn ghānimīn*—an expression as old as al-Wāqidī, op. cit., I, 756) from the hunt, but in shame if they shoot nothing. He has also some interesting notes on the Bedouin beliefs about Jinn in animal form in the Empty Quarter.

[381] "The Ritual Hunt," 189. Cf. *Sheba's daughters*, 443. There is some discussion also in A. Jamme, "L'inscription ḥaḍramoutique Ingrams I et la chasse rituelle sud-arabe", 99 *seq.*, and A. J. Drewes, "Some Ḥaḍramī inscriptions", op. cit., 93–94, whose new reading gives us "the Valley (*sirr*) of ^{c}Irmā".

[382] Cf. *Prose and poetry*, introd., 35. For *khushsh-hā*, enter it, one can also say *khudh-hā* in Ḥaḍramawt.

[383] Ibn al-Athīr, *Usd al-ghābah* (Cairo, 1285–86), II, 296; Ibn Sa^{c}d, *al-Ṭabaqāt al-kubrā* (Beirut, 1957–68), IV, 422; Al-Wāqidī, op. cit., 84, 86, 93, 228, 540, 544, 659.

[384] ^{c}Alī b. ^{c}Aqīl has mentioned boundary disputes, above, p. 17. I have not heard that the different Quarters of Tarīm have separate hunting mountains, but only that the routes to them when lying through the town are sometimes in dispute. It would seem that different villages do quarrel about hunting areas.

[385] W. H. Ingrams, "A Journey to the Sei^{c}ar Country and through the Wadi Maseila", *Geographical Journal* (London, 1936), LXXXVIII, VI, 546.

[386] *Daṯînah*, II, 1475: "Je crois donc que les cornes de bouquetins aux *ḥuṣūn* sudarabiques sont une réminiscence de l'antiquité orientale. Mais bien entendu, je ne saurais rien affirmer de précis n'ayant trouvé auprès des indigènes du Sud aucun appui pour mon hypothèse."

[387] Nūr al-Dīn, ^{c}Abdullāh b. Ḥumaid b. Sallūm al-Sālimī al-^{c}Umānī, *Jawhar al-niẓām fī ^{c}ilmay al-adyān wa-'l-arḥām* (Cairo, 1345 A.H.), 162. He also defines *wass al-kalb ay ighrā'u-hu bi-'l-ṣaid.*

[388] *Mukhaṣṣaṣ*, VIII, 31.

[389] "The 'Ta'lab Lord of Pastures' Texts," *B.S.O.A.S.* (London, 1955), XVII, 154–56; M. Höfner, "Ta'lab als Patron der Kleinviehhirten", *Serta Cantabrigiensia* (Wiesbaden, 1954), 29–36; A. Jamme, "L'identification de Ta'lab au dieu lunaire", *Bibliotheca orientalis* (Leiden, 1956), XIII, V–VI, 182–86. Glaser 1210 dealing with the shrine of Ta'lab, was re-translated by A. F. L. Beeston, "Two south Arabian inscriptions: some suggestions", *Journal of the Royal Asiatic Society* (London, 1937), 59–78. This inscription is of considerable interest to the present study, but it appears to me that it needs re-examination and revision in the light of the Hunt described here, and the probable connection of the pre-Islāmic Hunt with such sanctuaries as that of Ta'lab.

[390] R. B. Serjeant, "Some irrigation systems in Ḥaḍramawt".

[391] *Iklīl X*, op. cit., 17 *seq.* Cf. *Iklīl VIII* (*Al-Iklīl, al-juz' al-thāmin*), edit. Nabih Amin Faris (Princeton, 1940), 66–7.

[392] The pass (*naqīl*) of al-Ghūlah is marked just west of the road from Raidah to Khamir through, or just north of al-Bawn to which it is the natural limit, and half-way approximately between these two points, on the map said to have been made by the Russians and published in Arabic in reproduction by both Royalists and Republicans. The ancient road zigzagging up al-Ghūlah's steep mountain-side is still in evidence, but the new Chinese road has replaced it.

Cf. Joseph Werdecker, "A contribution to the geography and cartography of north-west Yemen (based on . . . the exploration of Eduard Glaser . . .)", *Bulletin de la Société Royale de Géographie d'Egypte* (Cairo, 1939), XX. Muḥ. al-Akwaᶜ, in his notes to *Iklīl I*, op. cit., I, 223, mentions the interdicted pasture (*ḥimā*) of al-Bawn, and also the *ḥimās* of al-Raḥabah (near Ṣanᶜā') and Hamal/Himil, N.E. of Ḥajjah, adding that Ḥimyar used to call (pasture) for horses and cattle *maḥjar* (pl. *maḥājir*), "and these are many in the Yemen up to this age."

393 A. Jamme, "*La religion sudarabe* . . . ", 273.

394 *Ṣifat Jazīrat al-ᶜArab*, op. cit., 82.

395 Turkish General Staff map -يمن ولايتي خريطة سي
1: 1,250,000 in Turkish script.

396 Op. cit., 109, and cf. above, p. 8. It is Sa'd of W. Maṭirah who are so described.

397 Op. cit., 86, 111.

398 Loc. cit.

399 E. Graf, *Das Rechtswesen*, op. cit., 182, *Schutz*. The citations are from North Arabia, but this is immaterial.

400 Cf. above, pp. 35 *seq*., and footnotes 147, 157.

401 *Prose and poetry*, 73, 76, 79. I have noticed this in many other unpublished Banī Mighrāh poems, and have detected references to floods and rains in many classical *qaṣīdahs* in the conventional opening verses.

402 *Al-Waqā'iᶜ*, 73, عسى رحمة لحيث الزمان اصله يحضر , and 80–81.

On p. 111, are the following verses:

إذا شى قتْل عند القبايل وَآهْل لوْشارْ
تشوفهْ في فرخْ كنّ عنْدهْ عيد لأَفْطارْ
عسى رحْمهْ بها ينْجلي همّي ولآكْدارْ

Possibly much more information on beliefs and practices regarding the Hunt could be derived from this *dīwān* which I have scrutinised fairly carefully; but without explanation of the obscure words and commentary by a competent Ḥaḍramī informant, much is lost to the reader.

403 The winged horse was also known. ᶜĀ'ishah had a *faras lahā janāḥān riqāᶜ*, a (toy) horse/mare with patchwork(?) wings. Abū Dā'ūd, *Sunan* (Cairo, 1952), II, 581. Solomon, she said, had winged horses! Cf. A. Grohmann, Göttersymbole und Symboltiere auf südarabischen Denkmälern", *Denkschriften der Kais. Akad. d. Wissenschaften in Wien*, Phil.-Hist. Klasse (Wien, 1914), LVIII, 1, 69, for confronted winged sphinxes from ᶜAmrān. Cf. figure a winged beast from Ma'rib.

404 Ibid, 264. Jāḥiẓ, *Ḥayawān* (Cairo, 1944), VI, 198, says that the Aᶜrāb (which I now prefer to render as "tribal Arabs") considered/made Suhail an ᶜ*ashshār* transformed (*musikh*) into a star, and al-Zuharah (generally rendered as Venus) a harlot woman transformed into a star, and her name was Anāhīd. The similarity between the words ᶜAthtar/ᶜAstar and ᶜ*ashshār*, a collector of tithes, is obvious.

Ibn al-Athīr, *Nihāyah*, III, 97, quotes the Tradition, "If you meet a tithe-collector (ᶜ*ashir*) kill him". This he explains as "If you find anyone taking the tithe as the people of the Jāhilīyah used to take it continuing according to religion (*muqīm-an* ᶜ*alā dīni-hi*), then kill him on account of his *kufr*".

^{c}*Ashshār* is the same as ^{c}*āshir*. Suhail is the star that marks the end of summer (*qaiẓ*); in the Persian Gulf it marks the beginning of the shipping season. In Ḥaḍramawt, cf. *Prose and poetry*, 164, No. 57, Sa^{c}d al-Suwainī says,

Sihail comes with night rain in the darkness,
Sihail that (thunders) night-long, heedless.

Suhail then brings the rains of *kharīf* with which the inscription tells us ^{c}Athtar watered Saba'. I suggest that the mythology reported by Jāḥiẓ with regard to Suhail is a post-Islāmic memory of the pre-Islāmic god ^{c}Athtar.

405 J. Ryckmans, "Deux importants ouvrages de la Sammlung Eduard Glaser", *Bibliotheca orientalis* (Leiden, 1967), XXIV, III/IV, 143.

406 *Ḥaḍramoût*, op. cit., 736, quoting Glaser, *Abessinier*, 82. Ṣirwāḥ is discussed by al-Hamdānī, *Iklīl* I, edit. al-Akwa^{c}, 140.

407 I have also come across this word in the recently published volumes of the *Iklīl* of al-Hamdānī. At Ḥuqqat Hamdān in 1972 I saw *balaq* white limestone. ^{c}*ithribī* red stone, of the colour of ^{c}*ithrib* flowers, and *ṣamm* and *ṣawrab*, types of stone without holes in them, as contrasted with some types of volcanic stone. Al-ḥajar al-Ḥabashī is much used today in buildings in Ṣan^{c}ā'.

408 A different photograph of this same piece appears in W. L. Brown and A. F. L. Beeston, "Sculptures and inscriptions from Shabwa", *Journal of the Royal Asiatic Society* (London, 1954), plate XXII, Fig. 2. Cf. Grohmann, Göttersymbole und Symboltiere . . . , op. cit., 33.

409 "The Moon-God on Coins of the Ḥaḍramaut," 623. I am indebted to Dr. Walker also for his report on coins found by R. A. Hall and J. S. L. Pressly. There are new coins with the epithet Shaqr, the Moon-God and a winged caduceus, another type with a bull and the names Sīn and Shaqr, both names of the Ḥaḍramī Moon-God, and a third type with an eagle and Shaqr. I have wondered if the caduceus is perhaps to identified either with the *bairaq* of South Arabian saint cults, or the hunting-pole, or, at least, if the ancient South Arabians associated this emblem on their coins with one or the other. Cf. A. F. L. Beeston, "Notes on old south Arabian lexicography", *Le Muséon* (Louvain, 1951), LXIV, 130. Shaqr is an epithet of the Qatabanian God. Cf. also J. Walker, "A New type of south Arabian coinage", *Numismatic Chronicle* (London, 1937), V, XVII, 260–79.

410 *Prose and poetry*, 128, 1.5, *ḥumsh al-siyan*, black of locks. Cf. T. Nöldeke, *Delectus* (Berlin, 1890), 107, line 4, where *ḥamsh al-lithāt* reads better as "black of gum", giving *ḥamsh* this sense, traditional in Ḥaḍramawt, and not, "having little flesh". The line compares the base of the gums with crushed antimony which of course is black.

411 *Al-Imtā^{c} wa-'l-mu'ānasah* (Cairo, 1944), III, 189. It may of course be objected that al-Tawḥīdī is a 4th/10th-century author in Iraq, not Arabia.

412 *Al-Shāmil*, 91.

413 "Hūd and other pre-Islāmic Prophets," op. cit., 148. Other curious names are wells in the Jewish part of Medina called al-Buwailah and al-Ḍarrāṭah, the mountains Musliḥ and Mukhrī of the tribes Banu 'l-Nār and Banū Ḥurāq—al-Wāqidī, op. cit., 380, 511. Cf. F. Wüstenfeld, *Das geographische Wörterbuch des . . . el-Bekri* (Göttingen–Paris), 1876, 559.

414 "Giraffe hunting among the Humr tribe," *Sudan notes and records* (Khartoum, 1956), XXXVII, 49–60, a valuable account for comparative purposes. On the contrary, there seems to be little in common between the Arabian and Sudanese hunts on the one hand, and the data provided by Mohammed Mokri, *Le Chasseur de Dieu et le mythe du Roi-Aigle* (Wiesbaden, 1967), either in concept or practice.

415 Ibid, 56 *seq.*

416 As Cunnison does not cite this word in Arabic script I can only guess, possibly incorrectly, that it comes from such as the classical Arabic verb *hakara*, *hukar*, what is withheld in the expectation of its becoming dear (Lane, *Lexicon*). *Hukr* would therefore, I suppose, mean "with-holding". If so, the sense is close to that of *Imtana*ᶜ ᶜ*alai-him qatl al-ṣaid*, of the *Bug͟hyat al-mustars͟hidīn*, 255, of the Saiyid ulema of Ḥaḍramawt.

417 Two verses drawn from ᶜAbd al-Ḥaqq, *Al-Waqā'i*ᶜ, 94 and 102, show that also in the Ḥaḍramī Hunt, *ḥasad* must be eschewed:

بني مغراه مرّت ليالينا على زيْن
على شرْع النّقا ما نسايرْ حاسد آوْ شيْن

وسعفكْ مالك الْملْك منْ حاسد وشيْطانْ
اصنْ للحضّ سلّمْ على آهْله عدّ لزْمانْ

The first verses say: "We have passed our nights in a seemly way, following the path/rule of keeping out of wrong-doing, not taking as companions of the way envious or evil men."

The second two verses I have not read with Ḥaḍramīs, but the gist of them seems to be that you should let God be with you, not an envious person or Satan.

418 Compare verse 2 of the Banī Mig͟hrāh poem translated above, p. 40.

419 See J. Ryckmans, "Un rite d' *istisqâ'* au temple sabéen de Mârib", *Annuaire de l'Institut de Philologie et d'Histoire Orientales et Slaves* (Bruxelles, 1973), XX, 379–88, for pre Islāmic rain-making, and my "Cultivation of cereals in Rasūlid Yemen", *Arabian Studies*, (London, 1974), I, 32. Ya'qūbī, *Tārīk͟h*, I, 254, alludes to the motive of *istisqā'*, seeking rain as a cause for setting up idols to worship in pre-Islāmic Arabia. Bajīlah, a Qaḥṭānī tribe (op. cit., 256), even have a *talbiyah* indicating that, in coming on pilgrimage, they seek rain.

Labbaika 'an Bajīlah   Fī bāriq-in wa-m(a)k͟hīlah

The latter half-verse asks for lightning and signs of rain.

SUPPLEMENTARY NOTES

Professor Beeston has generously sent me what he describes as "a tentative interim rendering, pending a more detailed investigation which I hope to publish fairly soon," of inscription R 4176 (cf. my foot-note 389). Even with his qualified support of his new version it is too important to omit.

"Ta'lab has prohibited all ibexes (*'arwy*, Ar. *arāwī*) from being hindered from feeding, in order that they may grow fat with off-spring; and Ta'lab has prohibited the peasantry of any (game-) reserve (*mḥrm*), mountain area (*rymn*) or (hunting) location (*mntt*) from driving out the herds which frequent (those places), for those (places) are a *ḥaram*: and it is not lawful for (the folk) Sam'ay to fail in their responsibility for the hunt of Ta'lab (*ṣyd T'lb*). Moreover Ta'lab has prohibited the wasteland (*'lb*) from (being the scene of) intercourse with women on the seventh day of the month dhû ṢRR, because (then) Ta'lab's *qṣd* go out (*tfr*) to Thûmat and to Utmân, and assemble (*hṣr*) at the enclave (*ḥrmt*) of Utmân, the *qayl* of MḌNḤN having summoned (*nš'*) the *qṣd*."

He has referred me to H. v. Wissmann, *Zur Geschichte und Landeskunde von alt-Südarabien* (Vienna, 1964), 307 for T͟hūmah. The high mountains with their steep sides begin immediately above T͟hūmah, north-east of D͟hū Marmar.

Professor Jacques Ryckmans writes also, "Une récente publication russe m'apprend la découverte d'une nouvelle inscription sud-arabe mentionnant la chasse, trouvée dans une *passe de montagne*. Ce serait la troisième inscription de ce genre trouvée dans un pareil endroit (les autres étant Naqīl Šiġa' et 'Aqāba Fatūra)."

From A. M. Hassan, *The poetry of Kus͟hājim* (London Ph.D. thesis, 1973, 219) I note (what had previously escaped me) as relevant to the hunting verse of the Ḥaḍramī poet 'Abd al-Ḥaqq and others, that, "The poet [Kus͟hājim] was sentimentally attached to *ṭarad* [the chase] more particularly in his old age. When he was no longer able to take part in *ṭarad* he would recall nostalgically his former days when he went hunting in the desert." It may be then, that the plaint that one is too old to hunt is a conventional motive of hunting verse going back a very long way indeed, and still followed by such poets as Bū S͟haik͟h (*Prose and poetry*, op. cit., English pref. 25),

On the *jōl* ahead the lads I'd fain be treading.
Age clutcheth my limbs, marrow to water turning.

GLOSSARY

Note: The Glossary is arranged according to the word-order of the Roman alphabet and takes no account of the signs for *hamzah* and c*ain*. Cross-referencing is provided as an aid to distinguishing words derived from a common root, but no distinction is drawn between classical and dialectical words. Nouns are mostly given in the singular followed by their plural(s) in brackets, but many plurals are entered separately as well. Verbs are entered in the perfect followed by the imperfect tenses, except in two cases.

Abū, first star of season, 12.
Abū (pls. *abwā & ubwah*), headman, 15, 27, 28, 29, 30, 33, 55, 60, 106; *abu 'l-ḥaḍar*, 28; *abu 'l-ḥāfah*, 46; *abu 'l-khibrah*, 27; *abwā al-Qaniṣ wa-'l-ḥāfah*, 44; see *buwwah*.
abwā, see *abū*.
c*ādah* (pl. c*awā'id*), custom, 19, 47.
ādamī, man, 39.
adgham, see c*aib*.
c*adhbah*, tail, of turban, 103.
aḍrās (s. *ḍirs*), teeth, 110; see *taḍāras*, *ḍāris*.
adwār, see *dawr*.
afrāḥ, festivals, 32.
aghrā al-kalb bi-'l-ṣaid, to set dog on game, 40; see *Mighrāh*, Index No. I, and *mughrā*.
aḥkām al-qanāṣah, decisions of hunt, 16; see *qanāṣah*.
aḥwarī, see *rashā*.
c*aib*, defect, shame, etc., 17.
*al-*c*aib al-adgham*, the "black shame", 61; see *mu*c*aiyab*.
*al-*c*ain*, evil eye, 82, 93; c*ain al-*c*Arab*, ditto, 82; c*ain al-saw*, ditto, 93.
c*aiyān*, look-out man, 103; see c*iyānah*.
c*aiyar*, *yi*c*aiyir*, make derogatory remarks about, 28.
akhta', *yukhti'*, to miss, of a shot, 14.
akhwāl (s. *khāl*, *q.v.*), maternal uncles, 39.
c*ākif*, worshipping, 92.
c*ajm*/c*ajim*, top half of haunch, 97; see *qaṣmah*.
c*ajz*, rump, 55.
alaba, hunt, chase, rain, 76.
c*alam*, a mark, 103.
*a*c*lam* c*alā*, give notice of, 57.
c*ālī*, pounding stone, 17.
am = *al*, 102.
*a*c*mām*, paternal uncles, 39.
c*āmid*, living in, inhabitating, 47.
c*ammārah*/c*ammāriyah* (pl. c*ammārī*), 46, 101.
amn, security, 62.
c*ānī*, messenger, 44, 53.
anmar min, more of a leopard than, 38; see *nimr*.
anṣāb/*nuṣub*, stones, standing stones, 92.
anwā ḥājah, *qaḍā-hā*, to perform something, 103; see *manwī; nīyah*.
c*aqabah*, pass, 52.
c*āqil* (pl. c*uqqāl*), headman, 92, 111.
c*aqīrah*, animal for sacrifice, 94.
*aqnaṣ al-*c*Arab*, most hunting of the Arabs, 8, 75; see *qāniṣ*, etc.
c*arbūn*, pledge, 15.
arkān al-Islām, the "Pillars" of Islām, 14.
arsh, fine for wound, 106.
c*arūs*, bride, 20. bridegroom (pl. c*arāwis*), 105; see *mu*c*arris*.
arwā (pl. *arāwīy*, *urwīyah*), ibex, mountain goat, 86.
*aṣābi*c, fingers, 93.
asās, see *sās*.
*ash*c*ar*, mark a sacrificial animal, 97.
c*āshir* c*ashshār*, tithe collector, 113, 114.
ashkhaṣ, *yushkhiṣ*, to raise, 43.
c*ashshār*, see c*āshir*.
c*ashwī*, evening ceremony, 29.
aṣl, "basis", 8.
c*atārīr*, see c*atrūr*.
aṭrāf al-jabal, fringes of mountain, 29; see *ṭarīq*.
c*atrūr* (pl. c*atārīr*), short road in mountains, small trickle after rain, 21, 94.
c*aṭṭal*, to spoil, cause to break down, 21.

^{c}*awā'id*, see ^{c}*ādah*.
awāqī, see *ḥullah*, *ūqīyah*.
awlād, see *walad*.
awqad, to heat (coffee), 51.
al-awwalīn, the ancients, people of long ago, 46.
ayah, 64.
ayāyil, see *iyyal*/*uyyal*.
^{c}*azam*, to go forth, 59.

Bā Fatīlah, matchlock, 55.
badā, commencer la guerre, 100.
badā - mā badā lak, what's come over you?, 12.
badan, *wa*^{c}*il b*., an old ibex, 98.
badan, meat given to *Manṣab*, 98.
badanah (pl. *budn*), sacrificial animal; ^{c}*alā dimā' al-budn*, 97.
badanah (pl. *badan*), = *wu*^{c}*ūl*, ibexes, 98.
baddā, to kill, 39.
baddā^{c} *al-qawāfī*, maker of the verses, 14, 29.
bādiyah (pl. *bawādī*), open country, deserts, 100, 110.
baiḍ al-na^{c}*ām*, ostrich eggs, 69.
bairaq, pole insignia of saint, 108, 114.
bait, temple, 92; tribal "house", 98.
bakarah/*bakrah*, column, pillar, set up for saint.
balaq̣, white limestone, 114.
baldah, village, 29, 44.
baqar, cattle, ibex, or game of deer family, 7, 71; see *bqr*.
baqqal, to plant, 17.
baqqārah, cattlemen, 88; see Index No. I.
baqqaw-hā, they spared it, 58.
bār, *rejected*, from *bari'a*, to be quit, free of, 14; see *barī'*.
barad, *yibrid* (*bardaw*), spend, pass, the heat of day, 53, 54.
barakah, luck, 23, 90; see *mubārak*, *tabārak*.
barī', clean, pure, quit of, 62; see *bār*, *birī*.
bāriq, lightning, 115.
bārūt, gun-powder, 96.
bas̲h̲s̲h̲ar (*-hu*) *bi-*, give good news of, to, 29, 30; see *bis̲h̲ārah*.
bās̲h̲ūrah (pl. *bawās̲h̲īr*), projection at corner of battlements, 39.
basīṭ, metre, 101.
basmala, say *bismillāh*, 73.
baṭn, tribal section, 8.
baṭṭah, leather bottle, 68.
baṭṭāl, *kalām b*., evil words, 38.
bawādī, see *bādiyah*.
bāz/*bāzīy* (pl. *buzāh*), falcon, hawk, 13, 90, 111.
bi-lā ziyādah wa-lā nuqṣān, neither more nor less, 47.
bi-mūjib, according to, 47.
bida^{c}, innovations, 19.
bidār ila 'l-qanāṣah, hastening to the hunt, 32.
birī (*min*), be free, exempt, quit of, 90.
bis̲h̲ārah, good news, gift or reward for good news, 27, 39, 53; see *bas̲h̲s̲h̲ar*.
bqr, meaning discussed, 95.
budn, see *badanah*.
bunduq (pl. *banādiq*), gun, 14, 96; see *laḥmah*.
bunduqīyah, bullet, 50, 103.
buqs̲h̲ah, coin-name, 67.
burj, sign of Zodiac, 72.
buwwah, office of headman, 60; see *abū*.
buzāh, see *bāz*.

da^{c}*ā*, *yid*^{c}*ī min*, = *nādā* ^{c}*alā*, to summon, 102.
da^{c}*ah*, freedom from trouble, easy circumstances, 62.
ḍab^{c}, hyena, 14.
dabbar, *yidabbir*, march, leave, 49, 50, 53.
ḍafā, couvrir, 101; see *ḍāfī*.
ḍa^{c}*fā*, see *ḍa*^{c}*īf*.
daf^{c}*ah*, impost, 102; see *daffa*^{c}*a*.
ḍafā^{c}*ir muraṣṣa*^{c}*ah*, plaits of hair woven together, 43; see *maḍfūr*.
ḍaffā, *yiḍaffī*, cover, *envelopper*, *entourer*, 101; see *ḍafā*.
daffa^{c}*a*, make pay an impost (*daf*^{c}*ah*, *q.v.*), 102.
ḍāfī (f. *yah*), wide, (stock epithet of hunting net), 45, 96; explained, 101; see *ḍafā*, *was̲h̲r*.
ḍa^{c}*īf* (pls. *ḍa*^{c}*fā*, *ḍu*^{c}*āf*, *ḍu*^{c}*afā*), poor, not bearing arms, clay-worker, 5, 27, 30, 46, 66, 107, 110.
ḍaim, opposed to *ḥaqq*, 17, 91; see *d̲h̲aim*.

dair (pl. *duyūr*), sugar and coffee, 47, 51, 102.
ḍallā, remain during the day, 105.
dallāl (pl. *dalal*), broker, 47, 49, 58, 102, 107.
damār, = *qatl*, slaying of game, 45, 101.
daqm/duqum (pls. *diqām*, *adqām*), mountain crest, peak, 11, 90,105.
dār (pl. *diyār*), dwelling house, family, 37, 78.
dār, *yidīr*, to make a round of, go round (marching), 102; explained as *yidarij* (*q.v.*).
darāhim bīḍ, silver coins, 67.
daraj, *yidarij*, = *yidīr* (*q.v.*) to go round, encircle, 102; see *darjah*.
daraqah (pl. *diraq*), shield, 96.
ḍāris, high land with jagged stones, 109; see *aḍrās*.
darjah, see *daryāt; daraj*.
daryāt, rounds, circumambulations, 102; see previous and *daraj*.
dasara, thrust, butt, 8; further senses, 88.
dasm, fat, 17; see *iddasam*.
dawām, always, 25.
dawār, circumambulation, place of an idol, 92.
dawlah, sultan, 20, 21.
dawr (pl. *adwār*), surrounding wall, 94, 101.
dhabḥ, sacrifice, 56.
dhabil, turtle-shell, 97.
dhail, tail, 55.
dhaim, taint, attaintedness, 15, 16, 17, 19, 20, 31, 59, 69, 70; = ᶜ*aib*, a defect, 17; = *ḍaim* (*q.v.*), 17; see *dhaiyam*, *tadhaiyam*, *mudhaiyam*.
dhaiyam, accuse of *dhaim*, attaint, 16, 56; see previous.
dhakāt sharᶜīyah, legal slaughtering, 59.
dhakkā, *yudhakkī*, despatch, kill, of an animal, 52.
dharā, to sow, 11.
dhikr Allāh, termination of poem by mentioning Allāh, 41.
dhirāᶜ, cubit, 28.
dhurah, millet, 36.
dihin, meat, fat, 17.
dīm, skin, 39, 55.
diqām, see *daqm*.
ḍiyādah, stalk of *ṭahaf* millet, 11, 90.
ḍiyāfah, entertainment, 39.
dimā', see *budn*.
dukhlah, ceremonial entry, 29, 54, 68; note on, 105.
dukhūn, incense, 59.
duqum, see *daqm*.

faddā, *yifaddī*, pay ransom (a sheep), 56; see *fidā*, *fidū*.
fahd (pl. *fuhūd*), lynx, 2, 70, 88; caracal lynx, 86.
faitah, natural death, 59.
fakhidh, thigh, 31, *al-f. al-ayman*, right thigh, 110.
fakhidh, section of tribe, 98.
faqaᶜ, to beat a drum, 46; see *faqqāᶜ*.
faqīh, man of religion, etc., 82.
faqīr (pl. *fuqarā'*), needy, man of (popular) religion, Ṣūfī, 82, 88; also *fekki*, 82.
faqqāᶜ, drummer, 50.
farᶜ, "branch" in legal or religious sense, 8.
farā'iḍ, religious duties, 20.
faras, toy horse with patchwork (*riqāᶜ*) wings, 113.
farfārah/farfīrah (pl. *farāfīr*), = *jubbah*, white coat, 21, 94; see *ṭawīlah*.
farīq, hunting party, 36, 37.
farraq, *yifarriq*, lay a contributary levy, 46; divide out a contributary levy among contributors, 101; see *firqah*.
faṣīlah, a tribal subdivision, 98.
fatāwā, legal opinions, 96.
Fātiḥah, opening *sūrah* of Koran, 46, 48, 50; see *khatam*.
Fatīlah, see *Bā*.
fattah, shredded bread, 46; see *khubrah*.
fekki, see *faqīh*.
fidā, sacrifice, propitiatory ransom, 93, 106; see *faddā*, *fidū*.
fidyah, sacrifice consecrating road, 93.
fiqrah, top part of neck, 55.
firqah, money levy, tax, impost, 101; see *farraq*.
fiṭām, diver's nose-stopper, 97.
fitnah, quarrel, 24.
Fiṭr, ᶜ*Id al-*, Feast of Fast-Breaking, 77; see *Lafṭār*.
fidū, sacrifice, 56; see *fidā*.

fuhūd, see *fahd*.
fuqarā', see *faqīr*.
furhud, young of ibex, 98.
futyā al-ṣaid, legal opinion in the case of game, 87.

ghaith, rain, 12.
ghalāq, conclusion, end, 55.
ghalaṭ, injury, 15.
ghanam al-jabal, mountain sheep, 86; see *rās*.
ghānimīn, see *sālimīn*.
ghawth, being whose aid is sought, 89.
ghāyib, absent (opp. of *ḥāḍir*, *q.v.*), 102.
ghazāl (pl. *ghizlān*), gazelle, 8, 86; *ghazāl al-Kaᶜbah*, 88.
ghirr, *qaniṣ al-*, slaying by chance hunting encounter, 27.
grtn, protection money (?), discussed, 76; see *jīrah*.

ḥabā'ib, see *ḥabīb*.
ḥabal, *yaḥbal*, to make a twist (*ḥabīl*, *q.v.*) of grass fodder, 11, 90.
habārīsh, roasted *sawād al-baṭn*, offal, 63, 108.
ḥabash, black building stone, 78, 114; see *ḥajar*.
ḥabaṭ, sacred enclave, 34, 35, 98.
ḥabb, corn, 99.
ḥabīb (pl. *ḥabā'ib*), honorific title of Saiyids, 18, 60, 107; *ḥabībī*, abbrev. to *ḥibī*, 109.
ḥabīl, twist of grass for fodder, 11, 90; see *ḥabal*.
ḥābiṭī, lower, 93.
ḥaḍar, craftsmen and small shop-keepers; 27; *abu 'l-ḥ.*, headman of *ḥ.*, 28; see *ḥaḍarī*.
ḥaḍarī, belonging to the *ḥaḍar*, villager, 27, 30, 56.
ḥadd, boundary, territory, 34, 37.
ḥadd, one, 15.
ḥaḍḍ, word of uncertain sense, 115.
ḥāḍir, present (used in formula), 102.
ḥaḍrat al-Nabī, his presence the Prophet, 46, 101.
ḥāfah (pl. *ḥuwaif*), quarter, ward, 15, 37, 58, 107; *abū/abwā al-ḥ.*, head-man/men of the quarter, 44, 46; *ḥ.* of *ḥawīk*, "weavers", 37.
ḥaffah, procession in line, 100; see *maḥaffah*.
hajar, village (possibly protected village), 111.
ḥajar, stone, 92; *ḥ. Ḥabashī*, black stone, 114.
ḥājib, excrescence on top of Jōl, 103.
ḥājir, drum, 46, 48.
hajīr, *wa-'l-hajīr*, hunters' cry, = *al-bidār ila 'l-qanāṣah*, 32.
ḥajj, pilgrimage, 6, 64, 67.
hāka, *yahūk*, to shout, 48, 52.
ḥakam, *yaḥkum*, to adjudicate, 57.
hakara, to be withheld, 115; see *hukr*.
ḥalāl, lawful, 106.
ḥalqah, circle, 103; link of a net, 56.
hamaz, to jump, 58.
ḥamdala, to say *al-ḥamdu lillāh*, 73.
ḥammal ᶜalā, to load a beast, 50.
ḥamsh al-lithāt, black of gums, 114; see *ḥumsh*.
ḥanaq, anger, rivalry against, 38.
ḥaqq, opposite of *ḍaim*, 17, 91; justification, 15.
ḥaqq, used with suffixes meaning, "belonging to", 15, 34, 35, 55, 93.
ḥaram, sacred enclave, 4, 7, 62, 69, 78, 87, 89, *ḥaram muḥarram*, 87; *ḥ.* and *maḥram*, 78; see Index No. III.
ḥarāwah, marriage, 55.
ḥasad, envy, evil eye, 82, 93, 115.
ḥasanāt, good deeds, 20.
ḥāsid, envious, 115.
ḥaṭṭ, off-load, 54.
ḥawīk, "weavers", artisan class as a whole, non-tribal class, 37, 99; *amīr al-ḥ.*, headman of *ḥawīk*, 99.
ḥawrā', see *rashā*.
ḥawṭah, sacred enclave, 4, 34, 43, 44, 45, 46, 47, 48, 49, 55, 69; see Index No. III.
ḥayā, rain, 99.
ḥazar, *yaḥzur*, to look to something, 50.
Ḥibī, abbrev. of *ḥabībī*, *q.v.*
ḥijārah, stone, 67; *ḥ. muḥaddadah*, jagged stone, 109.
hijrah, protection, 110, 111.
ḥilf, a pact, 108; see *ṭīb*.
al-ḥilqah, circle (of hunting party), 57; *ahl al-ḥ.*, people of the circle, 55.
ḥimā, interdicted pasture, 113.
ḥirz, amulet, 93.

hishmah, see *takhṣīr*.
ḥizmah, bundle, 51.
ḥubārā, bustard, 71; *ibn ukht al-ḥubārā*, "bustard's cousin", 112.
hujūj (s. *hijj*) *baqar*, yokes of oxen, 67.
hukar, see *hukr*.
ḥukm (pl. *aḥkām*), law, 19; judgement, 16; *ḥ. al-naṣaf*, judgement of justice, 94; see *qanāṣah*.
hukr/hukar, withholding, 82, 115; see *hakara*.
Ḥukūmah, (British) Government, 110.
ḥulal (s. *ḥullah*) *al-awāqī*, cloaks worth an *ūqīyah* (*q.v.*) of silver (?), 111.
ḥumsh al-siyan, black of locks, 114.
huqlah, sham play, 55, 105; see *muta-haqqil*.
ḥurq, burn, 14.
ḥuṣān, horse, 93.
ḥuṣn (pl. *ḥuṣūn*), fort, fortified house, 70, 112.

ibn ukht al-ḥubārā, "bustard's cousin" (name of bird), 112.
ᶜ*Id al-Aḍḥā*, Feast of the Sacrifices, 71.
ᶜ*Id al-Fiṭr*, Feast of Breaking of Fast, 77; pronounced ᶜ*Id Lafṭār*, 113.
ᶜ*iḍāh*, thorn trees, 87.
iddasam, to eat fat (i.e. meat), 17; see *dasam*.
ighrā', set (e.g. a dog) at game, 112.
iḥrām, a state in which what was lawful becomes unlawful, etc., 88.
ᶜ*ijrah* (ᶜ*ijar*), ring on horns, 29, 53, 57, 99.
ikhtabā, lay ambush, 92.
ikhtaṣar, = *yinādī*, to announce, 102.
ᶜ*ilb*, tree, 67.
ill, = *jār*, protected person, 76.
ᶜ*illāt*, circumstances, 34.
ᶜ*imārah*, tribe, 98.
imtall, = *ista*ᶜ*add*, to prepare, 72.
inkāf, rejection, 94.
inṣāf, doing justice, 94; cf. *naṣaf*, *naṣfah*, *naṣīf*.
iqrār, admission, confession, 57.
ᶜ*irqah*, narrow mountain road, 105.
ᶜ*irs*, see *ṣāḥib*.
*irtajaz min al-shi*ᶜ*r*, compose *rajaz* verses, 50; see *rajaz*.
ᶜ*irwah*, protection fee, 110, 111; see *ta*ᶜ*arwā*.

ishārah, see *shārah*.
ishtall, carry oneself off, 14.
*ista*ᶜ*ar*, to be sold at, 99.
iṣṭāb, to be hit by a bullet, 52.
iṣṭād (v.n., *iṣṭiyād*), to hunt, 90, 96.
istafṣal, to ask for particulars, 58.
istakbar, pick out a large one, 32.
istārath(?), *yistārith*, inherit, 111.
istasqā, *yastasqī*, beseech, invoke for rain, 36 (v.n. *istisqā'*, *q.v.*).
istikbir, imper, of *istakbar*.
istilām, acceptance (of evidence), 58.
istiqbāl, greeting, 29.
istiqrā', reciting Koran over sick person or animal, 20.
istisqā', invoking for rain, 115.
iṣṭiyād (v.n. of *iṣṭād*), *al-iṣṭiyād bi-shabak*, hunting with the net, 96.
*i*ᶜ*taṣab ra'yu-hum*, their mind is resolved, 49, 103.
ᶜ*ithrib*, name of plant with pink flowers, 114.
ᶜ*ithribī*, red coloured stone, 114.
*i*ᶜ*tibār*, = *burhān*, ᶜ*ibrah*, respect, consideration, 90.
ᶜ*itr*, sacrificial beasts, 92.
ᶜ*iṭr*, perfume, 108.
ᶜ*iwaḍ-an* ᶜ*an*, = *badal-an* ᶜ*an*, instead of, 107.
ᶜ*iyāl*, members of a quarter or ward, 106.
ᶜ*iyānah*, looking out, 103; see ᶜ*aiyan*.
*iyqā*ᶜ *mawzūn*, metrical harmony, 43.
iyyal/uyyal (pl. *ayāyil*), ibex, 2, 86.

jabbānah, cemetery, 67.
jabhah, forehead, 30.
*ja*ᶜ*d qaṭaṭ*, crisp curly hair, 80.
jaḍ r, *y jḍar* (sense unknown), 113.
jafnah, large bowl, 62.
jalabah, explanation of *khanabah* (*q.v.*), ewe, 100.
*jamā*ᶜ*ah*, company, family, 51.
jamālah, success, good fortune, 15, 50, 91; *dhikr*, *ḥusn al-ṣīt*, 100.
jambīyah, dagger, 29.
jamīlah, success at hunt, 14, 53, 54; = *fawz bi-taḥṣīl al-ṣaid*, 96; = *ẓafar*, 29; *tahnā-kum al-jamīlah*, congratulations on your success, 29.
jamm, much, 11.
jammālah, camel-men, 49, 50, 106.

jammar, to cense, 62.
jandal, stones, mass of stones, 70.
jār, see *ill.*
jarīdah, net-pole, 28.
jaw, sky, 93.
jawb (pl. *ajwāb*), shield, 96.
jāwīd, brave, noble, (perhaps for *ajāwīd*), 101.
jazlāt (s. *jazl*), large (of rings of horn), 99.
jifil, coffee-berry, 45.
jīrah, = *grtn* (*q.v.*), protection money (?), 76.
jubbah,=*farfārah* (*q.v.*), long white coat, 21; see *ṭawīlah*.
jufāt (s. *jāf-in*), rude (of tribesmen), 12.
jufsh, top ribs of beast, 31. Cf. *shirqat*.
jull, = *ṣaid*, game, 14, 91.
iuyūb (s. *jaib*), neck opening of garment, 8, 88.

kabb, *yikibb*, throw the hair loose, 109•
kabban, lay ambush, 92.
kabsh, ram, male, 6.
kāl yikīl, measure out, 10, 11.
kala', *fodder*, 89.
kalb, sort of wooden hook, 103. Cf. *kullāb*.
kam, a certain number of, 46.
kam min/*kammin*, how many a, 45, 90, 101.
karāmah, *yibaiyin karāmah*, manifest a miracle, 102.
karawān (pl. *karā*), bird resembling bustard, 72, 111, 112; see *khālah al-k*.
karr, faire un tour, 72.
kawr, skull, 30.
khabana, to hide, conceal, 92.
khaddā^{c}ah, ambushers, 28.
khadh-nī, took from me (= *akhadh*), 111.
khaibah, failure, 96; *khaibatain*, lit. two failures, 29.
khair, harvest, 90.
khāl, *khālah*, maternal uncle/aunt (special use of), 112.
khalā', open country, 74, 75.
khālah al-karawān, maternal aunt of the *karawān*, i.e. bustard, 72.
khalwah, "cell" of a saint or ṣūfī, 77.
khanab, game of mountain, 50, 103; *khanabah* expl. as *jalabah*, *shāh*, ewe, 100.
kharaj ^{c}induh, to fall to his share, 51; owe outgoings, 49.
khārib, destroyed, 15; see *sās*.
kharīf, "autumn" season, 114.
kharra, come from deserts to towns, 110.
khasar, *yikhsar*, to spend, 39.
khasārah, disbursement, 56; fine, 57; see *makhāsīr*.
khashm al-^{c}Arab, evil mouth of the Arabs, 82.
khatam al-Fātiḥah, conclude (recitation of) the *Fātiḥah*, 46.
khāṭir, *ṭībat kh.*, heart clear of sin, 15.
khaṭmah, see *khiṭmah*.
khaṭṭ al-sabīl, highway, 11.
khayāl, imagining, 94.
khibrah, party of hunters, 27, 99; *abu 'l-kh.*, headman of party, 27.
khimmah, one quarter of meat of game allotted to *Manṣab* and others (cf. pre-Islamic division of booty), 55, 106.
khitām, see *qaṣīdah khitām*.
khiṭmah/*khaṭmah* (pl. *khiṭam*), field of fire, mountains and plains, mountain pass, 100.
khiyānah, deceit, 15, 38.
khubrah (pl. *khubar*), date-cluster cover (basket-work); *khubar fattah*, baskets of shredded bread, 46.
khudh-hā, take it, used for *khushsh-hā* (*q.v.*), 73, 112.
khuṣār, anything eaten as a relish to bread, 31, 98; see *takhṣīr*.
khushm, the "nose" of a mountain, 33.
khushsh-hā withlāthī, enter it, by the triple (divorce), 73, 112.
kirā, hire, 56.
krw, to make her two legs revolve in running (she-camel), 72.
kūfiyah, cap, 93.
kufr, unbelief, etc., 113.
kulān, bridegroom, 67.
kullāb (pl. *kalālīb*), hook, 52; see *kalb*.
kullin, each one, 34.
kurā^c, trotter of beast, 39.

lā abā lak, may you have no father (imprecation), 12.
lā ^{c}*ād*, no more, 14.
labbaik(*a*), may you give help (?), 10, 89, 90, 115; = *labbaita*, 89.
labbaita, see previous.
Lafṭār, = *al-Fiṭr*, *q.v.*
laḥm, flesh, 17; *laḥmat al-bunduq*, successful hunter's share of meat, 33.
la^{c}*iba*, to dance, 43, 100; see *li*^{c}*b*.
lail, *al-lail yā* ^{c}*iyāl*, tonight men, 105; *al-lail yā Qaniṣ*, tonight huntsmen; phrases used to hurry one on, 53.
laqaf (?), *yilqaf*, ascend, 51.
laṭīmah, perfume, 108.
lawshār, see *washar*.
li^{c}*b*, play, 55; see *la*^{c}*iba*.
līd (*al-yad*), leg, 55.
liḥyah, beard (of ibex), 105.
lughah, dialect, 109.

mā shī bās, there is no harm in, 37.
ma^{c}*ārik*, places of battle, = ^{c}*atārīr* (*q.v.*), 94.
madārah, circle, 50.
maḍbī, see *maẓbī*, 108.
maḍfūr, plaited, 43; see *ḍafā'ir*.
madhbah, throat (of animal), 55.
maḍīq, narrow pass, 91.
madrūf, flute, 29; see *mudarrif*.
maghrah, red clay, 6.
maḥabbah, love of God, 8.
maḥaff, riding in circles, 72.
maḥaffah, procession in line, 39; see *ḥaffah*.
maḥājī, = *khanādiq*, trenches, 103.
maḥall, quarter, 24.
maḥaṭṭ, camp, 53, 57.
maḥḍarah, reception room, 45.
maḥfad, castle, fort, 75.
maḥjar (pl. *maḥājir*), (interdicted) pasture, 113.
maḥram, sacred enclave, 77; = *ḥaram* (*q.v.*), 78.
maiḥ (pls. *amyāḥ*, *miyāḥ*, *muyūḥ*), mesh (of net), 101.
maisarah, abundance, time of ease, 10.
maitah, that which has died of itself, unlawful carrion, 8, 20, 88.
ma^{c}*iz*, male goat, 45, 46.
majlis, salon, 42, 43.
makhāsīr, expenses, 56; see *khasar*, *khasārah*.
makhīlah, rain, 115.
malaq, occasion, 28; *maḥall wa-waqt*, 96.
manārah, minaret, 90.
manāsik, places of immolation, 92.
manqad, appeal judge, 7.
manṣab, spiritual and temporal lord of sacred enclave, Index No. I. and *passim*.
manwī, intending, 103; see *anwā*.
maqbūl, accepted, 110.
maqīl, afternoon (12 noon to 3 p.m.), 11, 90.
maqṭa^{c}, cut, spill-way from field, 105.
maqūd, well-ramp, 90.
marābī, see *mirbāh*.
marāh, woman, 93.
marāwis (s. *mirwās*), drum, 46, 48.
marba^{c}*ah*, = *marba*^{c}*ī* (*q.v.*)
marba^{c}*ī*(*yah*), animal (or perhaps its horns) with four finger-breadths between each ring of the horn, 101; also *marba*^{c}*ī*.
marba^{c}*īyah*, net, 45; cf. previous.
marbāt, see *mirbāh*.
marīyah, necklace, 93.
marzaḥah (pl. *marāziḥ*), rank(s) for singing and dancing, dancing squads, processions, 49, 50, 55, 102; *yishillūn m.*, form ranks for dancing and singing, 50; *yisuwwūn m.*, ditto, 53; *see raziḥ*.
maṣād, hunting place, 17; upper part of mountain, 91.
masaḥ, to massage, 93.
maṣārif, expenses, 46.
Mashāyikh (s. *Shaikh*), name of class of religious aristocracy, 35, 47, 97, 110, 111; *M. fuqarā'*, 110; *passim*.
mashṭūr, *qaṣīdah* with both half verses following monorhyme, 94.
masīd, = *masjid*, space around tomb or *khalwah* (*q.v.*), 77.
masjid, mosque, 77.
m ṣ y d , place where hunting nets are set up (?), 18.
maṭar, rain, 2, 36.
mathbūr, possibly same as pre-Islāmic *ṭbrw*, 110.
matnah, part of meat or flesh, 33.

maṭraḥ (pl. *maṭāriḥ*), camping site, 105.
maṭrūḥ, left aside, 19.
mawlā, lord, saint, also used in names of wards of quarters, etc.; see *mawla 'l-shabakah*.
mawt, *wa-'l-mawt*, death! (slogan on sighting game), 52.
mawwat, put to death, 52.
mawzūn, see *iyqā*^{c}.
mayassah, rump and tail-piece of animal, 55.
maẓbī/maḍbī, meat broiled on hot stones, 63, 68.
maẓlūm, wronged, 94; see *ẓālim*.
mib ^{c}*ād*, for *mā ba*^{c}*d/mā* ^{c}*ād* (?), no longer, 16, 91.
mibaddā, net, first net, 48, 51, 56, 102.
mid^c*ā*, see *mud*^{c}*ā*.
mijmar, substance used for censing, 52; see *mujmar*, *tajammar*.
mīr, emir, 21.
mirbā, sangar, breastwork, 103.
mirbāh/mirbāt/marbāt (pl. *marābī*), sangar, breastwork, narrow pass, 16, 52, 55, 91, 103.
mirsā, sangar, breastwork, 103.
mirwāḥ, departure, 49.
mishk, dark red colour, 6; see *mishq*.
mishq, red clay, 6.
miskīn (pl. *masākīn*), artisans, petty tradesmen, brokers (*dallāl*), 5, 14, 21, 22, 27, 28, 46, 48, 49, 53, 69, 101, 102, 106, 107, 110.
misrāḥ, going forth, departure, precedent (?), 30, 51.
mitrās, sangar, 55.
mi^c*waz*, waist-wrapper, 104.
mīzān, balance, scale, 102; see *ūqīyah*.
mu^c*arris* (pl. *ma*^{c}*āris*), = ^{c}*arūs* (*q.v.*), bridegroom, 55, 105.
mubārak, fortunate, blessed, 93.
mud^c*ā/mad*^{c}*ā/mid*^{c}*ā*, pillar erected to saint, 6, 7.
mudarrif, flute-player, 44; see *madrūf*.
mudd, measure (of corn), 99.
mudhaiyam, attainted, 15, 56; see *dhaiyam*, *tadhaiyam*.
mudhfif, mortal (wound), 106.
muḍwā, evening journey, 103.
mughādarah, trickery, 94.
mughaiyar, corrupted, 15.
mughrāh, a bitch set to hunting (?), 100; see *Mighrāh*.
muḥaddad, jagged, 109; see *ḥijārah*.
muḥarram, see *ḥaram*.
muḥāsabah, reckoning, 55.
muḥrim, one having entered the Meccan *Ḥaram* on pilgrimage, 86.
muḥtaram, respected, 110.
mujammi^c, unifier, uniter, 109.
mujmar, censing vessel, 62; see *mijmar*, *tajammar*.
mukarrib, ruler in sense of "unifier, uniter" (?), 109.
mukbin, man in ambush, 28.
mukharbaṭ, disordered, 15.
mulamma^c, see *washr*.
muqaddam, headman, 15, 27, 44; see *taqdimah*.
muqaddamah, forepart of the head, 30.
muqdum, top ribs, chest, ribs (of animal), 31.
murabba^c*ah*, square or oblong cabin, 103.
muraṣṣa^c*ah*, woven together, see *ḍafā'ir*, 43.
musaibilī, type of millet, 90.
musallibī, = *mujammi*^{c}, unifier, uniter, 109.
musikha, to be transformed, 113.
musinn, old aged, 98.
musliyah, *kilmah m.*, diverting words, 48.
musnad, pre-Islamic inscription, 17.
muta^c*aiyib fī*, shamed in respect of, 111; see ^{c}*aib*.
muta^c*assirah*, difficult (of circumstances), 101.
muta'aththir, affected (by some ill), 15.
mutadārik, metre, 96.
mutahaqqil, making play, 55, 105; see *huqlah*.
mu^c*tanī*, troubled, 100.
muṭarrib, herald, 99.
muttasirah, = *razīnah*, easy (of circumstances), 101.
muẓill, passing the heat of day in shade, 53.
muzmin, crippling wound, 106.
muzn, cloud, 99.

na^c*ām*, ostriches, 2, 69; see *baiḍ*.
nafakh, to blow on a pipe, 46.

nahb, robbing, 15.
nā'ib, officer (mil. term), 93.
na^{c}ish, weaving of hair, 109; see *tanwīsh*.
najdah, see *ṭalab*.
najdī, northern, 54.
naqā, *shar^{c} al-naqā*, the path/rule of keeping out of wrong-doing, 115; see *ṭib*, *naqī*.
nāqah, she-camel, 71.
naqar, part of an animal from a joint downwards, 30, 97.
naqī, clean, pure, with clean hands (fig.), 62.
naqīb, tribal chief, 73.
naqīl, pass, 112.
nāqiṣ, lacking (in honour, virtue, social standing, etc.), 15.
naṣaf, see *ḥukm*.
nasakh, *yansukh*, come (to a god) with sacrificial animals, 9.
naṣfah, *naṣīf Allāh* (*q.v.*), punishment of unjust person, 94.
nashshāsh, a beater, 96.
naṣīf Allāh, may God grant justice against, punish (the unjust), 21, 94; cf. *naṣaf*, *naṣfah*.
naṣr, victory (at hunt), possibly "support", 27.
naṣṣar, *yinaṣṣir*, chant/shout rallying song or cry, 29, 45, 52; see *tanṣūrah*.
naṭṭāḥ, that butts with the horns, 90.
nāẓir ṣadaqah, overseer of alms, 59.
ni^{c}āl, sandals, 97.
nidhr, votive gift or offering, 61, 97.
nikāyah, slaughter, 13.
ni^{c}mah, well-being, 36; see *rakhā'*.
nimir/nimr, leopard, 38, 70, 86; see *anmar*.
nisābah, men of same tribe or locality, 39.
nīyah, (good) intent, 50, 103; see *anwā*, *manwī*.
nūb, bees, 75.
nuqaṭ, diacritical points, 93.
nuṣub, see *anṣāb*.

qabā'iḥ, vile actions, 20.
qabā'il, see *qabīlah*.
qabīlah (pl. *qabā'il*), tribe, 19, 27, 31, 98, 111, 113; *^{c}alā qabīlah qabīlah*, tribe by tribe, 49.
qabīlī, tribesman, 111.
qadaḥ, bowl, 107.
qadīd al-ẓibā', strips of sun-dried gazelle meat, 64.
qahwā (?), *yiqahwī*, give or take coffee to, 48.
qahwah (pl. *qahaw*, perhaps for *qahāwī*), coffee, 102; *qahwat al-Qanīṣ*, coffee of the Hunt, 56; *ṭabakh al-q.*, to prepare coffee, 101.
qaiẓ, summer, 114.
qāmah, a man's stature (measure), 28.
qanaṣ, *yaqnaṣ*, to hunt, 5, 8, 14, 36.
qanaṣ, *ṣāḥib q.*, hunter, 5.
qanāṣah, hunting, 14, 16, 21, 30, 32, 33, 36, 38, 44, 90, 94; *ahl al- q.*, 27; see *aḥkām*.
qāniṣ (pl. *qunnāṣ*), hunter, 8, 17, 28, 30, 34, 88; used as a name, 33; see *aqnaṣ*, *Qiwainiṣah*.
qanīṣ, Hunt, hunting party, 14, 15, 19, 27, 30, 39, 46, 56-9, 94, 102; *ahl al-q.*, 16; *arbāb al-q.*, 19, 92; *q. al-ghirr*, *al-rumyān*, *al-shabak*, 24; see *abwā al-q.*, *awlād al-q.*; *qahwat al-q.*
qannaf, abstain (?), 99.
qanṣ, *shir^{c}at al-q.*, hunting law, 17.
qarā, *yiqrā*, recite, 93; also form *yirqī*, 93.
qarār, *hommes de métier*, 111.
qarn (pl. *qurūn*), horn, 30, 43, 67, 97; crown of head, 69.
qarṭūs (pl. *qarāṭīs*), squib, 55.
qaṣabah, pipe (music, inst.), 46.
qasha^{c}ah/qash^{c}ah, horns and forepart of head, 30, 97.
qaṣīdah (pl. *quṣud*), ode, poem, 46, 85; *q. khitām*, final (sung) ode closing a *soirée*, 47.
qaṣīr, falling short, 96; see *shar^{c}-ah*, and next entry.
qaṣīrah, failure, short-coming, 29.
qaṣmah, fragment piece, 106; piece of animal from knee to middle of leg, 55; *qaṣmat ^{c}ajim*, top half of back leg, 31.
qaṭaṭ, see *ja^{c}d*.
qaṭr al-samā', rain of heaven, 36.
qaṭrah, drop, 106.
qawāfī, verses, 14, 29; *baddā^{c} al-qawāfī*, maker of these verses, 29.
qawānīn (s. *qānūn*), laws, 15, 20, 60.

qawm, tribe, 6, 36, 98.
qaws muṭᶜimah, bow feeding its owner with game, 91; see *ṭuᶜm*.
qilt, pool.
qirih, main valley, 58, 107.
qirsh, Maria Theresa dollar, 28; see *riyāl*.
qirṭās, a paper, 100.
qism, share in meat, 27, 30, 55.
qitāl al-ṣaid, killing of the game, 56.
qubbah, dome, tomb of saint, 30, 77, 97.
quḥb, drought (?), 36.
qurā, villages, opposite of *bawādī*, 110.
quṣra, *ᶜajim/ᶜajm* (*q.v.*), 97.
quṣud, see *qaṣīdah*.
quṭb, net-pole, 28, 100. Cf. *ṭawᶜ*.

rā/rāᶜ, plant used for stuffing, 39, 100.
raᶜāyā, non-tribal class, 37.
rabb, God, 80.
Rabūᶜ, Wednesday, 46.
raᶜd, thunder, 11.
rādī, *châle*, piece of cloth worn round neck with the ends hanging loose, 42.
raḥmah, rain, 35, 99, 113; *r. sābighah*, abundant rain, 99.
raim, roof-top, 39.
ra'īs, chief, 39.
rajabah, ring on a horn, 96.
rajaz, metre, 11, 34, 90, 91; *r.* verses, 50, 53, 101; see *irtajaz*.
rakhā', well-being, 36; = *niᶜmah*, 90.
rāmī (pl. *rumyān*), gun, 27, 28, 51, 55, 56, 58, 106; archer, 95.
ramy bi-'l-bunduq, shooting with firearms/blowpipes, 96.
rānī, share of meat, 33, 55.
raqabah, neck, 55.
raqaṣ, *yarquṣ*, clap hands, 43,100,109.
rās, *r. ghanam*, head of sheep, 19, 106; *r. al-ṣaid*, head of game, 52.
rashā aḥwarī, gazelle, girl, wild cow, 71.
raᶜshah, ceremony, 21; ceremonial dances, 27.
rawᶜ, casting lots, 54; see *rawwaᶜ*.
rawwaᶜ, to cast lots, 54.
rawwāḥ, to go at night, 11.
raziḥ, dance, 20, 50, 55, 66; see *marzaḥah*.
razīnah, easy (of circumstances), 46; = muttasirah, 101.
ribāᶜah, *ahl al-r.*, men of same tribe or locality, 39.
rikāb, camels, 50.
rīm, white antelope, 86.
ri'm, antelope, 75; *riyām*, possible unrecorded plural of (?), 75.
riqāᶜ, patchwork, 113.
riṭl, pound (lb.), 62.
riyāl, Maria Theresa dollar, 28, 39, 59, 99, 110, 111; see *qirsh*.
rizq, provision, 82.

sāᶜ, *baᶜd al-sāᶜ*, now, then, 100.
sabᶜah, seven (circumlocutions employed for), 89.
sabb, abuse, 57.
al-Sābiᶜ, star-name, 64; see *Sābiᶜī*.
sābighah, see *raḥmah*.
Sābiᶜī, sort of millet, 64.
sabuᶜ, lion, leopard, lynx, etc., 24, 95.
ṣād, *yaṣīd*, hunt, 14; see *ṣaid*.
ṣadaf, *fī ṣ.*, behind, 52; explained, 103.
ṣadaqah, see *ḥilf*, *nāẓir*.
saᶜf-ak, in company with you, 115.
ṣaffaq, to clap, 109.
sāḥah, open space, 50, 55, 103.
ṣaḥārī (s. *ṣaḥrā'*), deserts, = *bādiyah*, 100.
ṣāḥī, unwounded, 58.
ṣāḥib ᶜirs, bridegroom, 103; see *ᶜarūs*, *muᶜarris*.
ṣahīrah, relation by marriage, 39.
ṣaid, game, object of the chase, 8, 10, 13, 15, 19, 28, 36, 39, 40, 45, 53, 59, 90-2, 96, 101, 103, 112, 115; *dhī yiqaiyid al-ṣ.*, 74; see *futyā al-ṣ.*; *rās*; *maṣād*; *ṣād*; *iṣṭād*.
ṣaid, *ṣīd*, 9, 90; see *ṣīd*.
ṣā'id, hunter, 89.
ṣaidah, *ṣ. ṣaghīrah*, small ibex, 58; *wiᶜl*, 95; *ism al-waḥdah* of *ṣaid* (?), 107.
ṣaif, summer season, 12.
sā'iḥ, itinerant, see *siyāḥah*.
ṣaiḥah, halloo, 14.
sail, flood, 11, 100.
salā, *fīhi s.*, he would like to, 100; see *sālī*, *muslī*.
ṣalāḥ, interests, welfare, 107.
ṣalaq (? vocalisation), ululation of women (*zaghārīt*, *q.v.*), 103; see *ṣallaq*.

sālī, enjoying, 46; see *salā*, *musli(yah)*.

ṣalīl, type of stone, 70.

sālimīn ghānimīn, lit. safe and bringing booty, 112.

ṣall, to proclaim, 73.

ṣallā, to pray, bless, 15, 30, 103; see *ṣallī*.

ṣallaḥ, to make, prepare (e.g. coffee), 55.

ṣallal, to say a formula such as *ṣallī ^{c}alaih* (?), 73.

ṣallaq, chant rallying song, shout at pitch of voice, 45, 52.

ṣallī ^{c}alaih (imperative), bless him (Muḥammad the Prophet), 29, 73, passim.

samā', heavens, 76; see *qaṭr*.

samāḥah, favour, 46.

samar, *yismur*, talk into the night, hold a *samrah*, 39; see *samr(ah)*, *summār*.

ṣamīl, club, 107.

ṣamm, stone without holes, 114.

samr/samrah, soirée, 45, 47, 55, 102; *yilqūn samrah*, they hold a *samrah*, 51; see *samar*, *summār*.

samsarah, hostelry, 68, 104.

ṣanam, idol, 92.

saqā, *yisqī*, to send rain, 12; see *saqqā*.

ṣaqar, hawk, 17.

saqaṭ, to go down, 52; see *saqqaṭ*.

saqqā, *yisaqqi*, to water, irrigate, 11; see *saqā*.

saqqaṭ, to fell, 57.

saraḥ, to go forth, 54.

sāriḥ, going in the morning to work, 11.

sās, *asās*, foundation, basis, 15, 91; *sās-uh khārib*, his foundation, basis is destroyed, 15.

sawād, black colour, 101.

sawād al-baṭn, = *habārīsh*, offal, 63.

ṣawārīkh, rockets, 91.

ṣawrab, stone without holes, 114.

sayyāḥah (s. *sā'iḥ* (?)), itinerant hunters (?), 8; see *siyāḥah*.

shā, future particle, 67.

sha^{c}ā'ir Allāh, the rites of God, i.e. the *ḥajj*, 97.

sha^{c}ar, *yish^{c}ar*, give notice, 29.

sha^{c}b, tribe, 31; confederation, 89, 98; *sha^{c}b/shi^{c}b*, 85.

shabā, *yashbū*, to go up, 21.

Sha^{c}bān, month called *wi^{c}l/wa^{c}il*, 98.

shabak (pl. *shibāk*), (hunting) net, 14, 27, 34, 50, 74, 101; *ahl al-sh.*, net-men, 28; *aṣḥāb al-sh.*, ditto, 37; *Mawla 'l-sh.*, ditto, 55; see *iṣṭiyād*.

shabakah, net, 8.

shabar, *yishbur*, measure with hand-spans, 93.

Shabwānī, name of dance, 32.

shāh, ewe (said to mean *khanabah*, *q.v.*), 100.

shahāmah, endurance, liveliness, 90.

shaḥm, fat, fleshmeat, 17; see *laḥm*.

shaibah (pl. *shībān*), old man, 46, 52, 53, 99.

shain (opposite of *zain*), evil, disgrace, 115.

shall, *yishill*, take, raise, etc., 50; see *shill*, *ishtall*.

shānn (pls. *shanan*, *shannānah*), a beater, 28, 51.

sha^{c}r, hair, *nāshirat al-sh.*, (woman) with loosened hair, 66.

shar^{c}, law (?), applied to *ḥilf* (*q.v.*), 108; *sh. Allāh*, Islamic law, 19; *shar^{c} al-naqā*, path, way of avoiding wrong-doing, 115.

shar^{c}-ah qaṣīr, *il fait fi de son honneur*, 96; see *shir ^{c}ah*.

shārah/ishārah, sign, 12, 90.

sharḥ, dance, 35, 36, 39, 99.

sharīk, partner, 90.

shariq, *^{c}ajm/^{c}ajim*, (*q.v.*).

shawwāf, look-out man at sea, 103.

Shawwāl, month called *wi^{c}l/wa^{c}il*, 98.

shayāṭīn, devils, evil spirits, 93.

shi^{c}b (pl. *shi^{c}āb*), mountain pass, 27, 31, 44, 56, 59, 60, 100, 105.

shiḥḥ, scarcity (?), 36.

shiḥnah, rivalry, 38.

shiḥrah, = *^{c}atrūr*, short road in mountains, etc., 94.

shill, imperative of *shall* (*q.v.*), 100.

shir^{c}ah, see *qanṣ*.

shirqat al-qāṣir, top ribs of beast, 31.

shiwār, counsel, 21; see *tashāwar*.

shu^{cc}ār (s. *shā^{c}ir*), poets.

shu^{c}arā' (s. *shā^{c}ir.*), poets.

shuqur, sweet basil worn in turban, 39.

ṣīd (pl. of *aṣyad*, 89; see *ṣaid*.

siddah, gate, 94.

sīnah (pl. *siyan*), locks or ringlets of hair, 80, 114; see *ḥumsh*.

sirr, valley, 112.
sittah samḥah, expression used for number seven, 89.
siyāḥah, going about as a devotee, or plural of *sā'iḥ* (?), 88.
siyāq, sense uncertain, perhaps meaning, "an advance, something given in advance", 111.
ṣud^{c}, split, fissure (physical feature), 58, 107.
ṣufiyat, to be purified (of Hunt), 107.
suḥaibī, kind of millet (*setaria italica*), 11, 12, 90.
sulaḥfāh, ^{c}*aẓm al-s.*, turtle shell, 97.
summār, those attending a *samrah* (*q.v.*), 47.
sunkar, sugar, 47.

ṭa^{c}*ām*, corn, *dhurah*, 36, 88.
ta^{c}*arwā*, to send an ^{c}*arwah* (*q.v.*) protection fee, 111.
ta^{c}*ashbak fī*, to entangle oneself in, 34.
ṭabakh al-qahwah, to prepare coffee, 101.
ṭabaq, round palm-leaf tray or platter, 102.
tabārak, *yitbārak*, to obtain blessing, good fortune, 29; see *barakah*.
taḍāras al-binā', the building became uneven, etc., 110; see *aḍrās*.
tadhaiyam, attainted itself, 59; see *dhaiyam*, *mudhaiyam*.
ta'dīb, punishment, 57.
ta^{c}*dīl*, division, 55.
tadkhīn, censing, 61.
ṭāf, *yaṭūf*, circumambulate, 24.
tafāḥush, indecency, 20.
tafkīr baṭṭālī, evil thought, 94.
ṭāghūt (pl. *ṭawāghīt*), temple(s), idol(s), 87; *ṭāghūt*, tribal law, 92.
ṭahaf, kind of millet (*eragrostis abyssinica*), 11, 12, 90.
taḥaiyāl, trickery, 21, 94.
ṭahārah, lavatory, 61.
ṭahhar, purify, 107; see *taṭhīr*, etc.
taḥt, used to mean "at, by", 100.
tahwīd, Hūd song, 9.
tais, male goat, 97.
ṭaiyab, to perfume, conciliate, become reconciled, 62; see *taṭyīb*, *ṭīb*, *ṭībah*.
tajammar, to cense, 62; see *mijmar*, *mujmar*.
takbīr (pl. *takābīr*), saying "*Allāhu akbar*", 21.
takhfīf, mitigation, 59.
takhmīr, veiling, 6.
takhṣīr al-hishmah, making the *khuṣār* (*q.v.*) of respect, 31.
ṭala^{c}, to go up mountain, 103; see *ṭalla*^{c}.
ṭalab najdah, demand for aid (technical term), 111.
talbiyah, type of verse commencing *labbaika* (*q.v.*), 9, 10, 12, 13, 90, 115.
ṭāli^{c}*ī*, upper, 93.
ṭalla^{c}, to appoint, 60.
tamāshah, Engl. tamasha, 55.
tamāwīr, see next.
tamwīr (pl. *tamāwīr*), *khayāl*, *tafkīr baṭṭālī*, imagining, evil thought, 21.
tanadhdhar, to make votive offering of a sheep, 69, 70.
tandīd, to raise voice in disapproval, 94.
tanṣūrah, rallying cry, 38; see *naṣṣar*.
tanwīsh, weaving the hair, 109; see *na*^{c}*īsh*.
taqdimah, headmanship, 60; see *muqaddam*.
taqdūm, sangar, 52.
ṭaraf, see *aṭrāf; ṭarīq*.
tarātīb, dispositions, 54.
ṭarīq al-ṭaraf, way of the mountain edge, 50.
tashāwar, *yitshāwar*, to consult together, 27; see *shiwār*.
taslūm, payment, 59.
taṣrīḥ, declaration, 60.
taṭhīr, purification, 62; see *ṭahārah*, *ṭahhar*.
taṭyīb al-Ka^{c}*bah*, purification, perfuming of the K., 62; see *ṭaiyab*, *ṭīb*, *ṭībah*.
ṭaw^{c}/*ṭū*^{c} (pl. *aṭwā*^{c}), pole of hunting net, 16, 19, 20, 28, 106; *ḍarab*, *yiḍrib al-ṭaw*^{c}, set up net-poles, 28; *ta'dīb bi-'l-ṭaw*^{c}, punishment by (beating with) net-pole, 57; see *quṭb*.
ṭawāf, circumambulation, 71; see *ṭāf*.
ṭaw^{c}*ah* (pl. *ṭaw*^{c}), net-pole, 45, 50, 100.
ṭawīlah, long coat, 94; see *farfārah*.
tawshīḥ, chorus, refrain, 11.
tazaiyad ^{c}*alā ḥadd bi-shī*, cheat one over something, 15.

t(a)zammal, to sing *zāmil* (*q.v.*) verses, 53.
thawb, boy's smock, 93; length of cloth, 110.
thawr, bull, 67, 68.
al-Thawr, star-name, Taurus, 68.
thib (imperative), *ijlis*, sit, 18; *qum*, rise, 92; see *wathab*.
ṭīb, perfume, 62; *ᶜala 'l-ṭīb wa-'l-naqā*, in friendship and sincerity, 108; *ḥilf ṭ.*, pact of *ṣidq*, *sharᶜ* and *ṣadāqah*, 108; see *ṭaiyab*, *taṭyīb*, *ṭībah*.
ṭībah, expiation, reconciliation, 62; *ṭībat khāṭir*, clearing the heart of sin, 15; see *ṭīb*, etc.
tijārī, merchant, 47.
ṭīn, clay (pellet), 96.
ṭuᶜm, bait, 17, 19; see *qaws*.
turs, shield, 96.
ṭuss, coffee-pot, 55; ordinary (metal) pot, 64.

ubwah, headmen, 100; see *abū*.
ᶜūd, aloes, 62; *al-ᶜūd al-ṭīb/ṭaiyib*, 108.
ᶜuddah, equipage, 13.
ᶜuqbuh, following it, 54.
ūqīyah (pl. *awāqī*), weight of silver, 111; *ūqīyah mīzān*, weighed ounce, 47; see *ḥulal*.
ᶜuryān(ah), naked, 66.
ᶜushūr, tithes on crops, 36.
uyyal, see *iyyal*.
ᶜuzūbah, = *qanāṣah*, going forth to hunt, 90.

wā lamsak wīk, cry of hunters with no known meaning, 45.
wadak, meat, 88.
waḥsh, wild animals, 13.
waᶜil (pls. *awᶜāl*, *wiᶜlān*), ibex, 98; *al-waᶜil al-musinn*, old ibex, 98; *walad al-waᶜil*, young of ibex, 98; *Shaᶜbān* and *Shawwāl* so called, 98.
waᶜl, place of refuge, 98; name of tenth month, 98; see *Shawwāl*. *Shaᶜbān*.
waᶜl/wiᶜl (pls. *awᶜāl*, *wuᶜūl*, *wiᶜlān*), ibex, 7, 14, 27, 28, 36, 39, 48, 69, 74, 86, 90, 91, 95, 97, 98; *wiᶜl* = *ṣaidah*, 95; *wiᶜl*, warrior, hero, 92; *awᶜāl* expl. as "angels", 98; *Shaᶜbān* and *Shawwāl* called *wiᶜl/waᶜil; Shawwāl* called *waᶜl*, 98; see *badan*, *badanah*.
walad (pl. *awlād*), member of a ward/quarter or hunt, 56, 60; *awlād al-Qanīṣ*, members of hunting party; *see wulīd*.
walī, saint, 98.
waqaṣ, *rester tantôt ici, tantôt là*, 108; see *waqṣ*, *waqṣah*.
waqf, object held in trust for public use, 106.
waqṣ, odd numbers (of cattle), 108.
waqṣah, chance division of meat, 63; see *waqaṣ*.
washr (pls. *awshār*, *wushūr*), hunting net, 45; *al-wushūr al-ḍāfiyah*, wide nets, 101; *washr mulammaᶜ bi-'l-sawād*, net shining black, 101; *lawshār* = *al-awshār*, 113.
wasm, brand mark, 95, 110.
wass al-kalb, to set a dog at game, 112.
wathab, *yathib*, rejoin, remain, 31; see *thib*.
wibār (s. *wabr/wabar*), coneys, hyrax, 17, 91.
wijh al-ṣalāḥ, earnest of uprightness, 60; discussed, 107.
wiswās, evil promoting, 19.
withlāthī, see *khushsh*, 73, 112.
wō habūh, hunter's cry (meaningless), 52.
wulīd, man, fellow, 28; see *walad*.

yaᶜill-uh, may be, perhaps, 21; = *ᶜill-uh*, *ᶜasā*, or *laᶜalla* (?), 94.
yā-nā, = *jā-nā*, he came to us, 96.
yiddī, colloquial form of *addā*, *yu'addī*, to give, 12.
yirqī, see *qarā*.

ẓaby (pl. *ẓibā'*), gazelle, 2, 7, 17, 87; see *qadīd*.
zād, provisions, 50.
zād al-tikrār, to be repeated, 57.
zafan, to dance, 46.
ẓafar, success, 27, 29, 60; *jamīlah*, 29.
zaff, ceremonial procession with dancing and singing, festivity, 29, 30, 37, 55, 58, 59, 60, 68, 71, 96, 101, 105; *z. al-bukrah*, morning procession, 55.
zaffa bi-, to make a ceremonial procession for, 58.
zaghārīt al-nisā', ululations of women = *ṣ l q* (*q.v.*), 103.
ẓahar ᶜalā, to go up on top of, 52.

zahīyah, joy, 45, 101.
zain, what is good, decorous, etc., opposite of *shain*, 115; see *zīnah*.
zā'ir, pilgrim, 29.
zajā, *y zjī*, perhaps the same as *zajā*, *yazjī*, to be vigorous, 99.
zakāt, tax, 36.
zalal, misdemeanour, 57.
ẓālim, one who acts unjustly, 94; see *maẓlūm*.
zāmil, marching song, 12, 29, 39, 53, 54, 105; see *tazammal*.
zawād, provisions, 38, 49.
zīnah, ornament, 6; see *zain*.
ziyārah, pilgrimage, visitation, 9, 29, 38, 72.
ẓuhār, net, second net, 48, 51, 56, 102.
zumrah, party, "pack", 19.
zurbiṭānah, arquebus, blow-pipe, squib (?), 14, 91.

I.

INDEX OF PROPER NAMES OF PERSONS, TRIBES ETC.

Note: No account is taken of the titles *amīr*, *mashāyikh*, *qāḍī*, *saiyid*, *sādah*, *shaikh*, *sharīf*, *sulṭān* and *abū/bū*, *ahl/hal*, *al*, *āl*, *bin/ibn*, *banū/banī*, preceding proper names, although these titles be inserted: e.g. *Mashāyikh Āl Bā Ḥumaid*, is listed under *Bā*. Names commencing ^{c}*Ayāl*, *Bā*, *Bal*, *Dhū*, are however listed under these words. Where words such as *Shaikh* are personal names, not titles, they follow the normal alphabetical order. Ancient pre-Islamic South Arabian names from inscriptions are capitalised, e.g., YHB'R.

^{c}Abbāsid, *see* Caliph.
^{c}Abd al-Baqar, 66.
^{c}Abd al-Ḥabīb, 107.
^{c}Abd al-Ḥaqq, hunting poet of Dammūn, 7, 18, 32, 40, 41, 76, 77, 79.
^{c}Abd al-Ḥaqq al-Baghdādī, 87.
Āl ^{c}Abd al-Qādir, of Āl Buraik, 110.
^{c}Abd al-Qawī Gharāmah, 22, 27.
^{c}Abd al-Wāsi^{c}, 1.
^{c}Abdullāh b. ^{c}Alī al-Ḥaddād, 19.
^{c}Abdullāh Bā ^{c}Alawī, 19.
Shaikh ^{c}Abdullāh Bā Qādir, Manṣab Ṣa^{c}īd, 34–7.
^{c}Abdullāh b. Jud^{c}ān, 62.
^{c}Abdullāh b. Muḥammad Bā ^{c}Abbād, *see* al-Qadīm.
^{c}Abdullāh b. Sālim Bakhḍar, 57.
^{c}Abdullāh b. ^{c}Umar, 90.
Shaikh ^{c}Abdullāh b. Yā-Sīn, dome of, 48, *sāḥah* of, 55.
^{c}Abdūn, 40; sons of, 41; *see* Sulmān b. ^{c}Abdūn.
^{c}Abūd of al-Ghuraf, 17.
^{c}Ād, tribe, 36, 98.
Aden Government, 111.
Aḥmad Muḥammad ^{c}Alī al-Ḥakīm, 7.
Shaikh Aḥmad b. Sa^{c}īd Bakhḍar, 43.
Aḥmad b. Zain al-Ḥabshī, 22.
Ahl Aḥmar, 98.
Ahmed Fakhry, Prof., 64, 66, 68.
al-Aḥrār, Yemeni Liberal Party, 36.
Ibn al-^{c}Aidarūs, 63.
^{c}Ā'ishah, 113.
Āl ^{c}Ajjāj, of Qa^{c}ūḍah, 33.
al-Akwa^{c}, *see* Ismā^{c}īl and Muḥammad al-Akwa^{c}.
Hal ^{c}Alāhah, 37.
Saiyid ^{c}Alawī b. Ṭāhir al-Ḥaddād, 12, 71, 81.
Saiyid ^{c}Alī b. ^{c}Aqīl, 17, 18, 29.
^{c}Alī al-Bu^{c}sī, Yāfi^{c}ī, 101.
^{c}Alī b. Ḥamad b. ^{c}Awaḍ, 11.
^{c}Alī b. Ḥusain al-^{c}Ubaidī, *naqīb*, 75.
Shaikh ^{c}Alī al-Khaṭīb, Ṣāḥib al-Wi^{c}l, 38, 69; b. Miḥimmid, 38.
^{c}Alī b. Miḥimmid, *see previous.*
Āl ^{c}Alī b. Sa^{c}īd, 47:
Bin ^{c}Alī b. Sa^{c}īd, Mawlā Nuṣairah, 47.
^{c}Alī b. Sumaiṭ, 93.
^{c}Alī b. Umbārak Bā Miftāḥ, 58.
Amīn ^{c}Abd al-Mājid, 42.
Amīr of Ḍāli^{c}, 110.
^{c}Āmir b. ^{c}Abd al-Wahhāb, 2, 86.
Āl ^{c}Āmir Muḥammad, 55.
^{c}Āmirī (pl. ^{c}Awāmir), 30, 34.
^{c}Amr b. ^{c}Abd al-Jinn, 9–10.
^{c}Amr b. Zaid of Khawlān, Ḥimyar tribe, 89.
^{c}Amrīyūn, *see* ^{c}Umrīyūn.
al-Ānisī, 71.
^{c}Aqārib (sing. ^{c}Aqrabī), 8.
^{c}Aqrabī, *see previous.*
Āl ^{c}Aqīl, of Āl Buraik, 110.
A^{c}rāb, tribal Arabs, 110, 113.
Arabians, South, 114.
Arabs of Kordofan, 82.
Arabs of Tihāmah, 8.
Arḥab, tribe, 75.
Arḥabīs, tribesmen, 75; two groups of, 75.
Ibn al-^{c}Ariqah, archer, 73.
al-Arwām, 96.
As^{c}ad Tubba^{c}, 34.
Aṣḥāb, *see* Bin Ḥalfūṣ, Bin Hādī.
Ashrāf, 111; of Fu^{c}ur, 81.

ᶜAskūl, poet, 48.
Ibn al-Athīr, 23.
Ahl ᶜAthtar, 35.
Āl ᶜAwaḍ of Āl Bā Ḥumaid, 47.
ᶜAwaḍ b. ᶜAbd al-Ḥabīb b. Saᶜīd, 57–58.
Āl ᶜAwaḍ b. ᶜAbdullāh of Āl al-Ṣiqair, 47.
ᶜAwaḍ Ṣāliḥ b. Biqīᶜ, 96.
ᶜAwāmir, *see* ᶜĀmirī.
ᶜAwlaqī (plur. ᶜAwāliq), 12, 110; Sultan, 111; tribes, 111.
ᶜAwlaqīs, expel Yemenis, 111; tax Shabwah, 111.
Aws, 62.
ᶜAyāl Siraiḥ, 75.
ᶜAyāl Yazīd, 75.
Ayman b. B t ᶜ b. Hamdān, 17.
Azraqī, 6, 89.

Bā Akhḍar (Bakhḍar), Mashāyikh, 42, 107; *see* ᶜAbdullāh b. Sālim.
Bā ᶜAwḍah, Ḥimyar, 11.
Āl Bā Farfārah, nickname, 21.
Bā Hārūn, hagiologist, 27, 67.
Mashāyikh Āl Bā Ḥumaid, 42, 47.
Bā Jarād, poet, 28, 101.
Bā Marḥūl, Mashāyikh, 34.
Bā Nāfiᶜ, 12; *see* ᶜUbaid Bā Nāfiᶜ.
Bā Qādir, Manṣab, 38; *see* ᶜAbdullāh Bā Qādir.
Āl Bā Qalāqil, 59, 60.
Bā Raḥmah, Mashāyikh, 35.
Bā Rashaid, 33.
Āl Bā Wazīr, Mashāyikh, 54.
Bā Ziyain, 67.
al-Badū, name of Āl al-Ṣiqair, *q.v.*
Baggarah Ḥumr tribe of Sudan, 82.
Baḥraq, 97.
Baiḥān, *see* Sharīf.
Baiḥānī, i.e. of Sharīfs, 111.
Bait al-Qiwainiṣah, 33.
Bajīlah, 115.
Balādhurī, 17, 34.
Bal-Faqīh ᶜAlī, *see* Āl al-Faqīh ᶜAlī.
Bal-Ḥārith, 8.
Bal-ᶜUbaid, 71; confederation, 110.
Baqqārah, Cattle-men, 66–68.
Baqqārah, Sudan, *see* Baggarah.
Bedouin, 12, 33, 49, 63, 98, 106.
Bedu, 106.
Beeston, Prof. A. F. L., 1, 31, 35, 65, 69, 70, 71, 72, 73, 74, 76, 84, 85, 86, 110.
Beja, 96.
Bin, *see under name following.*
Bū, *see under name following.*
Āl Bū Bakr (ᶜAwlaqīs ?), 111.
Saiyid Sir Bū Bakr b. Shaikh al-Kāf, 43.
Āl al-Shaikh Bū Bakr b. Shaikh, Saiyid family, 33, of ᶜĪnāt, 18.
al-Bundarī, 6.
Āl Buraik, Mashāyikh of, 97, 110–111, Manṣabs of, independent of Quᶜaiṭīs, 110; also Bin Buraik and Ahl im-Buraik.
Shaikh Buraik of Ahl Shabwah, 97.
Buraikī Shaikh, tomb of, 97.
Buraikī informant of al-Sakhāwī, 97.

Cahen, Prof. Claude, 23.
Caliph, ᶜAbbāsid, 13; Umaiyad, 12.
Christians, of Najrān, 111.
Cunnison, Ian, 82, 83, 115.

al-Dawlat al-Kathīrīyah, 94.
Day, Stephen, 96.
Dhaibān b. ᶜAliyān b. Arḥab, 75.
Dhaibānī tribe, Arḥab, 75.
Dhū Dhaim, 16.
Dhū Riyām, 75, as eponym, 76.
Doe, Dr. Brian, 9, 110.
Doughty, C., 68.

Egyptians, occupy Yemen, 78.

Fakhry, *see* Ahmed F.
al-Faqīh ᶜAlī, 35.
Āl al-Faqīh ᶜAlī, houses of, ᶜAqīl, Muḥammad, Jazal, Yā-Sīn, 37.
Āl Faraj, Mashāyikh, 47.
Farīq, *see under name following.*
al-Fāris, poet, 21.
al-Farrā’, 98.
Fiᶜir, *see* Fuᶜur.
Fuᶜur, Ashrāf, 87.

Gharāmah, *see* ᶜAbd al-Qawī.
Glaser, E., 74, 75, 76, 77, 112.
Governor of Aden, 94.
al-Ghūl, see Maḥmūd ᶜAlī.

Ibn Ḥabīb, 9.
al-Sharīf al-Habīlī b. Ḥusain, 110.
Ḥabshī Saiyids, 23.
Ḥaḍar, Headmen of, 27, 30.
Bin Hādī, Aṣḥāb or Farīq, Hunting Party, 37, see al-Qadīmah.
al-Hādī ila 'l-Ḥaqq, 97.
Shaikh Hādī b. Ṣāliḥ Bā Ḥātim, 14, 42, 101.
Ḥaḍramawt al-Ṣaid, 34.
Ḥaḍramī chronicler, see Shanbal.
Ḥaḍramīs, 94, 99, passim.
Hal, see under name following it.
Ḥalfūṣ, shaikh of ᶜAqīl of Āl al-Faqīh ᶜAlī, 37.
Bin Ḥalfūṣ, the Aṣḥāb or Farīq of, Hunting Party, 36, 37.
Hall, R. A., 114.
Hamdān, 8, 75, 114.
al-Hamdānī, 8, 10, 16, 17, 31, 34, 41, 66, 75, 76.
Āl Ḥāmid, Saiyids, 107.
Bin al-Ḥāmid, see next entry.
Ibn al-Ḥāmid, Ḥasan, Manṣab, 60.
al-Ḥāmidī, see previous entries.
Ḥamzah b. ᶜAbd al-Muṭṭalib, 5.
Ḥamzah ᶜAlī Luqmān, 22–23.
Ḥamzah Ḥusain al-Fiᶜir, 87.
Banu 'l-Ḥāriṯ, see Bal-Ḥāriṯ.
al-Ḥasan b. Yaḥyā, Saif al-Islām, 10.
Ḥāshid, 8; Ṣayad of, 34.
Hāshim, 98.
Ḥimyar, 9, 10, 11, 13, 18, 31, 34, 37, 89, 109, 113.
Banī Ḥishaiṣḥ, 63.
Ibn Hishām, 4.
Höfner, Prof. Maria, 76.
Hūd, Prophet, 9, 29, 36, 64, 81, grave of, 23, 25, 26.
Bin Hūd, pre-Islamic Prophet, 97.
Ḥumr tribe, 82, 83.
Bin Ḥumr, name of ibex, 52, 105, 108.
Ḥumūm, 81.
Hunter, F. M., 68.
Banū Ḥurāq, 114.
Hurmuzī, 69.
Ḥusain Ḥaidarah al-Quṭaibī, 93.
Āl Ḥuṣn, tribes, 47, 51.

al-Ifranj, 96.
Imām of Yemen, 110; of Zaidīs, 36; grants or withholds rain, 36.

Imāms, see Rassid.
Ingrams, W. H. & Mrs., 1; W. H., 72, 74, 111.
Hal Isrā'īl, Mashāyikh, called Bin Sarayīl, 35.
Qāḍī Ismāᶜīl al-Akwaᶜ, 89.

al-Jāfān, Farīq of, Hunting Party, 36.
Āl Jaᶜfar b. Badr, three tribes of named, 47.
Jāḥiẓ, 17, 43, 114.
Jahm, 75, 78.
Jahmīs, 63.
Jamme, Prof. A., 18, 70, 77, 110.
Āl Bā Jaray, 41.
Ibn al-Jawzī, 87.
Jibrail Jabbur, Prof., 98.
Johnston, Capt. Julian, 98.
Ibn Jubair, 6.
Jurhum, 88.

Kaᶜb al-Ṣā'id, 8.
Ibn al-Kalbī, 9.
Karab, see Kurab.
al-Kārim, 69.
Kārimī merchants, 69.
Āl Kaṯhīr, 102.
Kaṯhīrī, Government, 42; and see al-Dawlat; Sulṭāns, 20, 21; and see Sulṭān Miḥsin; Tarīm, 32; K. state, 22.
Kaṯhīrīs, 96; take al-Ghuraf, 28.
Kensdale, W. E. N., 64–66.
Khaiwān b. Zaid, 16.
Āl Khaṭīb Shaikh, see ᶜAlī al-Khaṭīb.
al-Khaṭṭābī, traditionist, 62.
Khawlān, of Ḥimyar, 89.
Khazrajī, 2, 62.
Kinānah, 10, 31, 98.
Kindah, 90.
King (tribal), of Ḥaḍramawt, 70, 73.
Kuhlān tribe, 89.
Āl Kulaib, 41.
Kurab/Karab tribe, 110, 111.
Kuwaib, 7.

Lambton, Prof. A. K. S., 86.
Landberg, Comte C. de, 34, 35, 38, 74, 77.
Lane, E., 40, 61, 75.
Liberals, Yemeni, see al-Aḥrār.
Luqmān, see Ḥamzah.

Madhḥij, 10.
Madḥij, *see previous.*
Maḥmūd cAlī al-Ghūl, Prof., 1, 6, 86, 87, 92, 111.
Majusian, 86.
al-Makārim, for Kārimī (*q.v.*), 109.
Abū Makhramah, 20.
al-Makkī, 43.
Banī Mālik, 101.
Malikshāh, 6.
Manāhīl, 33, 110.
Manṣab (pl. Manāṣib), 60, 106; of Āl Buraik, 110; of Āl Ṭuyūrah, 47–102, *passim;* tithes paid to, 36.
al-Manṣūr, cAbbāsid Caliph, 13, 22.
Maslamah . . . al-Khaiwānī, 17.
Mawla 'l-Ḥawṭah, 37, 38.
Mawla 'l-Khulaif, 16.
Mawlā Madūdah, 59, 60.
Mawla 'l-Qubbah, unknown saint, 38.
Mawla 'l-Rawḍah, 37, 38.
Mawla 'l-Sūq, 16.
Mawla 'l-Ṭuyūrah, cUmar b. cAbd al-Kabīr, 54.
Banī Mighrāh, hunting dogs, 21, 40, 46, 92, 100, 115.
Sulṭān Miḥsin al-Kathīrī, 20.
Minaibārī, *see* Munaibārī.
Mircī b. Birik b. Sacīd, 57–8.
Mucādh b. Jabal, 105.
Mubārak cAbdullāh al-Ṭawsilī, 74.
Bū Mubārak, 60.
al-Mubarrad, 12.
Muḍar, 31.
Muḥāriq b. Shihāb b. Qais al-Tamīmī, 17.
Muḥammad, Prophet, 5, 36, 62, 73; *see* Prophet.
Muḥammad (addressed by cAbd al-Ḥaqq), 41.
Muḥammad al-Akwac, 34.
Shaikh Muḥammad b. Bū Bakr Bā Ḥumaid, Manṣab of Āl Ṭuyūrah, 47–102; called b. Abī Bakr, etc., 48.
Muḥammad Kūfān, his *murabbacah*, 51.
Muḥammad b. Sacīd al-Wāḥidī, Wāḥidī State Secretary, 37.
Muḥammad al-cUbaidī, 75.
Ibn al-Mujāwir, 2, 8.
Āl Munaibārī, four tribes of named, 47.
Munaibārī/Minaibārī, 102.
Musaibilī b. Sacīd b. cUbaidullāh, 58, 107.

Mashāyikh Āl Nādir, 47.
Nahd, 33.
Āl Nājiyah, 41.
Banu 'l-Nār, 114.
Bin Nāṣir, *see next following.*
Bū Nāṣir al-Fāris, 94; *see* al-Fāris.
Sulṭān Nāṣir al-Wāḥidī, 11, 37.
al-Nucmān, of Ḥīrah, 62.
al-Nuwairī, 96.

Pharaoh, 71.
Philby, H. St. J. B., 5, 6, 10, 33, 39, 68, 70, 78, 110.
Pirenne, J., 109.
Portuguese, 95.
Pressly, J. S. L., 114.
Prophet (Muḥammad), 4, 6, 7, 16, 19. 23, 36, 41, 62, 66, 87, 93, 101, 10 111; *see* Muḥammad.

Qāḍī of Mūdiyah, 96.
al-Qadīm cAbdullāh b. Muḥammad Bā cAbbād, 59.
al-Qadīmah, name of Bin Hādī Farīq, 37.
Qaḥṭānī, 115.
Qanaṣ b. Macadd, 34.
Āl Qāniṣ, 33.
Qarā, tribesmen, 95.
al-Qardacī, 111.
al-Qāsim b. Aḥmad al-Rassī, 72.
Qāsim Munaṣṣar, 63.
Qaṭmīr/Qiṭmīr, ancestor of hunting dogs, 32.
al-Qiwainiṣah, 33.
Qucaiṭī, Shabwah pays tax to, 111; slave, 73.
al-Qucaiṭī, *see* Saif b. Ḥusain.
Qucaiṭīs, 32, 96; Dammūnīs of, 32; territory, 32; Āl Buraik independent of, 116; *see* 110, 111.
Qumaishīs, 98.
Quraish, 5, 7, 8, 62, 90, 98, 109.
Quṣaiy, 89, 98, 109.
Banī Qushair, Sādah/Saiyids, 102.
Āl Quṭaiyān, Kurab, 111.

RB ŠMS, 73.
Āl Rabīc, of Āl Buraik, 110.

Raemakers, Mrs. M. de Sturler, 101.
Raḥaiyam, Shaikh (^{c}Abdullāh), variously referred to as "my shaikh", "my Tarīmī shaikh, 14, 15, 20, 27, 32, 72, 108.
Rassid Imams, 72.
Republicans, 112.
Riyām, *see* Dhū Riyām.
Royalists, 78, 112.
Rubaiya^{c} b. Salīm, poet, 16, 91.
Russians, 112.
Ryckmans, Prof. G., 67, 72.
Ryckmans, Prof. Jacques, 77.

Sa^{c}d tribe, 76.
Abū Sa^{c}d, 36.
Sa^{c}d b. Mu^{c}ādh, *naqib*, 73.
Sa^{c}d al-Suwainī, 17, 100, 114.
Ṣadif/Ṣuduf, 34.
Ṣāḥib al-Wi^{c}l, *see* Shaikh ^{c}Alī al-Khaṭīb.
Saibān, 81. Cf. Kawr/Kōr Saibān, Index No. III.
Ṣaid, *see* Ṣayad, 34.
al-Ṣaid, 34.
Ṣā'id, 34.
al-Ṣā'id, *see* Ka^{c}b.
Shaikh Sa^{c}īd, of Daw^{c}an, 12.
Ibn Sa^{c}īd al-Maghribī, 88.
Shaikh Sa^{c}īd b. ^{c}Umar Bā Wazīr, 54.
Saif b. Ḥusain al-Qu^{c}aiṭī, 30, 91, 100; *see* Saif al-Qu^{c}aiṭī.
Saif al-Islām, *see* al-Ḥasan b. Yaḥyā.
Saif al-Qu^{c}aiṭī, see Saif b. Ḥusain.
Saiyids, 5, 18, 23, 93, *passim*, feud with Mashayikh, 18; of 'Īnāt, 33.
al-Sakhāwī, 97.
Ṣalāḥ b. Ṣāliḥ al-Qāniṣ Bā ^{c}Ajjāj Āl Qāniṣ, 33.
Ṣāliḥ, Prophet, 76.
Sālim b. ^{c}Alī b. Firaij, 58.
Sālimīn b. Sa^{c}īd b. Minaibārī or Munaibārī, 57, 58.
Saljūq, 6.
Sam^{c}ay tribe, 92; *see* SM^{c}Y.
Ṣamīl, headman, 59–60.
Bin Sarayīl, *see* Hal Isrā'īl.
Ṣayad/Ṣaid/Ṣīd, 34; Ṣayad tribe, 75.
al-Ṣayad, 8; of Ḥāshid, 34.
Shaikh mi-'l-Qubbah, unknown saint, 38.
Bū Shaikh, 41.
Shaikh b. ^{c}Abdullāh b. ^{c}Alī, 67.
Shaikh b. Muḥammad Jazal al-^{c}Azzānī, of Āl al-Faqīh ^{c}Alī, 37.
Āl Shamlān, 47.
Shanbal, chronicler, historian, 42, 95.
Sharīf of Baiḥān, 23.
Sharīf Rāshid, Dr., 87.
Shī^{c}ah, 25.
Bin Shihāb, poet, 101.
Sh r ḥ ' l B t ^{c}, discussed, 35.
Ṣīd, *see* Ṣayad.
Ibn Sīdah, 74.
Hal Sifālah, 37.
Āl al-Ṣiqair, three tribes of named, 47; Āl ^{c}Awaḍ b. ^{c}Abdullāh of, called al-Badū, 47.
Siraiḥ, *see under* ^{c}Ayāl.
SM^{c}Y, tribe, 92; *see* Sam^{c}ay.
Snell, Major I., 66.
Solomon, 113.
Somalis, 69.
South Arabians, 114.
Ṣubaiḥīs, 9.
Ṣuduf, *see* Ṣadif.
Amīr Suḥaim, Āl Thānī, 2.
Banū Sukhaim, 76.
Sulaimān b. ^{c}Abd al-Malik, Caliph, 12.
al-Ṣūlī, 86.
Sulmān b. ^{c}Abdūn, poet, 48, 102.
Bin Sumaiṭ, Saiyids, 93.
Sunnīs, 25.

Ṭabarī, 13.
Ṭāhā Muḥammad, of Bā Ḥumaid (*q.v.*), 42.
Ta'lab Rīm/Ri'm, 75; as eponym, 76.
Tamīm, 42.
Tawfik, Prof. M., 64.
Tawḥīdī, 80, 114.
Abū Tha^{c}labah al-Khushanī, 87.
Āl Thānī, 2.
Thaqīf, 4, 87.
Thesiger, W., 63.
Thomas, Bertram, 63.
Tritton, Prof. A. S., 70.
Turks, 75.
Turkish soldiery, 24.
Āl Ṭuyūrah, Mashāyikh, 47, 53.

^{c}Ubaid, Bā Nāfi^{c} Shaikh, 12.
Abū ^{c}Ubaid al-Bakrī al-^{c}Awnabī, 17.
^{c}Ubaid Surūr al-Jābirī, 22.

ᶜUdhar b. Saᶜd, of Hamdān, 75.
Ukaidir, 7, 88.
Umaiyad Caliph, 12.
ᶜUmar, 5.
ᶜUmar, ancestor of Mawlā Ṭuyūrah (*q.v.*), 105.
Shaikh ᶜUmar b. Ḥasan Bā Ḥumaid, 42.
ᶜUmar al-Miḥḍār, 67.
Umbārak ᶜUmar Hishmān, 58.
ᶜUmrīyūn, 8.
ᶜUrwah b. Masᶜūd, 6.
Usāmah b. Munqidh, 2.

Wāḥidī, sultan, 11, 35, 37; sultanate, 35, 92; territory, 37; tribes, their Ḥimyar descent, 10, 37.
Wāḥidīs, 35.
Walker, Dr. J., 30, 70, 80, 114.
al-Wāqidī, 6, 66.
Wissmann, Prof. H. von, 2, 71, 81, 98, 100, 102, 105, 107.
Āl Wuᶜail, 34.

Yāfi'ī, poet, 101; source, 110; tribal ruler, 22; ruler of al-Khilaif, 22; source, 110; tribal ruler, 22; tribe, 110.
al-Yāfiᶜī, author, 88.
Yāfiᶜīs, of Tarīm, 22, 27.
Yaḥmī Ill, for YḤM'L, *q.v.*
Yām, 110.
Bin Yamānī, of Tamīm, 43.
Saiyid Yaᶜqūb Bakr, Prof., 73.
Yāqūt, 9, 20, 62.
Yazīd, *see under* ᶜAyāl.
YD'L BYN, 73.
Yemeni, Liberals, *see* al-Aḥrār; poet, 36.
Yemenis, 111.
YHB'R, 73.
YḤM'L, 76.
Yūsuf . . . b. ᶜAbd al-Barr, of Cordova, 64.

Zaid b. ᶜAbdullāh b. Dārim, 18.
Zaid Dhū Dhaim b. Qais, 16.
Zaidī, 72; Imām, 36; state, 36; tribes, 36.
Zarānīq, 1.
Āl Zīmah Umbārak Āl Jaᶜfar b. Badr, 51.
al-Zubaidī, 14.
al-Zubairī, Muḥ. Maḥmūd, attacks Zaidī imāmate, 36, 39.
Zuhairī, Arḥab tribe, 75.

II.

INDEX OF GODS AND SUPERNATURAL BEINGS

Allāh, called Driver of Wild Cows, 88.
Anāhīd, name of al-Zuharah (*q.v.*), 113.
^{c}Astar, variant of ^{c}Athtar, 77, 113.
^{c}Athtar, 69, 73, 74; with variant ^{c}Astar, 77, 113; name resembles ^{c}ashshār, 113, 114; pre-Islāmic god, 114; divinity of irrigation, 77; hunt of, 111; waters Saba', 77, 114; Ahl ^{c}Athtar, 35.

Ba^{c}l Aw^{c}ālan, Lord of Ibexes (*q.v.*), 7.
Ba^{c}l Aw^{c}āl Ṣirwāḥ, *Maḥram* of, 77.
Ba^{c}lat, *see* Shams.

Dhū Samay, Lord of Baqar-um, 67, 88.
Driver of Wild Cows, epithet of Allāh, 7, 67; *see* Lord, ditto.
ḍSMWY, god, 61.

ḤLFN, god, 61, 70.

Iblīs, 99.
Ilmaqah/Ilumqah, Lord of Ibexes, 7, 74.
Ilumqah, *see previous.*

al-Lāt, 6, 81.
Lord of Cattle, 67.
Lord of Ibexes, 7, 74, 77.
Lord of Pastures, *see* Ta'lab.
Lord of Wild Cows, 88.

Mawlā Maṭar, saint of rain, 38.
Michael, *see next.*
Mīkāyīl, Michael the Archangel, 11, 12.
Moon God, 6, 64; Ḥaḍramī . . ., 114; Shaqr, 70, 114; crescents emblem of, 6.
Muḥarriq, pre-Islāmic god, 35.

Nā'ilah, legendary woman, 66.
al-Nasr, god, 9, 13; in Saba', 9; peaks identified with, 9, 10.

Qatabanian god called Shaqr, 114.

al-Rabbah, the Lady, goddess, 6.

Sa^{c}d, god, 10.
Sā'iq al-Baqar, *see* Driver.
Satan, 115.
Shams, Lady (Ba^{c}lat) of Maifa^{c}, 12, 35, 36.
Shaqr, Moon God, 70, 114; epithet of Qatabanian god, 114; emblem of, 70; name on coins, 114; temple of, 70, 78.
Sīn, Moon God, 80, 114; Ḥaḍramī Moon God, 114; effigy of, 80; hair of, 80; name discussed, 80.

Ta'lab, Lord of Pastures, god name, 74–76; his *chasse*, 92; *grtn/jīrah* impost taken by, 76; interdicted grazing land of, 75; pilgrimage administered by SM^{c}Y / Sam^{c}ay tribe, 92; at Riyām, 75: sanctity of his property, 76; shrine of, 112; symbolic animals of, 74.

al-^{c}Uzzā, peak of, 10.

Venus, identified with al-Zuharah, 113; *stades* of, 77; star at zenith, 77.

al-Zuharah, harlot transformed to star, 113; *see* Anāhīd, Venus.

III.
GEOGRAPHICAL INDEX

Note: Al-, jabal, wādī are ignored in indexing geographical names.

^{c}Abdalu, 20.
^{c}Abr, Ḥuṣn al-, 9.
Abyan, 8, 93.
Aden, 22, 23, 36, 37, 69, 97; British withdrawal from, 36; historian, 82; Federation, 103; Protectorates, 101; Western Aden Protectorate, 94, 105.
Afghanistan, 7.
Africa, E., 97.
al-Aḥqāf, 45; name of Ḥaḍramawt, 101.
^{c}Aidīd, village and wādī, 22, 25; gate of, 67.
^{c}Ain al-Wu^{c}ūl, 98.
Wādī Bin ^{c}Alī, 59, 60, 107.
^{c}Alwā, of Ḥaḍramawt, 31; defined, 97.
^{c}Amrān, 113.
al-^{c}Ankūb, pass, 51.
Anṣāb, 62.
Arabia, 69, 109, 114; northern, 18, 68, 113; southern 4, 6, 7–10, 25, 31, 35, 36, 61, 62, 64, 65, 68, 69, 74, 82–84, 97, 100, 102; south-west, 23, 82; ancient A., 85; Holy Cities of, 64; *passim*. Arabian peninsula, 71.
^{c}Arafāt, 67, 68.
Arḥab, 18, 108; *see* Ṣirwāḥ.
al-^{c}Arshah, name of Dome of Āl Ṭuyūrah, 50.
Bīr ^{c}Asākir, 95.
Athens, 89.
^{c}Athtar, present-day place-name, 76.
^{c}Awlaqī country, 62, 68; Lower, 75; Upper, 74; ^{c}Awlaqī-Wāḥidī border, 38.
Jabal ^{c}Ayāl Yazīd, 75.
^{c}Azzān, 11.

Bā Ḥabl, pass, 51.
Bā 'l-Khashab, ^{c}*aqabah*, 52.
Bā Ṣifyāh, 54.
Bā Ṭarfāh, 54.
al-Bāb, Baghdād, 24.
Bāb al-Azaj, 24.
Baghdād, 23–25.
Baiḥān, 2, 23, 71, 72; Wādī Baiḥān, 30.
Bait b. Ḥuṣn, 102.
Bait Jubair, 67
Bal-Faqīh ^{c}Alī, Gabal, 35.
Balkh, 7.
Balkha^{c}, 9, 89.
Baqar-um (?), 67, 88.
al-Bawn, 75, 76, 112, its *ḥimā*, 113; Qā^{c} al-Bawn, 75.
Beirut, 98.
al-Bīr, pass, 53.
Bīr, *see* ^{c}Asākir.
Burūm, 38.
al-Bustān al-Kabīr, 24.
al-Buwailah, 114.
Byzantine Museum, 89.

Cambridge Museum of Ethnology, 101.
Cordova, 64.

al-Ḍabbā^{c}in, 76.
Ḍāli^{c}, 12, 110.
Dammūn, 5, 16, 32, 66, 86; Dammūn pass, 40.
al-Darrāṭah, 114.
Dathīnah, 61, 74, 92, 97.
W. Daw^{c}an, 12, 30, 107.
al-Dawm, pass, 53.
ḏDB^{c}NN, 76.
Jabal Dhaibān, 75.
Dhī Bīn, road, 76.
al-Dimnah, nickname of Shibām, 101.
Dirjāj, 93.
Dome of Shaikh ^{c}Abdullāh Yā-Sīn, 50.
Dome of al-Qadīm, 59.
Dome of Āl Ṭuyūrah, *see* al-^{c}Arshah.
Dūmat al-Jandal, 7.

East road, Ḥaḍramawt, 34.
Empty Quarter, 66, 72, 73, 112.

Fardjalāt, *see* Jabal Farj al-Lāt.
Jabal Farj al-Lāt, 81.

Ghamdān, Yemeni pronunciation Ghumdān, *q.v.*, 89.
al-Ghubairah, 53.
Ghūlah, of al-Bawn, 75, 112.

Ghumdān, 9; *see* Ghamdān.
al-Ghuraf, 17, 28.
al-Ghurfah, or al-Ḥawl, 107.

Ḥ., i.e. Ḥuṣn, *q.v.*
Ḥabbān, 35, 108.
Ḥabūḍah, 41.
Wādī Hadā, 97, 98.
Ḥaḍramawt, 1, 2, 4, 13, 16, 18, 19, 31, 33, 64, 90; Wādī Ḥaḍramawt, 34, 41; called al-Aḥqāf, 45, 101; ᶜAlwā and Qiblī of, 31, 97; Ḥ. al-Ṣaid, 34.
Ḥaḍramī areas, 73.
Ḥaḍūr, 34.
Ḥaid b. ᶜAqīl, 30, 88.
Ḥaidarābād, 14, 96; spelt Ḥaidarᶜabād, 28.
Ḥaifah, Arḥab, 108.
Hajar Kuḥlān, 2.
al-Ḥājib - al-Qārah, 52, 103.
Ḥajjah, 113.
Wādī Ḥalfā, 7.
Hamal/Himil, *ḥimā* of, 113.
Ḥamduh, 40.
Ḥaram, *see* Mecca.
al-Ḥaram, 5; in Jawf, 35.
al-Ḥaramain, 4, 86.
Ḥaramī areas, 73.
Wādī Ḥarīb, 72.
Ḥaṣāt al-Ḥadd, Dammūn, 32.
Ḥaṣāt ᶜUmar b. ᶜAbd al-Kabīr, Mawlā Ṭuyūrah, 54.
Ḥawīr, 47.
al-Ḥawl, i.e. al-Ghurfah, 107.
Ḥawṣī, *see* Mithwā.
al-Ḥawṭah, 35, 36, 37, 38, 99.
Ḥawṭat Aḥmad b. Zain al-Ḥabshī, 22.
Ḥawṭat al-Faqīh ᶜAlī, 35, 37, 98; *see* al-Ḥawṭah.
Ḥawṭat Hishaimah/Hushaimah, 54.
Ḥawṭat Ṭuyūrah, 43, 44, 48, 49, 55, 69; *see* Ṭuyūrah.
al-Ḥazm, of Jawf, 104.
Hijrat Ṣayad/al-Ṣayad, 75, 76.
al-Himih, 53, 54, 57, 58.
Himil, *see* Hamal.
Ḥimyar, Gibāl Ḥ., 37.
al-Ḥīrah, 62.
Hishaimah, *see* Ḥawṭat, Hushaimah.
al-Ḥisī, pass, 51.
Holy Cities of Arabia, 64.
Ḥudaidah-Ṣanᶜā' road, 100.
Ḥukūmah building, 78.
Ḥuqqat Hamdān, 114.
Ḥuraiḍah, 102.
Hushaimah, 44, 53, 54; *see* Ḥawṭat.
Ḥūṣī, *see* Mithwā.
Ḥuṣn al-ᶜAbr, 9.
Ḥuṣn b. Minaibārī, 102.
Ḥuṣn b. Qairān, 51.
Ḥusn al-ᶜUrr, 95.
Ḥūth, 17.

ᶜIjiz, 41, 102.
ᶜĪnāt, 18, 29, 32, 33.
Indonesia, 68.
Iraq, 114.
ᶜIrmā, 23, 71, 112, = ᶜRMW, 74.
al-ᶜIrqah, near Madūdah, 51, 54, 55.

Jabbānah, 67.
al-Jaᶜfarīyah, cemetery of, 24.
Jandal, 70, 71.
Jarandal, 71.
Jarb Haiṣam, cemetery, 107.
Java, 64.
Jawf, of Yemen, 35, 64, 108; *see next entry.*
Jawf Bin Nāṣir, 3, 104.
Jawhar Mosque, 5.
Jaww al-Kudaif, 71.
al-Jidfirah, 50, 51, 53.
al-Jidfirah, Baiḥān, 2.
Jinainah, 70.
Wādī Jirdān, 6, 70, 71.
Jōl(s), plateau-like mountain top, 13, 28, 52, 53, 73, 103.
Jōl of Bal-ᶜUbaid, 71.
Wādī Juᶜaimah, 44, 45, 49, 51, 103, 106; location of, 100.
Jubair, *see* Bait.
al-Juruf, 53, 54.
Juwwat Āl ᶜAwaḍ b. ᶜAzzān, 53.

Kaᶜbah, 5, 6, 7, 20, 36, 62, 66; gazelle of, 88.
Jabal Kadūr, 18, 35, 98; of Bā Marḥūl, 34.
Kawkabān, 6, 78.
Kawr/Kōr Saibān, 38, 81; *see* Saibān.
al-Khabar, Wāḥidī-ᶜAwlaqī border, 38.
Khailah, Tarīm, 27.
Khaiwān, 17.

Khamir, 112.
Kharibat Āl ^{c}Alī, 64, 66, 68, 102, 103, 104.
Wādi 'l-Kharid, 75.
Khawlān, 6.
Khawr al-^{c}Umairah, 8.
al-Khishash, 40.
Khiṭmah Bā ^{c}Abbād, 53.
al-Khiṭmah al-Qiblīyah, 44.
al-Khiṭmah al-Sharqīyah, 44, 50, 54.
al-Khuraibah al-A^{c}līyah, 54.
al-Khurbah, 54.
Khushm al-Qāniṣ, 33.
al-Khutt, 44, 45.
Kibrān, of Bin Sarayīl, 98.
al-Kitāf, 10.
Kōr, *see* Kawr.
Kordofan, 82.
Kūfah, 6.
al-Kutur, pass, 51.

Lamāṭir, 35, 98.
Lihyah, 34, 98.
Wādī Liyyah, 87.
Luthail, *see* Shi^{c}b.

Ma^{c}a 'llāh, of Saibān, 105.
al-Madār, 17, 18.
am-Madārah, 92.
Madbī, 35, 98.
Madīnat Rasūl Allāh, 62; *see* Medina.
Madūdah, 14, 15, 16, 17, 20, 23, 31, 41, 42, 44 seq., *passim*; important in early Islām, 41.
al-Maḥābishah, 78.
Maḥfid, Lower ^{c}Awlaqī, 75, 94.
Maḥjir-Ma^{c}n frontier, 90.
Maḥmā Ta'lab, 75, 76.
Mahrah country, 25, 74.
Maḥram Ba^{c}l Aw^{c}āl Ṣirwāḥ, 77.
Maḥram Bilqīs, 63.
Maifa^{c}, 12, 35, 36.
Wādī Maifa^{c}ah, 80, 97.
Malaya, 64.
al-Ma'mūnīyah, 24.
Ma^{c}n, *see* Maḥjir.
Manārat al-Qurūn, 6, 87–88.
Manārat Umm al-Qurā, 88.
al-Manẓarah, 24.
Maqṭa^{c} al-Duqum, 54.
Marḥabā, 54.
Ma'rib, 2, 113, 115.
Maryamah, 14.
al-Masjid al-Kabīr, Ṣan^{c}ā', 89.
Masjid al-Kabsh, 109.
Masjid al-Wi^{c}l, 69.
Maṭāriḥ, 54.
al-Mathnā, 111.
Wādī Maṭirah, 113.
Maṭman al-Ghazālah, *see* Mawṭi'.
Ma^{c}wān, 111.
Mawṭi' al Ghazālah, 87.
Mawza^{c}, 8.
Mecca, 4, 6, 7, 8, 36, 61, 62, 66, 88, 89, 90, 108; Ḥaram of, 91, 92.
Medina, 4, 62, 69; al-Madīnah, 88; Jewish part of, 114.
Milan, 69.
Mirwath, 31.
al-Mishṭah, 96.
Mithwā Ḥūṣī/Ḥawṣī, 51, 54.
Mūdiyah, 73, 74, 96.
al-Muḥarriq, of Bā Raḥmah, 35; written Muḥarraq, 98.
al-Mukallā, 34, 69, 81.
Mukhrī, 114.
Murabba^{c}ah Muḥammad Kūfān, 51.
Musandam, 95.
Museum of Ethnology, *see* Cambridge.
Musliḥ, 114.
al-Muṭaiyabah, i.e. Mecca, 62.

Nā^{c}iṭ, of Arḥab, 75.
Najrān, 8, 25, 78, 79, 111.
Naqab al-Hajar, 38.
Naqīl Shujā^{c}, 72.
Nasr, in Saba', 9.
al-Nasr al-Qiblī, 9.
al-Nasr al-Sharqī, 9.
Nasrs, 70, 81, *see previous entries.*
al-Nuqūb, 110.
Nuṣairah, Ḥawir, 53.
^{c}NWDM, 70.

Oman, 74; *see* ^{c}Uman.

Persian Gulf, 2, 114.
Protectorates, *see* Aden.

Qā^{c} al-Bawn, 75; *see* al-Bawn.
Qā^{c} al-Ṣayad, 75.
Qabr Hūd, 23, 25, 26.
al-Qaḥalah, 78.
Qara, Jebel, 95.

al-Qārah, *see* al-Ḥājib.
al-Qarīn, 52.
Qarn al-Binā', 95.
Qarnāw, 3, 64, 66.
al-Qaryah, 24.
Qaryatain, 98.
Qasam, 41, 43.
Qaṭar, 2.
Qaṭuftā, 24.
Qaᶜūḍah, 33.
Qiblah, 51.
Qirfah, 35, 98.
Quᶜaiṭī territory, 32.
Qubbat al-Qadīm, 59.
Quzah, Dawᶜan, 30.

al-Raḥabah, *ḥimā* of, near Ṣanᶜā', 113; probably same as next entry.
al-Raḥbah, Yemen, 8.
al-Raḥbah, Iraq, 88.
Jabal al-Raḥmah, 67.
Raidah, 112.
al-Raiḍah, 17.
al-Rajjāl, pass, 51, 52.
Ramlat Sabᶜatain, 89; R. Saba'tain, 2, 9.
Ramlat Sabtain, 89.
al-Rawḍah, Wāḥidī, 35, 38, 99.
Wādī Rijām, 78.
al-Rimāl, The Sands, 72.
Riyām/al-Riyām, 18, 75, 76.
ᶜRMW, 73.
al-Rubᶜ al-Khalī, 73; *see* Empty Quarter.
Ruḍaimah, 51.
Rūḥī maᶜa 'llāh, 54.

Sabā, 77, 109; *see* next entry.
Saba', 9, 77, 89, 114; Nasr in, 9; Sands of the Two Saba's, 9.
Sabaean areas, 73.
Ṣaᶜdah, 17, 72.
Ṣāghir, 8.
Sāḥah of Shaikh ᶜAbdullāh b. Yā-Sīn, 55.
Sahara, 109.
Saibān, 105, *see* Kawr.
Ṣaid, sanctuary, 75.
al-Ṣaid, 88.
Ṣaᶜīd, of Wāḥidī, 31, 34.
Saiḥūt, 107.
Saiwūn, 22, 25, 41, 64, 74, 94, 97, 107.
Ṣanᶜā', 1, 22, 63, 68, 72, 78, 89, 104, 113, 114; Ṣ.-Ḥudaidah road, 100; Ṣ.-Ṣaᶜdah road, 17.
al-Saqāh, 35, 37, 98.
Wādī Sar, *see* Sarr.
al-Sarīr, Wādī Ḥaḍramawt, 41.
Wādī, Sarr/Sar, 100.
Shabwah, 9, 10, 13, 34, 70, 71, 73, 78, 79, 81, 97; long note on, 110–111.
al-Shāghī, 53.
Shaikh ᶜUthmān, village, 72.
Shajᶜūn, 41.
Shākir, 75.
al-Sharīrah, 98.
Sh hār, of al-Ṭā'if, 87.
Shiᶜb ᶜAidīd, 27; *see* ᶜAidīd.
Shiᶜb al-Ghanam, 51, 52.
Shiᶜb Luthail, 53.
Shiᶜb al-Rāk, 54, 57, 58.
Shiᶜb al-Ṣafāh, 54.
Shiᶜb al-Ṣaiᶜar, 54.
Shiᶜb al-Shaikh, 17.
Shiᶜb Āl Shamlān, 17.
Jabal al-Shiᶜbah, 2.
Shibām, of Ḥaḍramawt, 10, 58, 59, 62, 65, 97, 107; nicknamed al-Dimnah, 101.
Shibām Kawkabān, 6.
al-Shiḥr, 97.
Shujāᶜ, *see* Naqīl.
Jabal Shummat al-ᶜĀshiq, 81.
Singapore, 100.
Ṣiqair, 102.
Wādī Sirr, 78.
Ṣirwāḥ, of Arḥab, 75, 78.
Ṣirwāḥ, of Jahm, 63, 75, 77, 78, 114; temple at, 78; *ṭawāghīt*, temples at, 87; *see* Maḥram *supra*.
Somaliland, 64, 69.
al-Subaiᶜah, 6.
Ṣubaiḥī coast, 8.
Sūdah, of Arḥab, 76.
Sūdah, of W. Yemen, 78.
Sudan, 7, 17, 77, 88.
Sūq ᶜAbdullāh, 2.
Sūq al-Sulṭān, Baghdād, 24.
Syria, 89.

Ṭābah, *see* Ṭaibah.
Tadmor, 98.
Ṭaibah/Ṭābah, names of Medina, 62.
al-Ṭā'if, 4, 6, 87, 110.

Tāribah, 16.
Tarīm, 1, 5, 6, 14–16, 20–22, 25–27, 30–31, 33, 37–38, 41, 65–67, 72, 93–94, 96, 98, 103, 106–108, 112.
Tarīs, 41, 48.
Tawakhkharī, 51, 53, 54; meaning "hold back", 105.
Ṭawr al-Bāḥah, 71.
Thibī, village and wādī, 25, 26, 72.
Ṭībah, name of Zamzam, *q.v.*
Tihāmah, 1, 8.
Ṭuyūrah, 43–48, 54; *see* Ḥawṭah Ṭuyūrah.

^{c}Ukāẓ, 62.
^{c}Umān, 95; *see* Oman.
Umm al-Kurūn, 88.
al-^{c}Uqaiyiqah, 53.
al-^{c}Uqlah, 9, 70, 72, 73, 110.
al-^{c}Uraiqah, Tarīm, 27.
al-^{c}Urr, *see* Ḥuṣn.

Wāḥidī, country/sultanate, 11, 12, 18, 31, 34, 35, 38, 68, 92; is Ḥimyar, 37; W.-^{c}Awlaqī border, 38.
Wajj, 4, 87.

Yāfi^{c}, country, 110; Upper Y., 96.
Wādī Yashbum, 12, 90.
Yemen, 1, 4, 8, 9, 13, 35, 66, 88, 89, 97, 108; border, 78; eastern, 2, 32, 84; northern, 78; north-east, 64; Upper Y., 36, 43, 78.
Yemen Republic, 89.
Yinbakh, 34.
Yirmān, mountain, 86.

Ẓāhir al-Ṣayad, 75.
Zamzam, well, 62, 88; Ṭībah, name of, 62.
al-Zibb, mountain, 81.
al-Zubb, *see* al-Zibb.
Ẓufār, 95.